KYOTO AREA STUDIES ON ASIA
CENTER FOR SOUTHEAST ASIAN STUDIES, KYOTO UNIVERSITY
VOLUME 31

China's BRI in Southeast Asia

Concepts and Methodologies

KYOTO AREA STUDIES ON ASIA

CENTER FOR SOUTHEAST ASIAN STUDIES, KYOTO UNIVERSITY

The Nation and Economic Growth:
Korea and Thailand
Yoshihara Kunio

One Malay Village:
A Thirty-Year Community Study
Tsubouchi Yoshihiro

Commodifying Marxism:
The Formation of Modern Thai Radical Culture, 1927–1958
Kasian Tejapira

Gender and Modernity:
Perspectives from Asia and the Pacific
Hayami Yoko, Tanabe Akio and Tokita-Tanabe Yumiko

Practical Buddhism among the Thai-Lao:
Religion in the Making of a Region
Hayashi Yukio

The Political Ecology of Tropical Forests in Southeast Asia:
Historical Perspectives
Lye Tuck-Po, Wil de Jong and Abe Ken-ichi

Between Hills and Plains:
Power and Practice in Socio-Religious Dynamics among Karen
Hayami Yoko

Ecological Destruction, Health and Development:
Advancing Asian Paradigms
Furukawa Hisao, Nishibuchi Mitsuaki, Kono Yasuyuki and Kaida Yoshihiro

Searching for Vietnam:
Selected Writings on Vietnamese Culture and Society
A. Terry Rambo

Laying the Tracks:
The Thai Economy and its Railways 1885–1935
Kakizaki Ichiro

After the Crisis:
Hegemony, Technocracy and Governance in Southeast Asia
Shiraishi Takashi and Patricio N. Abinales

Dislocating Nation-States:
Globalization in Asia and Africa
Patricio N. Abinales, Ishikawa Noboru and Tanabe Akio

People on the Move:
Rural–Urban Interactions in Sarawak
Soda Ryoji

Living on the Periphery:
Development and Islamization among the Orang Asli
Nobuta Toshihiro

Myths and Realities:
The Democratization of Thai Politics
Tamada Yoshifumi

KYOTO AREA STUDIES ON ASIA

CENTER FOR SOUTHEAST ASIAN STUDIES, KYOTO UNIVERSITY

East Asian Economies and New Regionalism
Abe Shigeyuki and Bhanupong Nidhipraba

The Rise of Middle Classes in Southeast Asia
Shiraishi Takashi and Pasuk Phongpaichit

Farming with Fire and Water:
The Human Ecology of a Composite Swiddening
Community in Vietnam's Northern Mountains
Trần Đức Viên, A. Terry Rambo and Nguyễn Thanh Lâm

Re-thinking Economic Development:
The Green Revolution, Agrarian Structure and Transformation in Bangladesh
Fujita Koichi

The Limits of Tradition:
Peasants and Land Conflicts in Indonesia
Urano Mariko

Bangsa and Umma:
Development of People-grouping Concepts in Islamized Southeast Asia
Yamamoto Hiroyuki, Anthony Milner, Kawashima Midori and Arai Kazuhiro

Development Monks in Northeast Thailand
Pinit Lapthanon

Politics of Ethnic Classification in Vietnam
Ito Masako

The End of Personal Rule in Indonesia:
Golkar and the Transformation of the Suharto Regime
Masuhara Ayako

Grassroots Globalization:
Reforestation and Cultural Revitalization in the Philippine Cordilleras
Shimizu Hiromu

Conceptualizing the Malay World:
Colonialism and Pan-Malay Identity in Malaya
Soda Naoki

Violence and Democracy:
The Collapse of One-Party Dominant Rule in India
Nakamizo Kazuya

Bali and Hinduism in Indonesia:
The Institutionalization of a Minority Religion
Nagafuchi Yasuyuki

At the Edge of Mangrove Forest:
The Suku Asli and the Quest for Indigeneity, Ethnicity, and Development
Osawa Takamasa

Money-lending Contracts in Konbaung Burma:
Another interpretation of an early modern society in Southeast Asia
Saito Teruko

China's BRI in Southeast Asia:
Concepts and Methodologies
Yos Santasombat, Kian Cheng LEE, Decha Tangseefa

KYOTO AREA STUDIES ON ASIA
CENTER FOR SOUTHEAST ASIAN STUDIES, KYOTO UNIVERSITY
VOLUME 31

China's BRI in Southeast Asia

Concepts and Methodologies

Edited by
Yos Santasombat
Kian Cheng LEE
Decha Tangseefa

Kyoto University Press

TRANS PACIFIC PRESS

First published in 2025 jointly by:

Kyoto University Press
69 Yoshida Konoe-cho
Sakyo-ku, Kyoto 606-8315, Japan
Telephone: +81-75-761-6182
Fax: +81-75-761-6190
Email: sales@kyoto-up.or.jp
Web: http://www.kyoto-up.or.jp

Trans Pacific Press Co., Ltd.
[Editorial Office]
2-2-15-2F, Hamamatsu-cho, Minato-ku,
Tokyo, 1050013, JAPAN
[Registered Office]
PO Box 8547 #19682
Boston, MA, 02114, United States
Email: info@transpacificpress.com
Web: http://www.transpacificpress.com

© Yos Santasombat, Kian Cheng LEE, Decha Tangseefa 2025
Copyedited by Dr. Karl E. Smith, Melbourne, Australia
Designed and set by Ryo Kuroda, Tsukuba-city, Ibaraki, Japan

Distributors

World
Independent Publishers Group (IPG)
814 N. Franklin Street
Chicago, IL 60610, USA
Telephone inquiries: +1-312-337-0747
Order placement: 800-888-4741 (domestic only)
Fax: +1-312-337-5985
Email: frontdesk@ipgbook.com
Web: http://www.ipgbook.com

Japan
For purchase orders in Japan, please contact any distributor in Japan.

China
China Publishers Services Ltd.
718, 7/F., Fortune Commercial Building,
362 Sha Tsui Road, Tsuen Wan, N.T.
Hong Kong
Telephone: +852-2491-1436
Email: edwin@cps-hk.com

Southeast Asia
Alkem Company Pte Ltd.
1, Sunview Road #01-27, Eco-Tech@Sunview
Singapore 627615
Telephone: +65 6265 6666
Email: enquiry@alkem.com.sg

Cover photos (From the top):
Northeastern high-speed railway, Bangkok, Thailand (August 13, 2024).
Vietnamese protesters demonstrating against China moving an oil rig into disputed waters, London England (May 18, 2014).
High speed train from Laos to China stopping at Luang Prabang Railway Station, Laos (October 19, 2023).

Library of Congress Control Number: 2025931211

All rights reserved. No reproduction of any part of this book may take place without the written permission of Kyoto University Press or Trans Pacific Press.

ISBN: 978-1-920850-51-7 (hardback)
ISBN: 978-1-920850-52-4 (paperback)
ISBN: 978-1-920850-53-1 (eBook)

Table of Contents

List of Figures viii

List of Photos viii

List of Tables viii

Contributors ix

Preface xv

Introduction   *Yos Santasombat, Kian Cheng LEE and Decha Tangseefa* 1

1. Anthropology of Regionalization, Multi-sited Ethnography, and Voice Approach in BRI Research   *Yos Santasombat and Kian Cheng LEE* 23

2. Making Sense of BRI in Malaysia: Negotiating Volatile Political Situations   *Danny Wong Tze Ken* 51

3. Reconceptualizing Mobile Infrastructures and Infrastructural Temporality in the Transnational Cattle Trade   *Kengkij Kitirianglarp* 77

4. Chinese Loans for Infrastructure Development? Narratives of Railways, Highways, and China's Belt and Road Initiative in Vietnam   *Nguyễn Văn Chính and Đinh Thị Thanh Huyền* 105

5. Constructing the Field: Anthropological Infrastructure Studies on Transnational Railways in Laos and Thailand   *Panitda Saiyarod* 137

6. Shadow Zones: Fraudulent Infrastructure, the Alchemy of Sovereignty, and Destructive Economies in Shwe Kokko SEZ/KK Park and Thailand's EEC   *Pinkaew Laungaramsri* 175

7. The Belt and Road Initiative in Myanmar: A Review   *Ta-Wei Chu* 207

8. The Belt and Road Initiative from the Perspectives of Political Economy and Business Transnationalism   *Hong Liu* 233

9. Maximizing the Benefits of the Mekong Subregional Cooperation Frameworks   *Romyen Kosaikanont* 267

Index 299

List of Figures

Figure 3.1 Muse-Ruili and Boten-Mohan: Principal gateways to China 83
Figure 3.2 Map of actors and networks in the transnational cattle trade under the BRI 87
Figure 3.3 Roles and networks of brokers in the cattle trade 93
Figure 3.4 Apparatuses of temporality and vicious circle in the cattle trade 97
Figure 9.1 Mekong US Partnership at a glance 285
Figure 9.2 One Page Summary: ACMECS 293

List of Photos

Photo 5.1 Billboard in front of railway station in Vientiane, 2 June 2023 154

List of Tables

Table 2.1 Selected BRI projects in Malaysia 58
Table 4.1 Vietnam's total infrastructure investment need (2016–2040) 114
Table 4.2. Vietnam's foreign creditors as of 2021 119
Table 4.3 Foreign loans for expressway construction in Vietnam (2009–2022) 129
Table 8.1 Singapore's engagement with the BRI from 2020 to 2023 248
Table 9.1 Mapping cooperation frameworks in the Mekong subregion by areas of cooperation 282

Contributors

Ta-wei Chu is an assistant professor at the Department of Social Science and Development, Chiang Mai University. His research interests are security studies, hydro politics in the Mekong Basin and transdisciplinarity. His articles have appeared in *Wiley Interdisciplinary Reviews Water*, *Journal of Current Southeast Asian Affairs*, *Asian International Studies Review*, and *Asian Survey*. Currently, he is working on a research project focusing on Belt and Road Initiative (BRI) in Myanmar.

Kengkij Kitirianglarp is an associate professor of sociology in the Department of Sociology and Anthropology, Faculty of Social Science, Chiang Mai University, Thailand. He has been working on Marxist approaches to contemporary political and social issues. His publications include books and essays on social theory, sociology of labor, the Anthropocene, and ecological thought. His on-going field research seeks to elucidate the ecological wisdom of the Nagas.

Romyen Kosaikanont is assistant professor at the School of Management, Mae Fah Luang University. She is currently serving as the Centre Director of SEAMEO RIHED (Southeast Asian Ministers of Education Organization Regional Centre for Higher Education and Development). She received a PhD in International Development and Economics, University of Bath, and Master of Arts in Gender and Development, Institute of Development Studies, UK. Her main research interests cover the areas of international political economy of the Greater Mekong Subregion, gender and the future of work, internationalization of higher education in the GMS and the influence of China in the GMS. Her recent publications are *Chinese Capital Going Global: Thai-Chinese*

Industrial Zone and Labor Conditions in Thailand: Challenges and Prospects (2019), Gender and the Future of Work in Thailand: The 20 Years National Strategy and Thailand 4.0 (2019), *Partnership in Higher Education: Key to the Sustainable Development of the Southeast Asian Region* (2022).

Pinkaew Laungaramsri is a professor of Anthropology in the Department of Sociology and Anthropology at Chiang Mai University. Her research spans a broad range of topics including the politics of nature conservation, the right of upland communities, special economic zones and border studies. Her first book is titled *Redefining Nature: Karen Ecological Knowledge and the Challenge to Modern Conservation Paradigm* (2002).

Kian Cheng LEE, a Singaporean, holds a Ph.D. (Social Sciences), M.A. (Southeast Asian Studies), M.Th. (Asian Christianity), M.Div., M.A. (Biblical Studies), and B.Sc. (Physics). He is an assistant professor in the Faculty of Political Science and Public Administration while being affiliated with the School of Public Policy and Faculty of Social Sciences at Chiang Mai University. He is also a member of the board of the Asian Pastoral Institute Ltd. in Singapore. Kian Cheng's research interests concern Chinese business practices, transnational entrepreneurship, politics, cultural and citizen diplomacy, and Thai religious networks. Kian Cheng has published nine research-based articles in esteemed journals including Scopus-indexed journals such as *Journal of Chinese Overseas, International Journal of China Studies, Journal of Current Chinese Affairs* and *Identities*. In addition, he has published six research-based book chapters with Springer, Palgrave Macmillan and Edward Elgar Publishing, Inc. He can be contacted at kiancheng.lee@cmu.ac.th.

Hong Liu is the Tan Lark Sye Chair Professor of Public Policy and Global Affairs at the School of Social Sciences, Nanyang Technological University in Singapore, where he also serves as the University's Associate Vice President (International Engagement) and Director (Research and Executive Education) of the Nanyang Centre for Public Administration. He was previously the Chair of the School of Humanities and Social Sciences at NTU and the Founding Director of the Centre for Chinese Studies and Chair in Chinese Studies at the University of Manchester. Professor Liu's main areas of research include international political economy, Asian governance, Sino-Southeast Asian interactions, global talent management, and Chinese international migration. Professor Liu has published more than 25 books in English and Chinese as well as over 100 articles including in leading international journals such as *World Politics*, *Journal of Asian Studies*, *The China Quarterly*, *Journal of Contemporary China*, *Journal of Ethnic and Migration Studies*, and *Ethnic and Racial Studies*. His recent publications include *Research Handbook on the Belt and Road Initiative* (co-editor, 2021); *Changing Dynamics and Mechanisms of Maritime Asia in Comparative Perspective* (co-editor, 2021); *The Political Economy of Regionalism, Trade, and Infrastructure* (co-editor, 2022), and *The Political Economy of Transnational Governance: China and Southeast Asia in the 21st Century* (2022).

Chinh Van Nguyen is Professor and Head of Development Anthropology at the University of Social Sciences and Humanities, Vietnam National University, Hà Nội. He received his doctorate from the University of Amsterdam, the Netherlands. His recent academic interests focus on issues of ethnic minorities, development and migration.

Đinh Thị Thanh Huyền received her PhD in anthropology from Vietnam National University, Hanoi. She is currently a lecturer at the Department of Cultural Anthropology, University of Social Sciences and Humanities (USSH), Vietnam National University, Hanoi (VNU Hanoi). Her research focuses on cultural heritage, tourism and development.

Panitda Saiyarod is a lecturer in the Department of Sociology and Anthropology at Chiang Mai University. Before joining academia, she worked as a planning and policy analyst at Thailand's National Economic and Social Development Board (NESDB) from 2012 to 2015. Her research interests focus on the anthropology of infrastructure, regional development, cross-border trade, the socio-cultural impacts of Chinese influence in Thailand, and social change in contemporary Chinese society.

Yos Santasombat is professor of Anthropology, Department of Sociology and Anthropology, and Director, China-Southeast Asian Studies Center, Faculty of Social Sciences, Chiang Mai University, and Senior Research Scholar, Thailand Research Fund. His English language publication includes *Lak Chang: A Reconstruction of Tai Identity in Daikong* (Canberra: Pandanus Books, ANU, 2001); *Biodiversity, Local Knowledge and Sustainable Development* (Chiang Mai: RCSD, 2003, 2014); *Flexible Peasants: Reconceptualizing the Third World's Rural Types* (Chiang Mai: RCSD, 2008); *The River of Life: Changing Ecosystems of the Mekong Region* (Chiang Mai: Mekong Press, 2011); as well as the edited volumes *Impact of China's Rise in the Mekong Region* (Palgrave Macmillan 2015) *Chinese Capitalism in South-east Asia: Cultures and Practices* (Palgrave Macmillan 2017), *Sociology of Chinese Capitalism: Challenges and Prospects* (Palgrave Macmillan 2019), and *Transnational Chinese*

Diaspora in Southeast Asia: Case Studies from Thailand, Malaysia, and Singapore (Springer 2022).

Decha Tangseefa is associate professor of Political Theory, Center for Southeast Asian Studies, Kyoto University. His research fields lie at the nexus between migration studies and border studies, focusing especially on the Thai-Myanmar borderlands, where most of his publications on the following issues have been devoted: death & atrocity; refugees; music & youth; ethnicity; marginal migrant workers; community engagement; malaria elimination; and special economic zones. His most recent publication is the English and expanded version of *Light, Water and Rice Stalk: Cultural Fluency for Alterity* (Kobfai Publishing Project, 2020, second edition).

Danny Wong Tze Ken is currently Dean of the Faculty of Arts and Social Sciences, Universiti Malaya. He is also professor of History at the Department of History, Faculty of Arts and Social Sciences, Universiti Malaya where he teaches history of Southeast Asia and History of China. His research interests include the Chinese in Malaysia, China's relations with Southeast Asia and the history of Sabah. His more recent publications include, *Wang Gungwu and Malaysia*, (edited, Universiti Malaya Press, 2021), *One Crowded Moment of Glory* (Yang Ming Chiao Tung University Press, 2021) and *Lead & Grow: 115 Years of the Chinese Chamber of Commerce & Industry of Selangor and Kuala Lumpur* (Universiti Malaya Press, 2021).

Preface

Emerging from an ongoing collective project hosted by the China-Southeast Asian Studies Center, Faculty of Social Sciences, Chiang Mai University in Thailand and gathering essays by a host of Southeast Asian research scholars, this collection aims to unsettle received ideas about China's Belt and Road Initiative (BRI) by problematizing the existing concepts and approaches to academic research on the subject.

China's transformation into a capitalist world power has been one of the defining features of the 21st century. Over the past ten years, our team have conducted four research projects on the expanding economic and political role of China in Southeast Asia. The first project is a contemporary analysis of the *Impact of China's Rise on the Mekong Region* (2015). The second project focuses on the history and evolution of *Chinese Capitalism in Southeast Asia: Cultures and Practices* (2017); and *The Sociology of Chinese Capitalism in Southeast Asia: Challenges and Prospects* (2019). The third project examines contemporary Chinese transnational mobility through ethnographies of mobile Chinese subjects in Malaysia, Singapore, and Thailand, and their interactions with the ethnic Chinese communities in these countries (*Transnational Chinese Diaspora in Southeast Asia*, 2022). The fourth and ongoing project focuses on the impact of China's BRI in Southeast Asia. Our research objectives are (1) to assess the impact of China's BRI megaprojects in Southeast Asian countries with special focus on ethnographic case studies of special economic zones (SEZs) and high-speed train projects, (2) to compare and critically analyze the risks and benefits stemming from BRI megaprojects in Southeast Asia, and (3) to discuss policy implications and recommendations for regional development and balance of power and disseminate our findings through publications and international seminars on the BRI. This book is the first output of this research project, focusing on concepts and methodologies of BRI research.

Our team would like to express our deep gratitude to our colleagues for their comments on previous drafts of papers presented at various workshops. We would like to acknowledge in particular the contributions of Professors Suwanna Satha-anand, Rasmi Shoocongdej, Sirinan Kulchat, Worajit Setthapun, Karsidete Teeranitayatarn, Surichai Wankaeo, Achariya Choowonglert, Naruemon Thabchumpon, Chaiwat Meesantan, Simon Rowedder, Lee Lai To, Pittaya Suvakunta, Chusak Wittayapak, Jamaree Chiengthong and Kanokwan Manorom. Research and workshops have been made possible by financial and organizational support from the Program Management Unit for Human Resources & Institutional Development, Research and Innovation (PMU-B), Ministry of Higher Education, Science, Research and Innovation, Thailand.

I am most grateful for a generous visiting research fellowship from the Center for Southeast Asian Studies, Kyoto University. The time spent at the CSEAS was both joyful and productive. Special thanks are due to Professor Yoko Hayami, former Director, and Professor Fumiharu Mieno, present Director, my counterpart Associate Professor Decha Tangseefa, faculty members, staff and visiting research scholars at CSEAS for allowing me to be part of this exciting academic community. I would like to extend special thanks to the research liaison staff, especially Chiaki Abe, Motoko Kondo and Naoko Nishiyama as well as the Publications Committee, Editorial office at CSEAS, especially, Ms. Narumi Shitara for her kind assistance. Finally, Palaiwan Srisaringkarn deserves special recognition for her untiring organizational assistance to our project.

Yos Santasombat
Kyoto, 30 March 2025

Introduction

Yos Santasombat, Kian Cheng LEE and Decha Tangseefa

This book is part of an ongoing research project on the impact of China's Belt and Road Initiative (BRI) in Southeast Asia. Since its inception, the BRI has been shrouded in confusion and controversy. The Covid-19 pandemic and lockdowns from 2020 presented unique challenges for our understanding of BRI. Drawing on the extensive literature and our continuing empirical investigations of BRI projects in various Southeast Asian countries, this book outlines a conceptual and methodological experiment of mapping and analyzing the dynamics and implications of China's BRI, its international influence, and how its economic development trajectory impacts socio-economic and cultural realities on the ground.

A comprehensive literature review shows that most academic studies of the BRI have been based on macro analyses, top-down approaches, and theoretical deliberations (cf. Blanchard, 2021, see also Chapter One). Few empirical studies have examined BRI megaprojects' relationships with and impacts on local communities. Although studies such as Camba (2020; 2021; 2022) and Tritto and Camba (2023) have adopted a qualitative approach, we opine that they are generally confined to the perspective of limited state sovereignty. Against this backdrop, we attempt to identify the potential impact of BRI on the development of ASEAN countries by way of empirical research and case studies in various research sites to acquire first-hand ethnographic data on the risks and benefits of BRI projects at the local, national, and regional levels. To this end, this book argues for a research design that focuses on specific regions or countries while precisely identifying project participants and stakeholders.

The essays from a group of international researchers collected here share the conviction that China's BRI and its impact on Southeast Asia should be examined through a variety of perspectives such as transnational political economy, development studies, beyond state-centrism, state-corporate crime, an ontological turn, and geopolitical competition approaches. The method that differentiates our work from other BRI studies is multi-sited ethnography (Marcus 1995) where we explore how people navigate the complexity of making and struggling to maintain ordinary lives in the context of socio-economic, political, and institutional changes brought about by BRI projects. Using the ethnographic method, our researchers can discover in-depth qualitative data that are best obtained by using multiple research methodologies, including participant observation, interviews, focus groups and textual analysis to construct a holistic and contextual vision of specific BRI projects. Our researchers immerse themselves in both quantitative and qualitative data collected from their inquiries while performing iterative analyses to identify emerging issues.

Participant observation allows researchers to assess human and institutional behavior in real time. This information can strengthen the interpretation of data collected through interviews. Using open-ended questions, in-depth interviews aim to elucidate the informant's mental and experiential world. Individual interviews allow participants to tell their own stories while also allowing researchers to ask questions and seek clarification of participants' responses, and thus to follow new topics raised by the participants. Similarly, focus group discussions are useful for revealing relevant topics, with the group dynamics typically generating different forms of colloquial expressions and a broader range of critical data. Finally, textual analysis of project statements, information brochures, procedure manuals, and similar materials produce valuable data about operations, values, and mechanisms, which can in turn be examined to reveal themes and patterns underlying official discourses and narratives. Cumulatively, such methods can illuminate inconsistencies between official narratives and the lived-experience of individuals' and groups' actively engaged with projects at the local level.

This anthology presents nine chapters that problematize the BRI research corpus while offering new insights from a different conceptual framework. Of course, the various case studies and projects presented in this volume are neither exhaustive nor representative of the full-range of Chinese-Southeast Asian relations. On the contrary, they are significant sites of social, economic, political, security, and other salient issues that are relevant to understanding the BRI and its true impact in Southeast Asia. In Chapter One, Santasombat and Lee propose a methodological experiment in the anthropology of regionalization to adapt ethnographic practices to larger, more complex, and decentralized objects of study while at the same time listening to the marginalized subalterns speak via the voice approach (Spivak 1988). This paper problematizes the existing BRI research as trapped in homogenizing, bounded and dichotomizing perspectives, obliteration of socio-cultural voices, and a lopsided top-dominated representation. Instead, this paper argues for the adoption of an ethnographic approach. Against the backdrop of China's BRI expansionism, the ethnographic lens must be expanded from the conventional single-site fieldwork to multiple sites of observation that cut across dichotomies such as the local and the regional/global contexts. China's BRI cannot be adequately investigated by focusing on a single site of intensive observation. The term "multi-sited ethnography" refers to a mode of research, which collapses the distinction between the local site and the global system. Researchers observe situated local sites, and they study the BRI system directly on the ground. This requires a willingness to leave behind the bounded field-site paradigm.

In other words, while travelling from place to place and moving between media, researchers follow the thing (production), the metaphor, the plot, the conflict, the people, and their stories. Through these modes of construction, multi-sited ethnography allows us to engage with large-scale entities such as **BRI** without losing the intimate portrayal of people's collective experiences and subjectivities.

In Chapter Two, Danny Wong provides a conceptual framework to highlight the entanglement of China's **BRI** and Malaysian projects based on case studies of the East Coast Rail Links (ECRL) and the Forest City projects, with an emphasis on how they were shaped and how they were linked to the local stakeholders in Malaysia. Wong situates **BRI** in the context of national controversies related to the two projects and the impact these controversies had on how the **BRI** was perceived in the country. Two likely scenarios are identified: the first refers to how the **BRI** projects were shrouded in financial controversies, especially the ECRL, which was allegedly used to bail out the controversial 1MDB Fund; and the second refers to perceptions of the **BRI** as a Chinese takeover dominating Malaysian sovereignty. In the process, this paper examines the question of approaches to researching the **BRI** cases in Malaysia between 2013 and 2021. It emphasizes the election campaigns of 2018 and its aftermath – including a corruption scandal – that enormously impacted both projects directly, and Malaysia-China relations more generally. Further, this paper seeks to offer a viable approach to making sense of events during an uncertain period of political change in Malaysia.

As these projects in Malaysia and other countries are part of the larger **BRI** framework envisioned by China, the paper endeavors to elucidate China's overall vision of the **BRI**. It is only with a clear understanding of this macro view of the **BRI** that we can better appreciate the positioning of the **BRI** projects in other countries.

The micro views, on the other hand, require in-depth analyses of the BRI projects. In this vein, the East Coast Rail Link and Forest City were selected to demonstrate their importance vis-à-vis other BRI projects in Malaysia and Southeast Asia. Both projects have drawn much attention and criticism since their inception. Both have been linked to many issues including incurring high costs, subsumption of national interests, and questions about the projects' main beneficiaries. During the 2018 Malaysian general elections, questions were raised pertaining to ethnicity, foreign "domination," and the perceived loss of sovereignty to China via the BRI projects. There were also allegations of links between the projects and the 1MDB scandal involving the highest office in the country, as well as the chief promoter of BRI projects in Malaysia. These allegations raise questions about the possible ways of deciphering BRI projects and the way different Malaysian governments have approached these projects. The volatile political scenarios derailed some projects, in this case, particularly the ECRL project. Nonetheless, the projects eventually continued, albeit after some renegotiation.

Wong argues that the underlying factor sustaining the BRI projects despite the many challenges is *mutual dependency*. On the one hand, successive Malaysian political elites held on to the idea of Malaysia's dependency on the projects. They opined that Malaysia needed to maintain strong diplomatic, economic, and socio-cultural relations with China. As a result, they renegotiated the ECRL project to reduce the cost. On the other hand, this study demonstrates a possible mutual dependency from China's perspective. The importance of these projects to the success of the BRI made China willing to renegotiate and reduce the scale of the projects. The relief expressed on both sides when the ECRL project resumed was a clear indication of the mutual dependency of the two countries on the success of the BRI projects.

In Chapter Three, Kengkij Kitirianglarp discusses the impact of BRI's infrastructural development on the transnational cattle trade across Southeast Asia. Over the past two decades, the Chinese market's increasing demand for cattle has changed the pattern and trajectory of cross-border cattle trade in the Mekong region. Chinese cattle traders exert greater control over product quality, trade networks, and trade routes. The structural changes of cattle trade under flexible capitalism have no fixed form. In this situation, Chinese investors rely on several mechanisms to absorb surplus labor and resources. By interrogating the empirical contexts of restructured transnational cattle trade in the Thai-Laos-Myanmar-China borderlands, the paper proposes a need to reconceptualize infrastructural development under China's BRI where analysis should go beyond the fixed and material entities to include the mobile and immaterial aspects. In the cattle trade, Chinese entrepreneurs do not control the production processes from inside the border of Thailand and Myanmar where most cattle are raised, but from the outside by building logistic cattle stations in Laos. Chinese capitalism works like a machine absorbing and subsuming surplus produced by multiple actors from across the region without any direct involvement in the cattle production process. In this light, cattle trade infrastructure connotes a system controlling labor, time, and networks. Under the narrative of transnational connectivity, infrastructural development is an exploitative controlling mechanism that creates pernicious disparities by subsuming all production processes as well as informal local networks of farmers and brokers in the Mekong region.

The author argues that the transnational connectivity initiated by China's BRI effectively controls the whole region by establishing formal and material infrastructure, albeit indirectly operating through a brokerage system. Chinese capitalism enables local brokers to play a determinant role in the production processes by commanding the apparatus of time and helping to transfer surplus from local farmers to China. Chinese capitalism operates outside the labor and production processes, allowing locals to freely create surplus, while waiting at the border to accumulate that economic surplus. As a result, there are two layers of infrastructure within the BRI: first, the immobile and material infrastructure built by the Chinese investors in Laos; and second, the mobile and immaterial networks of infrastructure located in Thailand, Laos, and Myanmar. These two levels of infrastructural apparatuses work cooperatively in the region, enhancing the flexibility of Chinese investments in the cattle trade; nonetheless, they pose risks to the local farmers by increasing uncertainties. In other words, BRI's infrastructural development restructures the cattle trade, creating an economy in which local farmers are "trapped" in difficult trade networks. Seeing the BRI from below is to study the complex and intricately connected relations between the two levels of social relationship: the relation between the BRI infrastructures and the brokerage system; and the relationship between the brokers, as mobile infrastructural ones, and the farmers.

In Chapter Four, Nguyễn Văn Chính and Đinh Thị Thanh Huyền examine Vietnam's unique participation in China's BRI via the concept of "hedging strategy." Hedging is defined as an insurance-seeking strategy to limit risks in economic, political and security spheres. This paper aims to use BRI to explain how, when, and why weaker states like Vietnam hedge their relations with China. The authors argue that Vietnam's hedging behavior is governed by both international and domestic factors. While power fluctuations at the regional level can influence Vietnam to hedge, the predominant hedging factors are domestic in nature where political leaders seek legitimation.

Recent scholarship tends to associate BRI development in Vietnam with issues such as territorial disputes in the South China

Sea, low quality infrastructure projects and expensive loans. While these factors are undeniable, interviews with social groups who influence policy making reveal that Vietnam is pursuing a hedging strategy, choosing national security instead of unrestrained borrowing capital for infrastructure development. Vietnam's hedging strategy pursues a multilateral foreign economic policy and diversified capital sources to serve infrastructure projects instead of relying solely on the BRI and its financing. This policy is shaped by domestic politics in which intellectuals, professionals and activists play key roles. Analyzing the Vietnamese case, the authors argue that economic hedging is a strategy that small states adopt to maintain guardrails. Such mechanisms are created to protect from asymmetrical dependence on any great power. Economic hedging reflects the nature of economic statecraft, specifically small states' realization that great powers are always willing and able to use economic coercion in pursuit of their own interests.

Unlike some Southeast Asian countries, Vietnam's hedging strategy is influenced by a long history of territorial disputes with China. Hedging can entail complex engagement policies including a constructive hedge against potential risks that may come from business engagement or economic cooperation with China. This essay argues that hedging is the best way to understand Vietnam's participation in the BRI and its new foreign economic policy. Vietnam's hedging strategy emphasizes at least two main points. First, it involves a foreign economic policy that controls how much capital is borrowed from foreign countries. Second, it emphasizes multilateral foreign economic relations and diversifying sources for financing infrastructure development. On one hand, this policy seeks to enhance commercial openness with strategic foreign policy in "making friends with all countries" that Vietnam is pursuing. Yet, the policy promotes economic pragmatism in adopting a realist approach to foreign economic relations to protect Vietnam's national sovereignty from Chinese influence.

The paper contends that among the Southeast Asian countries who have signed on to China's BRI infrastructure project, Vietnam is the most reticent even though it has great need for infrastructure investment. The lack of trust in the bilateral relationship between the two countries and the influence of domestic politics are the top factors that dominate Vietnam's economic relations with China. Furthermore, Vietnam's domestic politics are strongly flavored by its bitter experience of borrowing capital from China for infrastructure development from 2000 to 2015. The severe effects of that failed experience have not yet been overcome. Meanwhile, Vietnam can approach other sources of capital for its infrastructure projects including loans from international Official Development Assistance (ODA) partners or mobilizing capital from domestic private sectors. In addition to the above factors, domestic politics has an important impact on Vietnam's foreign economic policy. The design and implementation of government policies is inevitably affected by differing development perspectives, interests of various social groups, and public feedback in general. Hence, to fully understand Vietnam's participation in China's BRI, special attention must be paid to internal politics and their influence on foreign economic diplomacy, particularly the policy for borrowing to invest in transport infrastructure.

In Chapter Five, Panitda Saiyarod presents a methodology for studying China's transnational railways in Southeast Asia as part of the BRI through case studies in Laos and Thailand. The author interrogates the merits of studying infrastructure with approaches and perspectives of the ethnographic methodology. The paper starts with a basic assumption that the completion of large, capital-intensive BRI projects is more complex than it is often portrayed. The paper proposes examining infrastructures supporting railway operations in terms of how they are adapted by the host countries and integrated into the social lives of the local people. Infrastructure is both relational and ecological. It means different things to different groups, and it is part of a composite whole comprised of actions, negotiations, technologies, and the environment. In exploring its impact on local communities, the railways are treated as both material infrastructure and an abstract concept. The paper argues that the "ethnography of infrastructure" is well-suited to study the dynamics, contingencies, and messy outcomes that characterize current **BRI** practices. By applying a dynamic ethnographic tool to examine infrastructure, our research sites are constructed through collaboration and intervention that requires constant reflexivity. The railway project is perceived as a platform where competition, negotiation and manipulation occur among the many actors striving to achieve their goals.

The ethnography of infrastructure is presented in this paper as a suitable methodology for examining how China's railways transform the social fabric of communities along the tracks. In addition to a bottom-up perspective, this research focuses on intangible or soft infrastructures that facilitate and support transnational railway construction and operations, such as ideas, knowledge, policies, practices, and technologies. The paper asks how they are woven together, transformed, translated, improvised, assembled, and disassembled in the host countries. The purpose of this paper is two-fold. First, the author hopes to contribute to **BRI** studies by providing concrete case studies of railway development in Thailand and Laos. Second, the paper seeks to push the methodological boundary concerning how to approach highly complex regional infrastructure. For instance, the author questions the appropriateness of empirical scales and units of analysis when studying transnational infrastructure: "How can we engage with voices and practices operating at different scales and in various sites, and how are they integrated, translated, improvised, reconciled, and (dis)connected?"

The paper is divided into four parts: (1) The first introduces China's transnational railway projects and the social life of railways for further exploration; (2) the second presents preliminary observations from the fields; (3) the third presents the relevant anthropological approaches and concepts, including railway ethnography, the politics of infrastructure and the technology of imagination; and (4) the fourth discusses the research tools and contributions of studying infrastructure ethnographically. The author then concludes by reflecting on the methodology and social intervention in the field.

In Chapter Six, Pinkaew Luangaramsri argues that Special Economic Zones (SEZs) play a key role in China's BRI. While massive connective infrastructure (including highways, fiber optic cables, railroads, oil and gas pipelines, ports, and airports) has been developed throughout Eurasia and Africa, its nodes of control have frequently morphed into SEZs. And Chinese funded special economic zones are often much more than nodes of political and economic power that serve China's strategic purpose in the region. Some BRI infrastructure projects have produced "shadow zones": an economic frontier where an obscure regulatory regime seeks to dissolve existing ecologies and social order to make way for a new form of unruly resource extraction and capital accumulation.

In line with the state-corporate crime concept (Whyte 2014, Ciocchini and Greener 2023), the author offers structural analysis of the impact of contemporary Chinese capitalism. To the author, understanding the harms of accumulation requires an analysis of the dynamic relations between the powerful Chinese state, regimes of permission in autocratic states of Southeast Asia, and the interests of corporations and subversive economy investors. In this analysis, the author unravels the cooperative and synergetic relationship between state power and corporations in the production of harm. Using case studies of Shwe Kokko SEZ and the recycling industry in the hinterland of the Eastern Economic Corridor (EEC), this paper argues that the proliferation of illegal and unhealthy economic activities in various zones operated by Chinese capital must not be viewed as isolated aberrations of China's growing economy in the region. The rise of shadow zones is rather a response to changing regional and global geopolitics in which the Chinese state is a key actor. These emerging zones are characterized by the following features. First, deploying the allure of infrastructure to mobilize capital, people, and socio-economic networks is concomitant with the creation of the zone. Second, the alchemy of sovereignty involving the various forms of frontier sovereignty that bend and suspend the rule of law has blurred the boundary between legal and illegal. Third is the "destructive economy" that benefits originators and their alliance network while causing drastic health, environmental, and economic damage, and turning the area into a hub of organized crime.

The paper offers an analysis of state-corporate power in Southeast Asia through the cases of two SEZs. While the two case studies may not be generalizable for a holistic understanding of China's BRI, the concept of shadow zones has shown that a certain set of dynamics around state power and the formation of circuits of extraction is characteristic of BRI accumulation in Southeast Asia. The case studies do offer a tentative generalization: Corporate profiteering takes a more harmful and unfettered formation in countries with regimes of permission riven with chronic problems of corrupted political processes. This conceptual framework reconnects locally experienced dispossession, injustice, ecological harm, and violence with the specific network of corporations and state capacities constructing neo-colonial resource extraction, exploitation, and capital accumulation.

Ta-wei Chu, in Chapter Seven, presents a literature review of China's BRI in Myanmar to demonstrate the limited explanatory value of state-centric frameworks. Chu argues that China has not been a unitary actor. On the contrary, China's state transformation has been fragmented, decentralized, and internationalized. In the late 1970s, China shifted from Maoist state socialism to state-led capitalism. The central government dispersed authority to numerous (often overlapping) agencies, ministries, and quasi-independent regulators. The result was a shift away from a top-down system of government towards a Chinese-style regulatory state model. In the regulatory-state model, China's party-state leadership offers vague hints and broadly semantic slogans instead of orders. To a noticeable degree, these actions have fragmented the political and governance system in China's party-state apparatus largely because many agencies now have overlapping jurisdictions. For example, eleven high-ranking government bodies get to oversee the country's oceanic and energy policies. What is more, these bodies have competed fiercely for budgets, power and resources while promoting and pursuing mutually incompatible goals.

Oftentimes, decentralization and internationalization are seen as the twin approaches to present China's state transformation. The central government decentralized power and resource control by delegating the making and implementation of policies to provincial governments. Provincial governments can seal international agreements, and they have fiscal authority. Thus, provincial governments in China have considerable interpretive leeway in their local application of foreign policy. This expression has been exemplified by the regional economic initiative Greater Mekong Subregion (GMS), water diplomacy in the Mekong, South China Sea policy, and the BRI. China is now a federal system characterized by constant bargaining between governmental tiers.

China's regulatory state has also impacted on state-owned enterprises (SOE). The central leadership's direct control of SOEs has reduced despite its continuing ability to influence them through personnel appointments, resource distribution, and policing malfeasance. In this light, SOEs, like provincial governments, have space to interpret the vague and broad slogans. This has inadvertently transformed SOEs into quasi-autonomous profit-seeking firms. Particularly after China's participation in the GMS in 1992 and its initiation of the "going out" strategy in 2000, SOEs have sought overseas markets. The internationalization of SOEs has given rise to new regulatory systems that focus on transnational economic expansion. More and more Chinese SOEs have pursued their own interests without considering China's national interests. The reckless behavior of some SOEs has become a major issue in their project-recipient countries, sometimes souring relations between the recipient country and the Chinese state. This is especially the case when SOEs withdraw from projects that cannot guarantee sufficient profits for the SOEs. In short, China's SOEs *do not* necessarily represent the Chinese state's interests. In Myanmar, the Ministry of Foreign Affairs, and high-ranking political leaders are involved with the Chinese SOEs in the BRI projects. Given the nature of China's regulatory governance, they have acted according to their own interests.

China's state transformation has problematized the argument that the BRI is Chinese grand strategy. First, some SOEs have withdrawn and discontinued their overseas projects, and some SOE-invested projects have caused tensions between China and the recipient states (from Europe to Africa). Chinese SOEs are the main Chinese actors to undertake BRI projects; therefore, if an SOE proves unwilling to implement a BRI project or if the SOE's preferred investments pose a threat to China's foreign relations, the Chinese government is unlikely to achieve its grand strategy, let alone challenge the Western-dominated world system. Second, the BRI has been fraught with vague and rhetorical slogans like "mutual benefit," "China dream," and "a community of shared destiny." Various involved ministries, provincial governments, policy banks, universities and think tanks have been contesting resources and funding. Thus, the fragmented BRI governance reflects that the BRI has not been a top-down sophisticated grand strategy but is instead an incoherent and inconsistent system.

This paper argues that a proper and rigorous analytical framework is needed to treat both China and Myanmar (and other partners in the BRI projects) as fractured actors. The involved actors (comprising SOEs, the Ministry of Foreign Affairs, and central leadership in China and the military junta, ethnic armed groups, and local communities in Myanmar) have used the BRI projects to maintain or enhance their interests and power. A fractured-actor framework reflects the nature of the BRI: It is not a sophisticated, top-down, and cohesive strategy, but is instead fraught with power struggles. The outcomes of these power struggles can shed light on why some projects could be re-launched (for example, the Letpadaung copper mining) and re-branded (for example, the Myitsone Dam), while other projects are sluggish (for example, the Kyaukphyu-Kunming Railway (KKR) and the Kyaukphyu Special Economic Zone (KSEZ). The fractured-actor framework can accommodate different actors' interaction, and it can deepen our understanding of the BRI projects in Myanmar.

Moreover, an effective analysis of the BRI in Myanmar must go beyond state-centrism. The Westphalian notion and hedging strategy would not provide a comprehensive understanding of the BRI projects in Myanmar, mainly because they limit analyses to the national level. One way to address this analytical problem is to transcend mono-disciplinary approaches (for example, International Relations). Theories in social science disciplines like anthropology, geography, and sociology can help because these theories place individuals and society as the key units of analysis. Integrating different theoretical knowledge from these disciplines can diversify the analytical dimensions of the BRI in Myanmar.

In Chapter Eight, Hong Liu takes the readers to a macro perspective by arguing for the importance of approaching the BRI from the perspectives of political economy and business transnationalism. The paper starts with an overview of recent studies on the BRI in the context of the changing political economy of Southeast Asia while calling for the systemic integration of political economy and business transnationalism approaches to analyzing the BRI. The paper then discusses Singapore's engagement with the BRI, delving into various policy initiatives after the Covid-19 pandemic started affecting the region in 2020. Liu presents two case studies of Sino-Singaporean business transnationalism – Pacific International Lines (PIL) and Nanofilm Technologies International (NTI) – to demonstrate the interweaving roles of the state and ethnicity in the BRI developments in the region. Case studies of Singapore-Chinese businesses operating in China demonstrate how the state, ethnicity, and culture remain crucial to the strategies of Sino-Southeast Asian businesses. In essence, these factors enable the businesses to capitalize on new opportunities and navigate the challenges of technological and geopolitical transformations.

Pacific International Lines (PIL) is a shipping company founded in 1967 by Teo Woon Tiong, who was born in China's Fujian province and relocated to Singapore in 1937. This case study reveals that PIL's entry into the Chinese market and its subsequent success was facilitated by Teo's close relationship with government officials, shipping agents, and customers. In 2017, PIL was ranked 15th among major shipping lines globally based on shipping capacity. During the 2010s, Singapore's competitive business environment, supported by strong and efficient government as well as bilateral and multilateral trade agreements, made the city-state an attractive partner for the BRI. PIL has been directly involved in China's BRI, and the transnational company has expanded its investment in new technologies and cooperation with Chinese companies and SOEs to develop a global supply chain system, linking China's domestic logistics networks with overseas networks.

Nanofilm Technologies International (NTI) was founded in 1999 by Shanghai born Shi Xu and is an example of a successful high-tech company. Shi actively participates in institutionalized social and business networking through the Singapore Huayuan Association (he is a former vice-president), which has been deeply involved in the BRI through institutionalized transnationalism. Formed by China-born professionals in 2001, this association serves as a medium for Chinese migrant businessmen and Singapore-born entrepreneurs. It serves not only to connect members through investment talks, business trips and networking sessions but also to integrate members with local communities through events organized with local People's Association.

These two case studies represent different economic sectors: shipping (PIL) and high technology manufacturing (NTI). Against the backdrop of the BRI, these companies offer flexible operating units through their respective corporate structures. Both companies are based in Singapore and were founded by China-born businessmen. While NTI was formed in the 1990s after China's opening, PIL started operations in 1967. The two companies differ not only in terms of their age, but their ownership and management are also different. NTI is owned and managed by first-generation migrants (or *xinyimin*) from China since the early 1990s, whereas PIL is managed by a second-generation ethnic Chinese businessman born in Singapore.

Liu employs these case studies to highlight the importance of conceptual ideas such as business transnationalism for understanding the BRI, both in Southeast Asia in general and in Singapore in particular. The key argument is: BRI is embedded in the local political economy that is shaped by diaspora business transnationalism in the context of a rising China and complex global geopolitics. The case studies of PIL and NTI demonstrate how the state, ethnicity, and culture remain crucial to the strategies of Singaporean Chinese businesses as they capitalize on new opportunities while navigating technological and geopolitical developments. These case studies reinforce the main characteristics of political transnationalism, showing how businesses continue to be conditioned by political forces. The growth of PIL and NTI enjoyed strategic support provided by the governments of Singapore and China. The state plays a central role in the emerging business transnationalism not only in terms of policy implementation, but the state has also directly participated in the transnational ventures of Chinese companies. Liu argues that business transnationalism is an increasingly important phenomenon that has not been given adequate attention in either international business studies or the transnationalism literature, especially with reference to the Chinese diaspora and their connections to the BRI. This chapter offers a contribution to the growing debates about political economy and business transnationalism in the context of the BRI and China's growing influence in Southeast Asia.

Romyen Kosaikanont, in Chapter Nine, discusses the Mekong Subregional Cooperation Frameworks against the backdrop of US-China rivalry. The purpose of this paper is two-pronged. First, it seeks to examine how the rivalry between China and the US is unfolding in the ASEAN riparian region through case studies of two multilateral cooperations: the Mekong US Partnership and China's Lancang Mekong Cooperation. The second aspect lies in the paper's quest to understand how the subregion can minimize risks while benefitting from this competition. Following China's announcement of the BRI in 2013 and its subsequent upgrade of the Lancang Mekong Cooperation (LMC) in 2016, the US has upgraded their Subregional Engagement of Lower Mekong Initiative to Mekong-US Partnership. The concept of "reciprocal influence" is utilized to explain the geopolitical competition in the Mekong Subregion. Kosaikanont argues that while China, as an emerging power implementing neighboring diplomacy through LMC, can be perceived as a "responsible great power," the US's recent reengagement in the region is a balancing strategy aimed to promote the "universal values" of good governance, the rules-based order, and respect for human rights.

Over the past decade, the development of the Mekong Subregion has been a site of significant geopolitical competition among super and emerging powers. For the US, reengaging with the Mekong Subregion after a long absence since the late 1990s is intended to contain China's influences among its neighbors. This is accomplished through close collaboration between the new Mekong US Partnership, extra regional partners, and the Mekong Subregion countries towards a vision of a better connected and economically integrated subregion. This initiative deliberately excludes China from the cooperation.

China, in contrast, is engaging in the region through the Lancang Mekong Cooperation. Although LMC self-presents as a comprehensive development cooperation framework, the author argues that one of China's objectives is to be perceived as a "responsible great power" engaged in a civilizing mission to develop all aspects of lives in the Mekong Subregion. By offering an alternative development model, China seeks to prove that it is possible to embrace China's peaceful rise.

As the Ayeyarwady-Chao Phraya-Mekong Economic Cooperation Strategy (ACMECS) is the only Mekong subregional cooperation framework comprising all five-member countries

– Thailand, Myanmar, Laos, Cambodia, and Vietnam – it is perceived to be a possible connector and agenda setter for the subregion. Using "reciprocal influence" as a concept with the cooperation framework as the smallest unit of analysis, the shared agenda with Mekong centrality can be seen as a way to respond to the US-China rivalry. The strategy could involve one of the following approaches, namely hedging, engagement, balancing or bandwagoning. This paper argues that the Mekong Subregion and its member states are not passive but are in fact negotiating for reciprocal influence to maximize the benefits of the geopolitical competition.

On the one hand, if the BRI can improve connectivity with infrastructural development for the Southeast Asia region, then the gigantic project presents an enormous economic opportunity. If China's foreign policy aims to create a stable external environment for domestic economic growth, then participation from countries in Southeast Asia is pivotal to the success or failure of China's ambitious undertaking. On the other hand, if smaller countries are ensnared into dependent relations with China, huge challenges arise. Recent disputes over the implementation of BRI between China and other Southeast Asian countries show that China should not assume that growth through infrastructure investments is an equally applicable economic imperative everywhere.

China's BRI is not only about infrastructural development around building railways, special economic zones, and seaports. The BRI brings opportunities in trade, engineering, agribusiness, and finance. Nonetheless, it also poses serious and fundamental challenges to the world economic order and international legal framework, in relation to both commercial and political disputes. The BRI also impacts foreign policy. Many Southeast Asian countries face a dilemma of being eager to both participate in China's BRI and maintain their status as traditional US allies.

They are often unsure how to make the next move and which superpower to side with on controversial issues, such as the South China Sea, military alliances, and global trade wars. After decades of neoliberal economic reform at home and a "going out" policy approach to the global economy during the late 1990s, China is again at a crossroads, asking itself where it might be heading. It is certain that BRI is central to President Xi's plans to geographically rebalance China's economy and global standing. Perhaps China will not alter the BRI's trajectory in response to criticism and feedback from its neighbors. However, Beijing should take note of how countries across Southeast Asia are reacting to the BRI and respond to their concerns. The challenge for China going forward as a responsible global power is as much about winning hearts and minds as it is showering foreign aid.

But before we can draw any conclusions about the risks or benefits, prospects or challenges of the BRI, projects and activities must be fully and systematically studied. This book offers critical suggestions about certain concepts and methodologies to help make sense of China's BRI and its impact on Southeast Asia. First, among other things, this book recommends that China's BRI should be examined through a variety of perspectives, including transnational political economy, development studies, non-state centricity, state-corporate crime, an ontological turn, and geopolitical competition approaches. Second, the method that differentiates our work from other BRI studies is a multi-sited ethnography, the in-depth qualitative process of exploring how people navigate the complexity of maintaining ordinary lives in the context of socio-economic, political, and institutional changes brought about by BRI projects. Third, it argues for a research methodology that focuses on the implications of project implementation: the economic and political costs and benefits of projects on the ground. These foci should lead us to heed the voices and perspectives of the local people.

References

Blanchard, Jean-Marc F. (2021) Belt and Road Initiative (BRI) Blues: Powering BRI research back on track to avoid choppy seas. *Journal of Chinese Political Science*, 26: 235–255.

Camba, Alvin (2020) The Sino-centric capital export regime: State-backed and flexible capital in the Philippines. *Development and Change*, 51(4): 970–997. DOI: 10.1111/dech.12604.

Camba, Alvin (2021) The unintended consequences of national regulations: Large-scale-small-scale relations in Philippine and Indonesian nickel mining. *Resources Policy*, 74: 102213.

Camba, Alvin (2022) How Chinese firms approach investment risk: Strong leaders, cancellation, and pushback. *Review of International Political Economy*, 29(6): 2010–2035.

Ciocchini, Pablo and Joe Greener (2023) Regimes of extreme permission in Southeast Asia: Theorizing state-corporate crime in the Global South. *The British Journal of Criminology*, 63(5): 1309–1326.

Marcus, George E. (1995) Ethnography in/of the World System: The emergence of multi-sited ethnography. *Annual Review of Anthropology*, 24: 95–117.

Spivak, Gayatri Chakravorty (1988) Can the Subaltern Speak? In Cary Nelson and Lawrence Grossberg (eds) *Marxism and the Interpretation of Culture*. Basingstoke: Macmillan, pp. 271–313.

Tritto, Angela and Alvin Camba (2023) The Belt and Road Initiative in Southeast Asia: A mixed methods examination. *Journal of Contemporary China*, 32(141): 436–454.

Whyte, David (2014) Regimes of permission and state-corporate crime. *State Crime*, 3: 237–246.

1 Anthropology of Regionalization, Multi-sited Ethnography, and Voice Approach in BRI Research

Yos Santasombat and Kian Cheng LEE

Abstract

The Belt and Road Initiative (BRI), a flagship foreign policy effort of President Xi Jinping, could potentially strengthen the world economic order, reshape global networks of trade, transport, and political ties within and between countries for decades to come. But since its inception, the BRI has been shrouded in confusion and controversy. The Covid-19 pandemic in the early 2020s presented new challenges for understanding the BRI. Drawing insights from an extensive literature review and our continuing empirical investigation of BRI projects in various Southeast Asian countries, this paper outlines a conceptual and methodological experiment to map and analyze the dynamics and implications of China's BRI, its growing international influence, its economic development trajectory, and its impact on socio-economic and cultural realities on the ground.

Keywords

China's BRI – anthropology of regionalization – multi-sited ethnography – voice approach

Introduction

This paper proposes a methodological experiment in the anthropology of regionalization (with special emphasis on processes of

Southeast Asian regionalism) that concerns the adaptation of ethnographic practices to larger and more complex objects of study (Marcus 1995) while at the same time engaging the voice approach that allows marginalized subalterns to speak (Spivak 1988). Against the backdrop of China's BRI expansion, ethnography must adapt from the conventional single-site fieldwork to multiple sites of observation that cross-cut distinctions such as the local and regional/global contexts. China's BRI cannot be thoroughly investigated by focusing on a single site of intensive observation. Our research develops instead an approach that acknowledges mega-concepts and narratives of China's redesigning regionalism and world order (Li 2019), traces cultural patterns across and within multiple sites of BRI megaprojects, and reconceptualizes aspects of BRI itself through the connections it suggests among different projects in Southeast Asia.

The term 'multi-sited ethnography' refers to a mode of research which collapses the distinction between a local site and the global system. Researchers identify systemic realities in situated local sites and study the BRI system directly on the ground. This requires a willingness to leave behind the bounded field-site and follow the thing (production), the metaphor, the plot, the conflict, the people, and their stories as they travel from place to place and move between different media. Through these modes of construction, multi-sited ethnography allows us to engage with large-scale entities such as BRI projects without losing the intimate portrayal of people's experiences and subjectivities. Designing BRI's multi-sited ethnographic research involves a search for *cultural logics* and *strategies of connection*, associations that are constituted within sites of the BRI system – states, markets, industries, media, and situated local communities.

This conceptual paper is organized as follows. The next section provides a literature review to problematize previous approaches to analyzing China's BRI, the participating countries and issues. Subsequently, this paper proposes a method for mitigating the research gaps through a conceptualization of the anthropology of regionalization where new analytic lenses of multi-sited ethnography, tracing connections, and listening to local voices are proposed. Finally, this paper concludes with an invitation to broaden the research methodology.

Problematizing existing approaches to BRI

This section problematizes previous approaches to BRI by way of a review of literature directly and explicitly related to the BRI. Of course, this review is hardly exhaustive given the burgeoning literature on the BRI in Southeast Asia and the rest of the world. Nonetheless, we attempt to organize this review according to the following categories: global perspectives, thematic perspectives, Southeast Asia (SEA) regional perspectives, and individual Southeast Asian (SEA) countries' perspectives. We conclude this section with a summary of the problematics and their implications to the development of our research methodology.

Global perspectives

We begin this literature review by considering China's BRI from a global perspective. To begin, the edited book entitled *Mapping China's 'One Belt One Road' Initiative* argues that China's BRI has been an open diplomatic invitation extended to all continents without neglecting any regions (Li 2019: 287). Rooted in an international economy approach, the book seeks to provide an overview of how the emerging world order will continue to take-on Chinese characteristics, albeit via complex, heterogeneous, continuous struggles, adjustments, and tensions (Li 2019: 24). Yet, the book admits a limitation in its own approach, which is using a uniform way to look at BRI-recipient countries, such as Central and Eastern European countries (Pavlićevic 2019: 272). This reduces the sharpness in appreciating particularistic distinctions across different national and local contexts. Hence, there is a need for "more methodological rigor" (Pavlićevic 2019: 273) in the study of the relationships between China's BRI and its recipient countries.

Sevilla's article titled "China's New Silk Route Initiative" discusses the political and economic implications of China's BRI for the Middle East and Southeast Asia (Sevilla 2017). In a promising note, Sevilla argues that China's BRI can facilitate trade transactions between Middle East countries with Europe, Asia and the Pacific despite the fierce competition posed by US, Europe and Russia to protect their interests in the Middle East, and the bilateral challenges posed by ASEAN countries' wariness towards China (Sevilla 2017: 105–106). Sevilla incisively delineates the different perceptions of Middle East and ASEAN countries towards China. The Middle Eastern countries, he argues, do not perceive any aggressive military intentions, viewing the BRI purely in terms of business activity and anticipating that China's increased presence in the region might position it to serve as a mediator in regional conflicts (Sevilla 2017: 89). The ASEAN countries, in contrast, are concerned that China's real intention may be much less benign, concerns that have been aggravated by sensationalized media and misinformation (Sevilla 2017: 91). While Sevilla's neat delineation and juxtaposition of geo-economic advantages and regional political dilemmas is commendable, the article might have inadvertently fallen into regional homogenization as well as territorial-based dichotomization. Therefore, it behooves us to adopt a methodology that examines differentiated, situated and connected local contexts while transcending traditional nation-state boundaries.

In "China's 'New Silk Roads'," Summers (2016) approaches the BRI from the perspectives of sub-national regions and networks of global political economy. Challenging the assumption that the BRI arose as a "geopolitical and diplomatic offensive" to extend China's political power and influence, Summers argues that the "silk roads" vision has its roots in sub-national ideas and practices (Summers 2016: 1628). Contra to perceiving it as a geopolitical maneuver, Summers ingeniously shows how China's BRI has emerged from a sub-national policy framework with a developmental mindset that is likened to an "omnibus program" supporting a wide-ranging set of policy goals (Summers 2016: 1639). Methodologically, this article traces the historical ideological underpinnings of BRI; however, we reckon that it falters in not tracing the dynamic transnational connections between people, places and products through variegated ethnographic case studies. Moreover, Zhou and Esteban (2018), in "Beyond Balancing: China's approach towards the Belt and Road Initiative," perceive the BRI as a strategic vehicle for softly countering the United States so as to move China from a "rule-taker" to a "rule-maker" status in the international order (Zhou and Esteban 2018: 487). Debunking the notion of a "China threat," the authors argue that the BRI engages in regional multilateralism to build coalitions and establish its legitimacy in pursuing "peaceful development" with the related countries (Zhou and Esteban 2018: 497–499). However, the article is China-centric and suffers from the absence of the multi-scalar voices from BRI-recipient countries.

Gabuev's (2016) "Crouching Bear, Hidden Dragon" metaphorically depicts the continuous jostling for power and influence between Beijing and Moscow in Central Asia while revealing the potential for mutual accommodation between BRI and the Eurasian Economic Union (EEU). Gabuev (2016: 61) identified the Chinese limiting factors as "top-down decision-making processes," "low involvement of the business community," and "China's preference to deal with states bilaterally." We surmise that our research methodology should respond to these paradigmatic gaps through deeper ethnographic work with voices from below. Finally, Rolland's (2017) "China's 'Belt and Road Initiative'" poses the question of whether BRI is overrated or a real game-changer. He argues that the BRI, as an important instrument in China's grand strategy, aims to solve China's fundamental geopolitical challenge and that this process will be impeded if Western scholars and policy-makers fail to comprehend the broader vision underpinning the BRI (Rolland 2017: 136). Hence, we contend that previous research has tended to make observations in isolation and has thus failed to see important connections between constituent components and the bigger picture.

In summary, this review of the literature on global perspectives establishes that BRI research has tended to fixate on the following: a uniformity in perspective, regional homogenization, territorial-based dichotomization, China-centricity, a top-down state-centric approach, and an overly narrow focus.

Thematic perspectives

This subsection reviews BRI-related literature from a thematic perspective. Tambo et al. (2019) look at China's BRI through the lens of public health measures' contributions to global economic growth and shared prosperity. They highlight the BRI's potential to both directly and indirectly impact development pertaining to health in more than 65 countries across Asia, Southeast Asia, the Middle East, Africa, and Europe (Tambo et al. 2019: 49). However, its bold claims on the value of the BRI's public health initiatives remain confined to a state-centric and institution-oriented framework.

On the theme of security and economy, Hallgren and Ghiasy (2017) present three country case studies – Belarus, Myanmar and Uzbekistan – to demonstrate how China engages in security cooperation and note that the three cases are not uniform (Hallgren and Ghiasy 2017: 1). The selection of geographically-diverse case studies provides a convincing account of distinct responses to complex economic and security challenges. Nonetheless, while attempting to assess local and cross-border security dynamics, they fail to go beyond structural state-centricity (Hallgren and Ghiasy 2017:1).

On the theme of the BRI's economic impact, Iqbal, Rahman and Sami (2019) opine that the diverse economic benefits delivered by the BRI throughout the world include trade, investment, job creation, transportation and other facilities (Iqbal, Rahman and Sami 2019: 15). Though the authors seek to provide an Asian perspective, the methodology is primarily based on analyzing online data (Iqbal, Rahman and Sami 2019: 1), which invariably ignores the voices of the affected economic subjects.

Xiong, Yang, Chen, Shi and Yuan (2019) conduct a thematic investigation of the environmental impact of the BRI with a specific focus on how increased overseas investment in coal power projects precipitated by BRI have created various environmental risks. With case studies of Indonesia and Vietnam, the authors have provided some comparative insights, yet their method was unable to trace the transnational connections between different coal power projects' sites and their environmental-related issues.

Finally, the edited volume entitled *Securing the Belt and Road Initiative* explores the themes of risk assessment, private security and special insurance along the new wave of Chinese outbound investments (Arduino and Gong 2018). It illuminates the inextricable ties between security, economics and governance in China's BRI (Arduino and Gong 2018: 8). While the authors claim to have adopted a holistic approach, we argue that they have not adequately addressed actual on-the-ground "people-to-people bonding" encounters where the Chinese companies, managers, and workers engage with local communities (Arduino and Gong 2018: 8).

From this brief review, we have identified lacunae in confined state-centricity, institution-based fixation, over-dependence on websites for data-collection, lack of transnational linkages, and overlooking the voices of "people-to-people" bonding.

Southeast Asian regional perspectives

This subsection reviews BRI-related literature focusing on Southeast Asia as a region. In "China's offensive in Southeast Asia: Regional architecture and the process of Sinicization," Suehiro (2017: 18) defines Sinicization as an attempt to create a China-led institutional framework and make the region more amenable to Chinese ascent. He carefully articulates the measured manner with which the Chinese have approached Sinicization, highlighting their preparedness to modify their approach in response to changing international circumstances. Suehiro examined the Greater Mekong Subregion Scheme (GMS) and the Nanning-based China-ASEAN (EXPO or CAEXPO) to reveal the caution China exercises as she navigates advancing Sinicization (Suehiro 2017: 129). Unfortunately, the over-emphasis on institutional/ organizational entities ignores the voices of the local people and communities in the recipient states and thus reveals little if anything about their response to the subtle but pervasive process of Sinicization.

Zha's (2018) "In Pursuit of Connectivity: China Invests in Southeast Asian Infrastructure" seeks to rectify the widespread but erroneous perception that the BRI is an extension of China's strategic and political influence. Zha argues that the Chinese government wants to share the infrastructure-related expertise with other countries (Zha 2018: 1). Refuting the accusation that the Hambantota port project in Sri Lanka is a "debt trap," Zha seeks to demonstrate the magnanimous intention of the Chinese company involved by citing its perseverance in building other economically vital projects, such as industrial zones and logistical networks for the local community (Zha 2018: 1). By way of conclusion, Zha exhorts host countries to reciprocate China's magnanimity by assuming responsibility for project financial governance, local labor usage and skills diffusion (Zha 2018: 1). While it is important to ensure the international community is accurately appraised of China's amicable approaches, we contend that Zha's is a one-sided approach that fails to reflect the ebbs and flows of trust in recipient countries, contrary to his own observation that "connectivity is a two-way process" (Zha 2018: 7).

Finally, Gong's (2019) "The Belt & Road Initiative and China's influence in Southeast Asia" argues that BRI has certainly extended Chinese influence in Southeast Asia, but not to the extent of forging a Sinocentric order. The merit of this article is its attempt to provide a self-reflexive Chinese perspective by highlighting the multi-dimensional domestic, regional and international factors confronting and impeding the BRI in Southeast Asia. However, methodologically, we need a closer look at the myriad and fluid socio-cultural interactions that constitute the international relations between China and the region.

Summarizing this sub-section, we noted several problems in the various research methodologies, specifically: an over-emphasis on institutions, organizations and other structured entities; a dearth of local voices from BRI-recipient states; the ebbs and flows of fluctuating perceptions; and social and cultural dimensions behind state-centered international relations.

Individual Southeast Asian countries' perspectives

Many scholars focus on individual countries in Southeast Asia, and their reactions to the BRI. Yeoh, Chang and Zhang (2018), for example, look at trade, investment and cooperation between China and Malaysia in the contexts of China–ASEAN integration and the 21st century Maritime Silk Road Construction (MSR). Exploring the prospects and challenges of China-Malaysia cooperation, Yeoh et al. (2018: 303–304) outline the Persatuan Persahabatan Malaysia–China (PPMC) in Malaysia as an example of "exemplary" people-to-people interactions. However, we contend that although formally a non-governmental organization, the PPMC is nevertheless state-driven, and that the authors' perspective is skewed towards the voices from above, such as the several political leaders they have quoted.

Punyaratabandhu and Swaspitchayaskun (2018) examine the political and economic challenges and opportunities confronting China–Thailand development under the BRI. While arguing that Thailand could become the central hub linking the ASEAN countries to one another and to outside the region, the authors outline what they perceive to be the main challenges facing Thailand: balancing America and Japan, dealing with allied countries in ASEAN, and managing conflicts and sovereignty issues between China and other countries (Punyaratabandhu and Swaspitchayaskun 2018: 333, 340). We note, however, that this state-centric perspective gives no consideration to other BRI-recipient countries or their potential collaboration.

Chen (2018) focuses on the development of Cambodia–China relations and raises concerns that the BRI poses risks to Cambodia's economic autonomy, political stability and national legitimacy (Chen 2018: 371). In a nutshell, Chen recommends that Cambodia seek aid from other countries (Chen 2018: 371) and suggests that China might work to earn Cambodia's respect by shifting focus from financially lucrative infrastructure projects to socially beneficial programs (Chen 2018: 381). While we appreciate Chen's concern that such projects generate tangible benefits for the local community, we criticize the absence of any supporting evidence with voices from below.

Tai and Huang (2018) investigate the Philippines's political and economic relationships with China under the BRI. Their main argument is that the BRI will be severely impeded by Philippines' internal policies, unstable political situation, and her strong relations with other powerful countries (Tai and Huang 2018: 367). Apart from revealing structural and institutional constraints, we problematize the article's failure to consider the local and transnational social actors, which limits understanding of BRI-related issues.

In contrast, Soong and Nguyen (2018) argue that Vietnam's economic interests in China's BRI must be offset against various political and security risks. Like several of the articles mentioned above, the authors suggest that Vietnam should enjoy the emergent market opportunities offered by the BRI while remaining cautious of the political and security risks (Soong and Nguyen 2018: 342). Methodologically, Soong and Nguyen over-emphasize the role of institutionalized entities, such as the AIIB (Asian Infrastructure Investment Bank), in the complex political positioning of Vietnam in the international arena (Soong and Nguyen 2018: 348).

In "China's OBOR Initiative and Myanmar's Political Economy," Li and Song (2018: 323) argue that Myanmar does not understand China's BRI, although it expects to benefit. The authors juxtapose perspectives to show how the BRI can serve both as an economic opportunity and a threat to Myanmar's national sovereignty and security (Li and Song 2018: 318). However, they do not consider how transnational mobile actors traversing between Myanmar and other countries contribute to the dilemma.

Kiik (2016) seeks to draw perspectives from nationalism and anti-ethno-politics to explain why "Chinese development" failed at Myanmar's Myitsone Dam. Our critique is that the author focuses solely on the ethnic Kachin group, and relations between the Kachin state, the Myanmar national government, and the Chinese government, while neglecting to consider the views of other ethnic groups related to the Myitsone Dam case. Furthermore, the failure to observe transnational ethnic connections ironically leaves the author subject to his own critique of China's "state-centric paradigm when facing foreign social worlds" (Kiik 2016: 374).

The review in this sub-section highlights the following research gaps: one-sided representation of voices from above; imbalanced China-centric perspectives; a neglect of mobile local and transnational social actors; over-emphasis on institutionalized entities; and a narrow and limited focus of ethnic representations.

Summary and implications to research methodology

To reiterate, this modest literature review is not exhaustive of the burgeoning literature related to China's BRI. Nevertheless, the succinct summaries of the four sub-sections above have identified the following problematics with BRI-related research: (1) a homogenized perspective of the region; (2) a territorial or nation-state bounded perspective that limits analysis and is prone to dichotomization; (3) over-emphasis on online data and institutions that drowns out social and cultural voices; and (4) over reliance on top-down voices. Given these limitations, we propose a research methodology that considers a balanced representation of voices from-above and from-below across multiple sites while recognizing that the success or failure of BRI projects is determined by dynamic interactions between a diverse array of self-interested actors that is not reducible to states, institutions, or geo-political boundaries.

Beyond the literature reviewed above, we posit that our research methodology can also be distinguished from other recent qualitative research studies. For instance, Camba (2020: 973) interviewed the "Philippine elites, members of the bureaucracy and civil society organizations ... members of the Chinese embassy in the Philippines, representatives of SOEs and private firms of different sizes" to explore how China's crisis of over-accumulation led to a Sino-centric capital export regime; among other things, Camba notes that Chinese investors began seeking opportunities in new territories with cheaper labor and resources. While Camba (2020: 992) is to be commended for exposing the illicit flow of flexible capital through focusing on the Chinese state and major private firms, our research extends the sociological elucidation of diverse impacts by adopting a multi-sited perspective. This methodology is supported by a corpus of literature reporting the findings of multi-sited qualitative research.

For example, Camba conducted multi-sited fieldwork in the Philippines and Indonesia, interviewing the "representatives of large-scale mining firms, local government officials, ASM [artisanal and small miners], local mayors, Chinese investors, and community representatives" (Camba 2021: 2). Camba also demonstrated how national regulations produced unintended consequences generated by the corresponding large-scale-small-scale relations in nickel mining of both countries, albeit in different forms. In another example, Camba conducted interviews with elite "Chinese firm representatives, presidential advisors, senators, parliamentarians, party members, oligarchs, Chinese ministry officials and embassy representatives, and think tanks of various countries" (Camba 2022: 2012). Though the fieldwork was based across "Metro Manila, Hong Kong, Singapore, Kuala Lumpur, and Jakarta," the focus was "the perception of Chinese elites toward the Southeast Asian leaders, as well as how Southeast Asian leaders reacted to the

Chinese actors" (Camba 2022: 2012). Finally, Tritto and Camba analyzed the volume of Chinese investments employed through in-depth interviews with "business executives, leaders of business associations, consultants, Chinese banks, and policy makers" across Indonesia, Malaysia, the Philippines, and Myanmar (2023: 437) and concluded that Chinese capital investments through BRI are heterogeneous as they are dependent on host country dynamics and interests (Tritto and Camba 2023: 450). However, while these examples can be commended for transcending geographical localities, our research attempts to go beyond approaches seeking to provide a singular coherent explanation for the different outcomes of the diverse cases being compared. Through tracing the lines of human and non-human mobilities and connecting the dots or nexuses of social, political, economic and cultural interactions, our research methodology seeks to reveal the interconnections between the different embedded actors and agencies across multiple and diverse sites.

Conceptualizing the anthropology of regionalization

Having problematized the prevailing approaches to China's BRI and its impacts on recipient countries, we turn now to an attempt to mitigate the identified research problematics through conceptualizing an anthropology of regionalization. We begin by pondering the genesis of the BRI in China's turn towards being an entrepreneurial state encouraging entrepreneurial selves. Then we examine a range of conceptual apparatuses with the potential to adequately compare and contrast complex social contexts by tracing connections through a versatile multi-sited ethnographic research orientation. Finally, we re-situate the dynamic interactions between the BRI and ASEAN identity while accentuating the saliency of the voice approach.

Entrepreneurial state, entrepreneurial self

In 1973, the renowned American sociologist Daniel Bell described a new post-industrial society dominated by the regime of management. Five years later China embraced free market neoliberalism and marked the birth of a new socialism aiming at governance of the state, economy, and science by an expert elite. Since the early 1980s, China has experienced rapid economic growth while its leadership principles evolved from communism to state-led capitalism. Management rationality permeates virtually all spheres of social life (Nadai and Maeder 2005: 7). Managerial thinking culminates in the entrepreneurial state; a culmination of rationalities and strategies for ruling others and the self. With the ascendance of Xi Jinping and the fifth generation of CCP leadership in 2013, managerialism characterizes the entrepreneurial self who rationalizes his or her life according to market imperatives and knows how to search for and seize available opportunities. The prevalence of this way of thinking drastically expands the ranks of urban professionals, for whom knowledge, expertise, adaptability, flexibility and mobility are prerequisites for success.

This managerialism provides the cultural logic of deploying the BRI to expand China's connections with the emergent world order. In the context of Southeast Asian regionalism, the BRI raises several questions: To what extent is this cultural logic applicable in different social contexts and integration platforms? Who is affected by this cultural logic and how has it manifested and been transformed in the process of implementation and expansion? In what ways are Southeast Asian regionalism and strategic stability enhanced or hindered by the BRI?

Comparisons, contrasts, and similarities

To address the questions above, we propose a methodological experiment in the anthropology of regionalization, adapting ethnographic practices to large and complex objects of study. Our multi-sited ethnographic methodology is comparative by nature, but it is more than that. As Marcus (1995: 102) noted, conventional comparisons in traditional ethnography "are generated for homogeneously conceived conceptual units;" one compares communities, locales, and peoples looking for contrasts and similarities. In multi-sited ethnographic research, the object of study is inherently fragmented and differently situated, and the comparisons take the form of juxtapositions of phenomena that have conventionally been treated as worlds apart. For example, our research analyzes Special Economic Zones (SEZs) through four ethnographic case studies (Kyaukphyu, Shwe Kokko, EEC, and Mong Cai) in three Southeast Asian countries (Myanmar, Thailand and Vietnam). We also study the effects of constructing high-speed rail links through case studies in four countries (Laos, Thailand, Vietnam and Malaysia). Our research objective is to elucidate the BRI's impact on Southeast Asia, so we studied many sites to distinguish regional/local variations. Comparing the findings from the different sites served to produce detailed pictures of similar processes in different places, which should in turn provide answers to other questions, the pieces of a puzzle being put together to form a more complete picture. Since the object of the study spans more than one social world, it cannot be reconstructed by exploring only one site. Thus, a multi-sited ethnographic approach is indispensable.

Our research treats the local and regional sites as interconnected rather than viewing them as distinct spheres or dimensions. Every ethnography of the BRI is an ethnography of the system. In contrast to conventional ethnography's focus on a single locale, multi-sited ethnography maps connections and linkages at the regional level. The basic methodology is to compare and contrast the data collected through observations and engagement from multiple sites. Continued attentiveness and engagement in the details of everyday life, listening, participating, feeling, and discovering become incredibly important.

Marcus (1995) proposed several "following" techniques for conducting multi-sited ethnographic research, most notably "follow the people" (pioneered by Malinowski 1922), which has found applications in migration studies (Grasmuk and Pessar 1991), diaspora studies (Rouse 1991; Yos 2022), and cultural studies (Gupta and Ferguson 1992).

"Follow the thing" is an extensively used ethnographic technique for constructing a multi-sited study environment. Broad general patterns can be identified by following the movement of objects, rights, and interactions (Malinowski 1922; Wallerstein 1991). Appadurai (1986) presented a template for using this strategy to identify systemic connections through ethnographic and speculative studies of the movement of objects in and through environments (Miller 1994; Mintz 1985). The multi-sited technique has been used most explicitly in tracing artistic works and influences, documenting the evolution of indigenous artworks (Myers 1992), emerging music genres (Feld 1994), and cultural preferences (Savigliano 1995; Silverman 1986). Latour's (1987; 1988). Mapping of people, machines, and creatures on the same plane of examination is among the most significant works that follow a research topic across numerous fields.

"Follow the metaphor" refers to tracing the "circulation of signs, symbols, and metaphors" that construct social correlates and ground associations in ethnographic research into language use, and its documentation in print, visual, and electronic media. One of the most significant benefits of this method is that when it applies complexity theory to a discursive organization, metaphorical linkages can be discovered. Some examples of this include knowledge creation, governmental institutions, and economic regulation (Martin 1994). Such an approach can identify potential locations of cultural production for ethnographic research to discover empirical connections between sites in the evolving landscapes of accumulation, circulation, and exchange.

"Follow the plot, tale, or allegory" is a strategy that involves recreating situated social environments in multiple sites from a single-sited framework (Brooks 1984). Many narratives heard during fieldwork at a single site can serve as a heuristic for constructing multi-sited ethnographic research. Such narratives and plots are rich sources of connections, associations, and suggested relationships for shaping research objectives. This method has found fresh life in studies of social memory that record disputes over collective definitions of reality (Boyarin 1994). Identifying a plot and comparing it to the ethnographic data from sites identified from a captivating story is an intriguing, mostly unexplored technique of organizing multi-sited research.

"Follow the life or biography" favors life tales. Biographies can provide ethnographic data for multi-sited research to produce and develop life histories. Life histories reveal changes in social contexts through a succession of narrated individual experiences. They can offer guidelines for delineating ethnographic spaces within systems shaped by categorical distinctions. Unexpected or novel associations that shape spaces, sites, and social contexts can be discovered in life history accounts.

"Follow the conflict" or the parties to conflicts is another means of mapping a multi-sited terrain for ethnographic research, mostly confined to research in the anthropology of law. In small-scale societies, this has been an established technique ("the extended case method") in the anthropology of law. This technique is more commonly used in the more complex public spheres found in contemporary society. The collection of studies edited by Sarat and Kearns (1993) includes excellent examples of inherently multi-sited work. Conflicts, disputes, and protest movements are also fundamental phenomena discussed in development studies and anthropology of environmentalism.

BRI, ASEAN identity, and voice approach

Regionalism is a reaction to global developments. Regions are not naturally given but are "dynamic settings for social interaction" (Söderbaum 2012: 18). As Hettne argues, regions "are created and recreated in the process of global transformation" (Hettne 1999: xv). This project examines Southeast Asia as a constructed region for conceptual analysis because of its relatively greater strategic significance for the Chinese state than elsewhere in the Global South (Bräutigam 2011; Gallagher and Porzecanski 2010). The following features have made Southeast Asia critically important to China: geographical proximity, gateway position linking the Pacific and Indian Oceans, transport hub, energy supply, resources for sustainability (long-term economic growth and prevention of external influence), ethnic Chinese connections, and projection of Beijing's positive global image and soft power (Lim et al 2017: 187–188). However, as our project transcends the geographical boundaries of state sovereignty, we have not sought to examine the specific details in each country of Southeast Asia. Instead, our researchers have examined the multi-scalar implications of projects and issues – nationally, transnationally, regionally, and globally. This is why we do not focus exclusively on either mainland or maritime Southeast Asia but include countries from both. Regions are intersubjective creations that connect identity and space; they are not fixed, but continuously produced and reproduced. The production of regional identities is a contest over contending images and meanings of the region. Hence, we view Southeast Asian regionalism and its organizations (such as ASEAN, AEC) as historically evolved constructs of specific political, economic, and social relations. The socially constructed perspective emphasizes the norms and values, shared practices, and beliefs that hold a region together.

Regional identity can be defined as "regional attachment, belonging or collective consciousness" (Zimmerbauer 2011: 246), but it is often established by supranational actors with vested interests in creating a regional image. Before establishing ASEAN in 1967, the countries of Southeast Asia had tried several times to establish organizations to promote regional integration and security under the guidance of the United States. These included, among others, the Southeast Asia Treaty Organization (SEATO) in 1954, the Association of Southeast Asia (ASA) in 1961, and MAPHILINDO, a group comprising Malaysia, the Philippines and Indonesia in 1963. Each set out to strengthen relations between countries in the region and to promote cooperation in security, economics, science, and culture.

Following the collapse of the Soviet Union in the early 1990s and China's rapid ascent as a global power, however, Beijing has taken advantage of the new regionalism, becoming a skilled practitioner of "commercial diplomacy" (Frost 2005: 95) to offset regional security anxieties with promises of economic cooperation (trade, investment, foreign aid), regionalization and global connectivity. Over the past decade, ASEAN's regional focus shifted from security to trade, investment, and increasing economic "connectivity" with China through the BRI. By the 2010s, ASEAN was celebrating connectivity as integral to building and strengthening the regional community. The organization perceived greater connectivity in terms of infrastructure, institutions and interpersonal relations to be essential for achieving its objectives of a more competitive and resilient region. Connectivity improves the lives of ASEAN citizens by enhancing economic and social development and thus providing more opportunities and boosting prosperity.

Importantly, however, this perception of an interconnected regional image may be more prevalent in China and among business investors than to the other sectors and inhabitants of the region. For example, although BRI projects provide opportunities for Southeast Asian businesses to profit and governments to build new infrastructure and improve connectivity, many local communities are experiencing displacement, relocation, and uncertainty. In Thailand for instance, although improved connectivity allows farmers to engage in new opportunities such as raising cattle or improving quality in its export fruit production, it has also increased imports of Chinese agricultural products which, in turn, increases competitive pressure on domestic producers. To investigate the diverse benefits, risks, and challenges experienced by different groups of stakeholders, our approach seeks to raise or amplify the voices of neglected and marginalized peoples. Several communities in northeast Thailand, for example, have raised their voices to protest the design of a high-speed rail project that might negatively impact their livelihoods. Other communities have sought to negotiate relocation plans that would minimize the risk to their livelihoods and security. The voices of local experiences can be polyphonic and ironic, are rarely if ever uniform or transparent. Nevertheless, attention to local voices can be a productive starting point for research that seeks to 'give voice' to the powerless and draw attention to the often ambiguous and contradictory effects that the BRI produces. Our voice approach pays serious attention to the border and in-between places, "conceived as a zone between stable places, since most metropolitan typifications suppress, exclude, even repress border zones" and rural communities (Appadurai 1988: 19).

Concluding remarks

This paper has outlined a methodological experiment in the anthropology of regionalization against the backdrop of China's BRI. To recap, we have criticized prevailing research methodologies for being trapped in homogenizing tendencies, bounded and dichotomizing perspectives, obliterating socio-cultural voices, and an over-reliance on top-down representations. Hence, this paper seeks to contribute to this specialized field within the discipline of international relations with multi-sited ethnography, "follow" metaphor of tracing connections and a comprehensive voice approach that incorporates the neglected actors. We invite readers to embrace holistic research methodologies and recognize the need to examine the many different perspectives on China's BRI.

References

Appadurai, Arjun (1988) Introduction: Place and Voice in Anthropological Theory. *Cultural Anthropology*, 3(1): 16–20.

Appadurai, Arjun (ed.) (1986) *The Social Life of Things: Commodities in Cultural Perspectives*. New York: Cambridge University Press.

Arduino, Alessandro and Gong, Xue (eds.) (2018) *Securing the Belt and Road Initiative: Risk Assessment, Private Security and Special Insurances Along the New Wave of Chinese Outbound Investments*. Singapore: Springer Nature.

Bell, Daniel (1973) *The Coming of Post-industrial Society: A Venture in Social Forecasting*. New York: Basic Books.

Boyarin, Jonathan (1994) Space, Time, and the Politics of Memory. In Jonathan Boyarin (ed.) *Remapping Memory: The Politics of TimeSpace*. Minneapolis: University of Minnesota Press, pp. 1–38.

Bräutigam, Deborah (2011) *The Dragon's Gift: The real story of China in Africa*. Oxford: Oxford University Press.

Brooks, Peter. (1984) *Reading for the Plot: Design and Intention in Narrative*. New York: Knopf.

Camba, Alvin (2020) The Sino-centric capital export regime: State-backed and flexible capital in the Philippines. *Development and Change*, 51(4): 970–997. DOI: 10.1111/dech.12604.

Camba, Alvin (2021) The unintended consequences of national regulations: Large-scale-small-scale relations in Philippine and Indonesian nickel mining. *Resources Policy*, 74: 102213.

Camba, Alvin (2022) How Chinese firms approach investment risk: Strong leaders, cancellation, and pushback. *Review of International Political Economy*, 29(6): 2010–2035.

Chen, Shihlun Allen (2018) The Development of Cambodia–China Relation and Its Transition Under the OBOR Initiative. *The Chinese Economy*, 51(4): 370–382. DOI: 10.1080/10971475.2018.1457317.

Feld, Steven (1994) From Schizophonia to Schismogenesis: On the Discourses and Commodification practices of 'World Music' and 'World Beat.' In Charles Keil and Steven Feld (eds) *Music Grooves*. Chicago: University of Chicago Press, pp. 96–126.

Frost, Stephen (2005) Chinese Outward Direct Investment in Southeast Asia: How big are the flows and what does it mean for the region? *The Pacific Review*, 17(3): 323–340.

Gabuev, Alexander (2016) Crouching Bear, Hidden Dragon: 'One Belt One Road' and Chinese-Russian Jostling for Power in Central Asia. *Journal of Contemporary East Asia Studies*, 5(2): 61–78. DOI: 10.1080/24761028. 2016.11869097.

Gallagher, Kevin P. and Roberto Porzecanski (2010) *The Dragon in the Room: China and the future of Latin American industrialization*. Redwood City: Stanford University Press.

Gong, Xue (2019) The Belt & Road Initiative and China's influence in Southeast Asia. *The Pacific Review*, 32(4): 635–665. DOI: 10.1080/09512748. 2018.1513950.

Grasmuk, Sherri and Patricia R. Pessar (1991) *Between Two Islands: Dominican international migration*. Berkeley: University of California Press.

Gupta, Akhil and James Ferguson (1992) Beyond 'Culture': Space, identity and the politics of difference." *Cultural Anthropology*, 7: 6–23.

Hallgren, Henrik and Richard Ghiasy (2017) Security and Economy on the Belt and Road: Three country case studies. *SIPRI Insights on Peace and Security*, 2017(4): 1–11.

Hettne, Bjorn (1999) The New Regionalism: A prologue. In Bjorn Hettne, Andrus Inotai and Osvaldo Sunkel (eds), *Globalism and the New Regionalism*. New York: St. Martin's Press, pp. xv–xxix.

Iqbal, Badar Alam, Mohd Nayyer Rahman and Shaista Sami (2019) Impact of Belt and Road Initiative on Asian Economies. *Global Journal of Emerging Market Economies*, 11(3): 260–277. DOI:10.1177/0974910119887059.

Kiik, Laur (2016) Nationalism and anti-ethno-politics: why 'Chinese Development' failed at Myanmar's Myitsone Dam. *Eurasian Geography and Economics*, 57(3): 374–402. DOI: 10.1080/15387216.2016.1198265.

Latour, Bruno (1987) *Science in Action*. Cambridge: Harvard University Press.

Latour, Bruno (1988) *The Pasteurization of France*. Cambridge: Harvard University Press.

Li, Chenyang and Shaojun Song (2018) China's OBOR initiative and Myanmar's political economy. *The Chinese Economy*, 51(4): 318–332. DOI: 10.1080/10971475.2018.1457324.

Li, Xing (ed) (2019) *Mapping China's 'One Belt One Road' Initiative*. Springer Nature: Switzerland AG.

Li, Xing (2019) China's Pursuit of the "One Belt One Road" Initiative: A New World Order with Chinese. In Li, Xing (ed.) Mapping China's 'One Belt One Road' Initiative. Springer Nature: Switzerland AG, pp. 1–27.

Li, Xing and Paulo Duarte (2019) Conclusion: The One Belt One Road in the Politics of Fear and Hope. In Li, Xing (ed.) *Mapping China's 'One Belt One Road' Initiative*. Springer Nature: Switzerland AG, pp. 279–289.

Lim, Kheng Swe, Hailong Ju, and Mingjiang Li (2017) China's revisionist aspirations in Southeast Asia and the curse of the South China Sea disputes. *China: An International Journal* 15(1): 187–213.

Malinowski, Bronislaw (1922) *Argonauts of the Western Pacific*. New York: Dutton.

Marcus, George E. (1995) Ethnography in/of the World System: The emergence of multi-sited ethnography. *Annual Review of Anthropology*, 24: 95–117.

Martin, Emily (1994) *Flexible Bodies: Tracing immunity in American culture from the days of polio to the age of Aids*. Boston: Beacon.

Miller, Daniel (1994) *Modernity: An ethnographic approach*. Oxford: Berg.

Mintz, Sidney (1985) *Sweetness and Power: The place of sugar in modern history*. New York: Viking.

Myers, Fred (1992) Representing Culture: The production of discourse (s) for Aboriginal acrylic paintings. In George E. Marcus (ed) *Rereading Cultural Anthropology*. Durham: Duke University Press, pp. 319–355.

Nadai, Eva and Christoph Maeder (2005) Fuzzy Fields: Multi-sited ethnography in sociological research. *Forum Qualitative Sozialforschung / Forum: Qualitative Social Research*, 6(3): Art. 28, http://nbn-resolving.de/urn:nbn:de:0114-fqs0503288.

Pavlićevic, Dragan (2019) A Power Shift Underway in Europe? China's Relationship with Central and Eastern Europe Under the Belt and Road Initiative. In Li, Xing (ed.) *Mapping China's 'One Belt One Road' Initiative*. Springer Nature: Switzerland AG, pp. 249–278.

Punyaratabandhu, Piratorn and Jiranuwat Swaspitchayaskun (2018) The Political Economy of China–Thailand Development Under the One Belt One Road Initiative: Challenges and Opportunities. *The Chinese Economy*, 51(4): 333–341. DOI: 10.1080/10971475.2018.1457326.

Rolland, Nadège (2017) China's 'Belt and Road Initiative': Underwhelming or Game-Changer? *The Washington Quarterly,* 40(1): 127–142. DOI: 10.1080/0163660X.2017.1302743.

Rouse, Roger (1991) Mexican Migration and the Social Space of Postmodernity. *Diaspora* 1: 8–23.

Savigliano, Marta E. (1995) *Tango and the Political Economy of Passion.* Boulder: Westview.

Sarat, Austin and Thomas R. Kearns (eds) (1993) *Law and Everyday Life.* Ann Arbor: University of Michigan Press.

Sevilla Jr., Henelito A. (2017) China's New Silk Route Initiative: Political and Economic Implications for the Middle East and Southeast Asia. *Asian Journal of Middle Eastern and Islamic Studies,* 11(1): 83–106. DOI: 10.1080/25765949.2017.12023327.

Silverman, Debora (1986) *Selling Culture: Bloomingdale's, Diana Vreeland, and the new aristocracy of taste in Reagan's America.* New York: Pantheon.

Söderbaum, Fredrik (2012) Theories of Regionalism. In Mark Beeson and Richard Stubbs (eds) *Routledge Handbook of Asian Regionalism,* Abingdon: Routledge, pp. 11–21.

Soong, Jenn-Jaw and Khac Nghia Nguyen (2018) China's OBOR Initiative and Vietnam's Political Economy: Economic Integration with Political Conflict. *The Chinese Economy,* 51(4): 342–355. DOI: 10.1080/10971475.2018.1457333.

Spivak, Gayatri Chakravorty (1988) Can the Subaltern Speak? In Cary Nelson and Lawrence Grossberg (eds) *Marxism and the Interpretation of Culture.* Basingstoke: Macmillan, pp. 271–313.

Suehiro, Akira (2017) China's offensive in Southeast Asia: Regional architecture and the process of Sinicization. *Journal of Contemporary East Asia Studies,* 6(2): 107–131. DOI: 10.1080/24761028.2017.1391619.

Summers, Tim (2016) China's 'New Silk Roads': Sub-national regions and networks of global political economy. *Third World Quarterly,* 37(9): 1628–1643. DOI: 10.1080/01436597.2016.1153415.

Tai, Wan-Ping and Yang-Fu Huang (2018) Political and Economic Relationships Between China and the Philippines Under the OBOR Initiative. *The Chinese Economy,* 51(4): 356–369. DOI: 10.1080/10971475.2018.1457328.

Tambo, Ernest, Christopher Khayeka-Wandabwac, Grace Wagithi Muchirid, Yun-Na Liu, Shenglan Tang and Xiao-Nong Zhou (2019) China's Belt and Road Initiative: Incorporating public health measures toward global economic growth and shared prosperity. *Global Health Journal* 3(2): 46–49. http://dx.doi.org/10.1016/j.glohj.2019.06.003.

Tritto, Angela and Alvin Camba (2023) The Belt and Road Initiative in Southeast Asia: A mixed methods examination. *Journal of Contemporary China*, 32(141): 436–454.

Wallerstein, Immanuel (1991) *Report on an Intellectual Project: The Fernand Braudel Center, 1976–1991*. Binghamton: Fernand Braudel Center.

Xiong, Minpeng, Xiaowen Yang, Sisi Chen, Fulian Shi and Jiahai Yuan (2019). Environmental Stress Testing for China's Overseas Coal Power Investment Project. *Sustainability*, 11(19), 5506. https://doi.org/10.3390/su11195506

Yeoh, Emile Kok-Kheng, Le Chang and Yemo Zhang (2018) China–Malaysia Trade, Investment, and Cooperation in the Contexts of China–ASEAN Integration and the 21st Century Maritime Silk Road Construction. *The Chinese Economy*, 51(4): 298–317. DOI:10.1080/10971475.2018.1457318.

Yos Santasombat (ed.) (2022) *Transnational Chinese Diaspora in Southeast Asia*. Singapore: Springer.

Zha, Daojiong (2018) In Pursuit of Connectivity: China Invests in Southeast Asian Infrastructure. *Perspective*, 2018(62): 1–9.

Zhou, Weifeng and Mario Esteban (2018) Beyond Balancing: China's approach towards the Belt and Road Initiative. *Journal of Contemporary China*, 27(112): 487–501. DOI: 10.1080/10670564.2018.1433476.

Zimmerbauer, Kaj (2011) From Image to Identity: Building regions by place promotion. *European Planning Studies*, 19(2): 243–260.

2 | Making Sense of BRI in Malaysia: Negotiating Volatile Political Situations

Danny Wong Tze Ken

Abstract

For a long time, Sino-Malaysia relations were shrouded by Cold War considerations, conditioned by Malaysia's historical experience of a mainly ethnic Chinese-led Malayan Communist Party which launched an armed insurrection against, first the British colonial administration, and after 1957, against the independent Malaysian government. It did not help that the Chinese state was supporting the Malayan Communist Party. Even after establishing diplomatic relations in 1974, bilateral relations between the two countries improved very little. Only after the MCP ended its armed insurrection in 1989 did relations between the two countries begin to improve. This coincided with China's modernization policy and the beginning of Chinese investment in Malaysia, which nevertheless lagged behind its investments in other Southeast Asian countries. The launch of the Belt and Road Initiative in 2013, however, sparked a remarkable turn-around, and Chinese firms began operating in Malaysia (and the rest of the world) in large numbers, with massive infrastructure and communication investments. In the process, Chinese firms took on projects such as the multi-billion ringgit East Coast Rail Links, Forest City, Malaysia City, and an oil pipeline in Borneo, to name a few. As these investments significantly increased, concerns emerged regarding the nature of the projects and how they were negotiated. Allegations were made of misconduct in the negotiations for these deals. Accusations of lopsided BRI project deals heavily favoring Chinese firms provided rich fodder for the Malaysian public to express concerns about the nation's many commitments during the campaigning for Malaysia's 14th general elections. This paper examines the effect of BRI projects on Malaysian domestic politics and how these in turn, affected Sino-Malaysia relations. To highlight changing attitudes over time, the paper will contrast how the BRI was perceived at the time of Malaysia's 14th and 15th general elections (held in 2018 and 2022, respectively).

Keywords

Belt and Road Initiative – Sino-Malaysian relations – investments – misconduct – perceptions

Introduction

Following President Xi Jinping's announcement of the Belt and Road Initiative (BRI) in 2013, many large projects commenced in Malaysia, a strong trading partner with close diplomatic ties. The projects were mainly for infrastructure development, energy resources, and to provide strategic connectivity under the overall BRI framework. Of the many projects, two stand out in terms of the scale of both the projects themselves and of their associated controversies: the East Coast Rail Link (ECRL) and the Forest City. The ECRL was implicated in the 1Malaysia Development Berhad (1MDB) scandal, in which then Prime Minister Najib Tun Razak and some of his closest confidants were accused of corruption, bribery and money laundering. Suggestions that the high price of the ECRL included funds to bail out Najib and 1MDB were mobilized by the opposition parties to criticize the government. At the same time, Forest City, a massive residential development intended to attract buyers mainly from China, raised concerns that Chinese nationals were dominating an ethnically-sensitive part of the country. Importantly, the negative public receptions of these two projects contributed to the downfall of a Malaysian government and significantly strained Malaysia-China relations.

This study examines the impact of the BRI in Malaysia by focusing on the ECRL and Forest City projects, especially how they were formulated and their connections to local stakeholders in Malaysia. The study will investigate controversies surrounding the two projects and the impact these controversies had on the BRI's reception in the country. It identifies two quite distinct concerns: the ECRL was plagued by financial controversies and allegations of local political corruption; and Forest City raised fears of the Chinese taking-over or dominating the country.

This study seeks to make sense of the impact of the BRI projects on both Malaysia and its relations with China, and to perhaps provide insights into how BRI projects could and perhaps should be managed.

This study also aims to address the question of how to research the BRI projects in Malaysia between 2013 and 2021, and particularly around the 2018 election campaign and its aftermath, where a corruption scandal appears to have had enormous impact on the projects and Malaysia-China relations. This study emphasizes the need to find a viable approach to understanding the events that impacted the projects during a period of political turmoil.

The Belt and Road Initiative

Chinese investments in Southeast Asia and Malaysia could be broadly divided into two phases: before and after the Belt and Road Initiative (BRI) in 2013. Prior to 2013, Chinese investments were mainly by state-owned enterprises who sought partnerships and joint-venture projects in prospective countries. These investments were typically small and exploratory in nature. This situation changed markedly with the launch of the Belt and Road Initiative in 2013.

Chinese President Xi Jinping launched the Belt and Road Initiative (BRI) as a mega project linking China with the rest of Asia and the world at large. Drawing inspiration from the ancient Silk Road, the new Silk Road forms a "belt" that connects China to Southeast, South and Central Asia as well as Russia and Europe overland. A maritime Silk Road meanwhile connects China with the maritime countries of Asia, the South Pacific, the Middle East, Africa and Europe (Xi 2014). From the beginning, the initiative was an overarching plan to link China to the world's markets and precious resources. Along with those obvious goals, the initiative also clearly envisages this improved connectivity delivering a common destiny for China and its partner countries (Wang 2016). As the BRI began to take shape, the Asian Infrastructure Investment Bank (AIIB) was established in 2016 to fund its massive projects. To date, there are 106 member countries in the bank, which could be interpreted as indicating support for the BRI (AIIB 2016).

Since 2013, the Belt and Road Initiative has attracted numerous Chinese companies to Malaysia to set up communication and transportation infrastructure. Chinese investment in the country rose steadily, increasing from RM920 million (0.9% of Malaysia's Foreign Direct Investment (FDI) flows) in 2010 to RM6,2 billion (9.0% of FDI) in 2017 and has continued to rise since then. The sharp rise of this investment is notable: from 2.0–2.2% in 2012–2014, when the BRI was launched, to 3.0% in 2015, 6.0% in 2016, and 9.0% in 2017.

This sudden influx of FDI changed the pattern and nature of investments significantly. Investments were no longer confined to state-owned enterprises and were no longer content with joint-venture projects. The new firms were interested in mammoth infrastructure development projects, especially pertaining to transportation (land, sea, air) and telecommunication, energy-related development, finance and banking as well as accommodation and support services. Some of the mega projects that were initiated included: the Kuantan-Qingzhou Industrial Parks, East Coast Rail Link, Second Penang Bridge, and the Mass Rapid Transit System in Klang Valley. To facilitate the flow of funds and services, major Chinese banks were invited to open branches in Malaysia, including Bank of China, Industrial and Commercial Bank of China (ICBC), and Asian Infrastructure Investment Bank (AIIB).

Since its inception, many BRI projects have launched in AIIB member countries. In Southeast Asia, Chinese companies, led initially by state-owned enterprises (SOEs) followed by government-linked companies (GLCs), began to descend on AIIB member-countries to work with local partners in initiating projects under the BRI framework, mainly infrastructure-related projects focusing on developing rail-links, hydropower plants, power grids, ports and port facilities, air-communication and urban development. Each project is seen as a dot that links to a wide range of similar projects in different locations to provide the connectivity envisaged by the larger initiative.

These projects were typically envisioned and completed by joint-ventures between Chinese companies and local partners, sometimes including government-related companies, and in some cases, state governments. The funding would come from various sources including Chinese financial institutions such as the China Export-Import Bank, the Bank of China, the International China Banking Corporation (ICBC) and the AIIB. Some projects involved local governments granting long term land concessions to Chinese partners. This *modus operandi* while effective in securing projects, began to attract criticism, most notably in terms of concerns about funding arrangements, the way projects were conceived, the heavy costs borne by the partner countries, and the terms of the land concessions.

To countries in the Southeast Asian region, including Malaysia, the BRI came through at least two channels. The first, was to be inducted into the foundation structure of the BRI, including being a member of the AIIB and expressing a willingness to participate in the BRI as part of its relations with China. The second, following the inclusion to be part of the BRI, was to work on the various projects that would be introduced in the country – including one that could strategically provide connectivity to the larger framework of the BRI.

Malaysia has been one of the most receptive of the many countries that have embraced the BRI. Kuik (2017: 652) argues that Malaysia's strategic location between the Indian and Pacific Oceans is crucial for China's ambitions to build a maritime Silk Road of the BRI. Finding itself the subject of China's attention, the Malaysian government welcomed the BRI with open arms, believing that Chinese investment and stronger trading ties would boost the Malaysian economy. "This is crucial for Malaysia, particularly at a time when the country is facing the dual challenges of shrinking foreign direct investment inflows and falling oil prices" (Kuik 2017: 653). Thus Malaysia's government embraced the BRI and was among the earliest to join the AIIB. It was quite vocal about its strong support of China and the BRI, even bringing some projects that were already underway before the BRI was announced under the BRI umbrella. Indeed, According to Kuik:

> Malaysia has forged the broadest range of connectivity cooperation with China in the ASEAN region. These include rail and port construction, port network, industrial parks, and other new forms of economic projects like digital free trade zones and setting

up of regional headquarters by Chinese mega corporations in Malaysia. (Kuik 2017: 652)

The next section will discuss selected BRI projects in Malaysia, in particularly the East Coast Rail Link and the Forest City.

BRI in Malaysia

In Malaysia, the BRI manifested in many forms but strongly biased towards infrastructure projects that provide connectivity and community-building. The earliest were in transportation infrastructure (railways, ports, bridges, and highways, among others) and communication facilities, as well as mining supply-chains, petroleum-processing facilities and electricity generation plants. These projects marked the beginning of a sharp rise in Chinese investments, by both state-owned enterprises (SOEs) and government-linked companies (GLCs) in Malaysia (Lim 2015).

In November 2016, Malaysian Prime Minister, Najib Tun Razak returned from China with 14 memorandum of understanding (MOU) agreements for China's direct investment valued at RM143.64 billion (US$34.4 billion). Attracting such a huge investment for Malaysia was a major achievement for Najib, who saw it as very important to "generate economic rents, reward businesses allies, and dispense patronage through company directorships and subcontracts to party members to strengthen his political position" (Gomez 2017).

These projects are quite diverse in nature, ranging from constructing communications infrastructure for railways and ports to oil and gas pipelines, and urban development. Some of the projects are new, conceived and initiated under the framework of the BRI. Several projects, however, were already underway and were expanded or upgraded via the BRI. One of these is the Kuantan

Table 2.1 Selected BRI projects in Malaysia

No	Project	Value (RM)	Major Partners
1.	East Coast Rail Link (ECRL)	55 billion 85% EXIM Bank (guaranteed by Malaysian Sovereign Fund)	CCCC 70% Malaysian 30%
2.	Forest City	247 billion	Country Garden 60% Malaysia 40% (Sultan of Johor 64.4%, Johor State Government 20%)
3.	Bandar Malaysia	200 billion Bank of China, ICBC, CIMB Bank, RHB	China Railway Engineering Company (SOE) Malaysia Iskandar Waterfront Holdings (Credence Resources & Johor State Government)
4.	Melaka Gateway	41 billion	China Shenzhen Yantian Port Group; Power China International, Rizhao Port Group KAJ Development & Melaka State Government
5.	Malaysia-China Kuantan Industrial Park & Port	6.5 billion	China 49% Guangxi Beibu Gulf ASEAN Investment Malaysia 51% Kuantan Pahang Holding, SP Setia and Rimbunan Hijau, IJM Kuantan
6.	Trans-Sabah Gas Pipeline	4.53 billion EXIM Bank 85% with Sovereign Fund Guarantee 15% CIMB	China 100% China Petroleum Pipeline Bureau
7.	Gemas-Johor Bahru Double-Tracking Rail Project	8.9 billion Malaysian Government	Malaysia 30% (company linked to Sultan of Johor) China 70% (China Railway Construction Company 40%, China Railway Engineering Company 30% and China Communication Construction Company 30%)
8.	Xiamen University Malaysia	1.3 billion Xiamen University	China 100% (Xiamen University) Sun Suria (Suria City Development)

Sources: Ngeow (2019a); Liu and Lim (2019); Lampton, Ho and Kuik (2020); Jones and Hameiri (2020).

Port and Industrial Park, which was initially conceived as a parallel port city to Qingzhou Port in Guangxi, which started construction in February 2013, before the BRI was launched. Another is Forest City, which commenced in 2006, but only took on its present form under the BRI.

An important characteristic of the BRI is found in the keyword "construction." Almost all these projects involve infrastructure development, and include major construction works. While infrastructure is important, many critics lamented the BRI's bias towards construction projects with little scope for technology transfer or human resources development (Loh 2017). There are exceptions, such as Xiamen University Malaysia and several projects initiated by Chinese tech companies, including Huawei. But their value pales by comparison to the large-scale construction projects.

As mentioned, these BRI projects significantly increased the level of China investments in Malaysia, from 2.0–2.2% in 2012–2014, to 9.0% in 2017. While Malaysia always prided itself on being one of China's major trading partners in ASEAN, the same could not be said of its ability to attract Chinese investment.

For the purposes of this paper, two projects stand out: the East Coast Rail Link (ECRL) and Forest City. While they are not the most expensive projects, they are crucial to making sense of the BRI in Malaysia. These two projects stand out for their prominence in the media – both from their promoters and the amount of press coverage (both positive and negative) that they received.

The East Coast Rail Link (ECRL)

The East Coast Rail Link (ECRL) aimed to connect the East Coast region of Peninsular Malaysia to the West Coast. The project involves constructing 640 km of railway from Kota Bharu in the

East Coast state of Kelantan to Port Klang, Malaysia's largest commercial port situated at the central Southwest of the West Coast of the Peninsula, just 40km from Kuala Lumpur, the commercial capital of the country. In the broader BRI context, the ECRL will join with a pan-Asian network of railways either already under construction or planned, connecting China with the Indochinese countries: Thailand, Malaysia and Singapore. Within Peninsular Malaysia, the rail will pass through some of the country's poorest rural areas of the East Coast. Apart from being a major conduit for connecting east and west, it was hoped that the project would stimulate economic growth in the eastern Malay states, as can be seen in Prime Minister Najib's declaration that, once completed, ECRL "can close [the] east-west coast economic divide" (*New Straits Times* 2016). For this purpose, the ECRL became a driver for Eastern Economic Region, which was initiated in 2007 to oversee economic development in the region. The project will create opportunities for Malaysian firms beyond providing a link for rural industries to major ports and cities under the BRI (Camba et al. 2023).

The project was estimated to cost RM55 billion, including RM46 billion to connect Kota Bahru and Gombak, just outside Kuala Lumpur, and RM9 to connect Gombak to Port Klang. The project was carried out by the China Communication Construction Company (CCCC) which holds a 70% stake in the project with the remaining 30% held by a number of Malaysian companies. The Chinese stake was financed by China EXIM (Export-Import) Bank through a soft loan of 3.5% per annum. The rest was financed by a sukuk Islamic bond through several local Malaysian banks, which is guaranteed by the Malaysian Sovereign Fund.

Construction of the ECRL began in 2017 and was expected to be complete by 2024. However, from the beginning, the project attracted a lot of attention. Critics voiced concerns about the costs as well as the rationale and wisdom of such a mega project. Nurul Izzah Anwar, a Member of Parliament, and the leader of the opposition party until 2018, exclaimed that China's investments in Malaysia had grown "too much, too fast, too soon" (Kuik, 2017: 653). Questions were raised about whether Malaysia needed a project such as the ECRL and how it fitted with Malaysia's own development plan (for instance, the 11th and 12th Malaysia Plans). Many questioned who the main beneficiary of these projects would be, expressing concerns that these projects, as Chinese initiatives intended to advance China's overall BRI strategies, would inevitably benefit the Chinese more than Malaysians.

At RM91.67 million per kilometer, many agreed with the construction executive who said "It could be the most expensive rail infrastructure project in the world in its class… It's a good project but not at this ridiculous price" (*The Edge Malaysia Weekly*, 7–13 November 2016; cf. Tay 2016). Another analyst confirmed that "there is an element of overpricing but I'm not sure what it is. State rail transport doesn't generally cost that much" (ibid.). These statements did little to shift public perceptions of the project or instill confidence. There was a widely held view that the high costs were largely due to the fact that the China Communication Construction Company (CCCC) had been directly appointed to construct the ECRL with no competitive tender process, and thus the costs at every point had been inflated.

A separate criticism was centered on perceptions that the potential for locals to benefit directly from the project was limited, especially in terms of jobs and business opportunities, because the project was 70% owned by the Chinese. Indeed, when construction commenced in 2017, the CCCC and its Chinese subcontractors generally brought their own workers from China, even for jobs that could be done by locals. Although these concerns were eventually addressed by limiting such practices, those first impressions strongly contributed to the public's negative perceptions of the project.

Forest City

Forest City originated as a residential project in the southern state of Johor, across the straits from Singapore. Strictly speaking, Forest City began as a private concern, initially conceived in 2006. It did not begin construction, though, until 2013, with BRI partners and financing. Costing RM100 billion, it was conceived as a 'futuristic urban development' project which would literally build a city, including offices, parks, hotels, commercial hubs, health facilities and schools as well as a massive housing development on four artificial islands over 14 square kilometers. A total of 250,000 units of housing for 700,000 people were planned, primarily aimed at buyers from China. The project has a 60:40 split between Chinese and Malaysian interests, with the Chinese property developer Country Garden holding the Chinese share (60%) and the Malaysian share held by the Sultan of Johor (64.4%) and the Johor state government via various investment arms (20%). It was expected to take 20 years for final completion.

The project did not involve the federal government, nor any guarantee of a sovereign fund, yet managed to become controversial for entirely different reasons. Country Garden, based in Guangdong, has four other construction projects in Malaysia, but Forest City was different – it is simply enormous and unprecedented. The problem that arose was that the project was primarily pitched at attracting Chinese nationals as investors and residents. Forest City was promoted across China's urban areas as a tropical paradise for retirees who had faithfully served their country.

From the beginning, the project was plagued with problems. One year after commencement, work stopped when concerns were raised about the Singaporean and Malaysian coastlines being affected by the reclamations to build the artificial islands. The project resumed in 2015, yet despite enormous efforts to promote the project, by the end of 2016, only 15,000 of the 250,000 residential units had been sold, and 70% of the buyers were Chinese nationals. Yet in January 2017, the Chinese government imposed currency controls, preventing its citizens from converting Yuan into foreign currencies to purchase property (ibid.). Despite some initial setbacks, though, the project remained on track.

Before the general elections of May 2018 the most prominent criticism was from the opposition party which was echoed by numerous civil society groups who were unhappy with a project that appeared to be exclusively for the benefit of foreigners. The fact that it would mainly benefit Chinese nationals, in particular, inflamed the racial sensitivities of a multiracial country in which an influx of large numbers of Chinese to live in Forest City could unsettle the perceived delicate balance of ethnicity in the country. Other concerns about the Forest City included allegations that the project had by-passed regulations, creating negative environmental and social impacts (Tritto and Camba 2023).

The 14th general election and the volatile political scene

Criticism of China and the BRI projects became more pronounced and passionate in the months leading up to the general elections of May 2018. In this contest for power, the opposition parties – the Parti Keadilan Rakyat, the Islamic Party of Malaysia (PAS), Democratic Action Party (DAP) and Parti Pribumi Bersatu – were finally able to join hands under the leadership of former Prime Minister Mahathir Mohamad and challenge the National Front (Barisan Nasional) under Najib Razak. Among the many issues raised were allegations of massive corruption involving the prime minister and the country's sovereign fund, 1MDB.

1MDB had significant investments in various BRI projects, such as the Bandar Malaysia Project, and was guarantor for others, such as the ECRL. Thus, as the 1MDB scandal grew, BRI projects began to be questioned. As previously mentioned, speculation was rife over whether the high costs of certain projects could be attributed to Chinese money being diverted to repay the 1MBD debt.

The ECRL for instance, was considered to be obscenely expensive to service a less developed region that was not likely to generate much economic benefit. It also brought severe criticism among politicians including Dr Mahathir, who expressed strong concerns about the way the transactions were arranged – which he felt was lopsided.

Mahathir's barrage of criticisms of the Najib Razak government during the election campaign was quite unprecedented in Malaysian politics, especially in bringing a foreign-related issue into the national election debate. Mahathir and his team attacked Najib Razak's purportedly close ties with China, accusing him of "selling the country to China." Mahathir was picking up on "popular disquiet" about the Chinese investment in Malaysia, and "turned it into an election issue" (Liz Lee 2018). Mahathir's election promise to reconsider Chinese contracts under the BRI if his coalition won the election had severe implications for the BRI projects and China-Malaysia relations.

Mahathir basically argued that Malaysia would not benefit from Chinese companies buying up land and building expensive infrastructure like the East Coast Rail Link, Forest City, and Bandar Malaysia. In fact, Mahathir and his team went further, stoking fear by reminding the Malaysian public of the debt traps reportedly experienced by other countries, such as Cambodia, Sri Lanka, and Laos, who had committed to long term loans that would take generations to pay off while granting land concessions, in some cases, for as long as 100 years.

While Najib attempted to defend himself by arguing that foreign investments do not threaten Malaysia's sovereignty, the rapidly increasing Chinese presence in the country remained a pressing issue in the public's view. Economically, many, including businessmen, felt that the presence of Chinese nationals employed by Chinese companies offered only limited benefits for local firms and the local economy. Chinese firms' reliance on Chinese workers and suppliers was a source of resentment among locals who did not see any tangible benefits of the Chinese presence or investments.

And, of course, concerns about the Chinese presence in the country were not limited to economic considerations; they touched on a sensitive matter of racial (or ethnic) imbalance, at least in the manner it was perceived. When it became known that more than 70% of the buyers of Forest City housing were Chinese, alarm rippled through local communities, including Najib's own UMNO party.

Another project in Kuantan, the capital of the eastern state of Pahang, provided Mahathir with additional ammunition with which to attack the government. This project commenced in 2013 with the construction of walls to enclose 1,219 acres of land cleared and dedicated for the first phase of the Malaysia-China Kuantan Industrial Park (MCKIP). Signs promoting the project were written in Chinese, as were the many motivational and nationalist slogans hung over the green safety nets that are typical of Chinese construction sites, earning the title "Great Walls of Kuantan" (*Malaysiakini* 9 October 2017). This impression was reinforced when the site acquired a reputation as a Chinese enclave, separated by walls from the rest of the Kuantan community. Security at the site was provided by mixed crews of local and foreign security personnel. Reports that a local state assemblyman and Mahathir himself had been denied entry by foreign guards (*Malaysiakini* 2017; Tritto and Camba 2022) added fuel to the fire. Although Tritto and Camba (2022) document the many alleged personal interventions by Najib to attract Chinese investments, including the appropriation of publicly owned land, those issues were not highlighted by Mahathir and critics of the MCKIP project.

In fact, the industrial park had great potential to realize its objectives, with many potential benefits for the local community. The main investor was Alliance Steel (US$1.5 billion), followed by Guangxi Shenlong Metallurgical, planning to invest US$526 million on clay porcelain production and Guangxi Beibu Gulf was to invest US$158 million in an aluminum factory (Gomez et al. 2020; Camba, Lim and Gallagher 2022). Despite the fact that the majority shareholder of the park was the Kuantan Pahang Holding Sdn Bhd,[1] the way the project was developing, with a massive Chinese presence monopolizing if not dominating the site made the 'Great Wall of Kuantan' a powerful symbol used by the opposition to criticize the government. The state government's efforts to respond to this criticism by explaining the nature of the operation were to no avail. The attacks continued, and appear to have been effective, led by Mahathir, the leader of the opposition.

Changes following the 14th general election

The change of government in 2018 severely affected bilateral relations between China and Malaysia, especially after the new

---

1 Kuantan Pahang Holding Sdn Bhd is a Malaysian public-private partnership comprising IJM Land Berhad (40%), Sime Darby (30%) and the Pahang Government (30%), while the Chinese owner (49%) is the Guangxi Beibu Gulf international Port Group Co. Ltd.

Malaysian government suspended the ECRL project and imposed restrictions on Chinese nationals purchasing properties in Forest City, with the explicit intention of ensuring it would not be seen as a Chinese-dominated city.

With the ECRL on hold, the new prime minister went to Japan to negotiate more attractive financing for the project. The suspension of the ECRL project caused severe anxiety among stakeholders, including the Chinese government. Feelers were sent and the project was renegotiated. It was finally revived in April 2019, albeit with a reduced cost and new stakeholders in Malaysia. The then Chinese Ambassador Bai Tian expressed relief at the project's resumption (*The Star*, 19 April 2019).

The impact of these projects on both Malaysia's political scene and its foreign relations, especially its bilateral ties with China, make a clearer understanding of the BRI projects in Malaysia imperative. These Malaysian BRI projects can provide crucial lessons to other countries trying to engage with and benefit from the BRI.

Examining events leading up to and following the general elections in 2018, it is clear that the controversies surrounding the ECRL and Forest City projects contributed to the fall of a Malaysian government. News of corruption, irregularities, etc, plus the fact that decisions were made mainly by political decision and less so by actual business consideration – raised many questions that were left unanswered. The public perception that Malaysia might be losing out to Chinese domination was stoked by the Mahathir-led opposition to cast doubt on the government.

As soon as it took office, in May 2018, the new Pakatan Harapan government, under Mahathir's leadership, began to shift directions and turned to an old acquaintance, Japan, with the hope of providing some balance to the Chinese presence. The Chinese, however, were willing to renegotiate the ECRL arrangements and construction resumed in April 2019. Was this a capitulation to the Chinese, perhaps indicating some degree of dependency on the part of the Malaysian government, regardless of creed and orientation, on the BRI projects? Or was it a matter of being so deeply invested already that there was no viable way to extricate itself from the deals? Suspicions of dependency seemed to be a constant, continuing even after the government changed again on 16 August 2021, when Muhyddin Yasin, the successor of Mahathir Mohamad and leader of BERSATU, who was leading the Perikatan Nasional Government, resigned and gave way to the return of Najib Razak's UMNO as leader of a Barisan Nasional-led government under the new Prime Minister, Ismail Sabri. Despite all these changes BRI projects in Malaysia were sustained.

Making sense of the BRI projects in Malaysia

Since the BRI was launched, many works have tried to explain President Xi's initiative. The Chinese government has churned out countless publications on the topic, including Xi's *The Governance of China* (2014), for instance, containing speeches that Xi delivered in Kazakhstan and Indonesia to launch the BRI initiative. Wang Yiwei's widely circulated work, *The Belt and Road Initiative: What will China Offer the World in its Rise* (2016), argues that the present initiative was inspired by the ancient Silk Road to drive the region's revival from the effects of its imperialist-dominated past. According to Wang, Xi's BRI will transcend the Marshall Plans. Wang asserts that the plan is part of China's dream, and offers great opportunities for the regions and countries involved to cooperate, to change the world and provide opportunities for global development.

Since its introduction, the BRI has received mixed reviews, ranging from positive portrayals like Wang's – a view not shared by many – to measured reactions by others. Many have expressed suspicions about the sincerity of the initiative and the possibility of hidden agendas. Some Western scholars have described the BRI as China's plan to take over the world's resources to feed its own insatiable demand for internal development. Bruno Macaes, for instance, sees the BRI as more than just a development fund; he believes that China is out to dominate the world, and argues that the BRI is its plan for a new world order (Macaes 2019).

As Chinese investment in the country became an increasingly important part of political discourse, reports began to link the Chinese projects to alleged corruption. Of particular interest was the alleged connections between the Malaysian sovereign fund 1MDB and the BRI projects. Opposition politicians, especially Liew Chin Tong, had a field day questioning how the projects were arranged and the likelihood they would become burdens for Malaysia (Liew 2017). The Chinese clearly wanted to distance themselves from the controversies surrounding the 1MDB scandal, and to avoid being seen as accessories to Najib and his cronies (Camba et al. 2023).

Questions about the BRI projects in Malaysia were certainly not confined to the ECRL, Kuantan Industrial Park, and Forest City. There are many issues relating to BRI projects in Malaysia that require close examination into the decision-making in initiating the projects, the various parties involved, and the ways they are managed by both Malaysian and Chinese stakeholders, among other things.

The conviction of former Prime Minister Najib Razak on corruption charges related to siphoning money from the 1MDB sovereign fund continues to cast a shadow over the BRI projects. As Najib was a strong champion of the BRI projects in Malaysia, many questions remain about possible Chinese involvement in the 1MDB scandal.

Nevertheless, as the country headed towards the 15th general elections, it was clear that the BRI projects were most likely going to stay. Between the short hiccup after the 14th general election in May 2018 and the resumption of the ECRL in 2019, mutual assurances and commitments were given by both the Chinese and successive Malaysian governments to see through the BRI projects. These projects constitute an important part of efforts to sustain a robust and fruitful Malaysia-China relationship.

In the 15th general elections in November 2022, there was a marked absence of discussion about China and the BRI projects by politicians clamoring for support. Gone were the heated sentiments expressed by the opposition parties in the 2018 election about the country's sovereignty being threatened by a potentially overwhelming Chinese presence via the BRI projects. While the renegotiation of the ECRL project might have alleviated some concerns about the expense, other BRI projects including the Forest City continued unabated. The conspicuous absence of the BRI projects as election issues in 2022 raises questions about whether they were merely convenient scapegoats for the parties then in opposition or were genuinely of paramount importance in 2018 as vectors for revealing the corruption in the then government. But perhaps it was rather that the politicians vying for power in 2022 recognized how much the criticisms of 2018 had strained Chinese-Malaysian relations and decided that relationship was too precious to risk again.

Concluding remarks

As integral parts of the larger framework envisioned by China, any assessment of these Malaysian projects requires a clear understanding of China's macro view of the BRI. The micro views require an in-depth analysis of the BRI projects – in this case, the selected cases of East Coast Rail Link and the Forest City, are identified to understand the importance of the two projects vis-à-vis other BRI projects in Malaysia.

Both projects had attracted attentions and criticism since their inceptions. Both were linked to many issues including high costs, whether they were in the national interest, and who would be the main beneficiaries of the projects. During the 2018 Malaysian general elections, questions were raised about ethnicity, concerns about foreign 'domination' and the perceived threat of losing sovereignty to China via the BRI projects. This study also showcased another BRI project, the Malaysia-China Kuantan Industrial Park, which was hotly debated during the 14th general elections.

The allegations of connections between the projects and the 1MDB scandal – implicating the highest office in the country, who was the chief promoter of the BRI in Malaysia – raises questions about how the BRI projects were handled by different governments in Malaysia, as well as questions about the effect the projects themselves had on Malaysian political campaigns and processes. The volatile political scenario certainly disrupted some of the projects, as we have seen in the case of the ECRL. Nevertheless, the projects ultimately continued, albeit with some renegotiation. The same could not be said of Forest City. The financial squeeze imposed by the Chinese government was further complicated by restrictions imposed on Chinese buyers, resulting in the project being abandoned; it has come to be known as a Chinese-built "ghost city" (Marsh 2023).

This raises questions about how the projects survived the many challenges that they faced. One possible scenario is that Malaysia's dependency on the projects and need to maintain strong bilateral relations with China, both diplomatically as well as economically and socio-culturally, compelled it to request a renegotiation of the ECRL project. Likewise, this study demonstrated that China also has a need for the successful execution of its BRI projects and was therefore willing to renegotiate their scale. Its expressed relief at the resumption of the ECRL project indicates some degree of mutual dependency for these two countries. In this sense, the level of Malaysia's perceived dependency is neutralized to some extent by China's dependency on the success of these projects.

References

AIIB (2016) *Connecting Asia for the Future: Annual Report and Accounts* https://www.aiib.org/en/news-events/annual-report/2016/home/pdf/Annual_Report_2016.pdf

Brown, Clare Rewcastle (2018) *The Sarawak Report: The Inside Story of the 1MDB Exposé*. Petaling Jaya: Gerakbudaya Enterprise.

Camba, Alvin (2021) Sinews of politics: State Grid Corporation, investment coalitions, and embeddedness in the Philippines. *Energy Strategy Reviews*, *35*: 100640.

Camba, Alvin, Terence Gomez, Richard Khaw and Kee-Cheok Cheong (2023) Strongmen politics and investment flows: China's investments in Malaysia and the Philippines. *Journal of the Asia Pacific Economy*, 28(3): 813–834.

Camba, Alvin, Guanie Lim and Kevin Gallagher (2022) Leading Sector and Dual Economy: How Indonesia and Malaysia Mobilised Chiese Capital in Mineral Processing. *Third World Quarterly*, 43 (10): 2375-2395.

Gomez, Edmund T. (2017) *Minister of Finance Incorporated: Ownership and Control of Corporate Malaysia*. Basingstoke: Palgrave-Macmillan.

Gomez, Edmund T., Siew Yean Tham, Ran Li and Kee Cheok Cheong (2020) *China in Malaysia*. Singapore: Springer.

Hutchinson, Francis E. and Tham Siew Yean (2021) The BRI in Malaysia's port sector: Drivers of success and failure. *Asian Affairs*, 52(3): 688–721.

Jacques, Martin (2010) *When China Rules the World: The Rise of the Middle Kingdom and the End of the Western World*. New York: Penguin.

Kuik, Cheng Chwee (2017) A Tempting Torch? Malaysia embraces (and leverages) BRI despite domestic discontent, *Asian Politics and Policy*, 9(4): 652–654.

Kumar, S. Y. Surendra (2019) China's Belt and Road Initiative (BRI): India's Concerns, Responses and Strategies. *International Journal of China Studies*, 10(1): 27–36.

Lai, Karen P. Y., Shaun Lin, and James D. Sidaway (2020) Financing the Belt and Road Initiative (BRI): Research agendas beyond the 'debt-trap' discourse. *Eurasian Geography and Economics*, 61(2): 109–124.

Lee, Liz (2018) 'Selling the country to China' debate spills into Malaysia's election. *Reuters*, 27 April.

Liew, Chin Tong (2017) Investments from China: Malaysia can afford to be – and should be – choosy. https://www.facebook.com/liewchintong.my/posts/investments-from-china-malaysia-can-afford-to-be-and-should-be-choosyinvestments/10154161909730911/ Accessed 13 January 2017.

Lim, Guanie (2015) China's Investments in Malaysia: Choosing the 'right' partners. *International Journal of China Studies*, 6(1): 1–30.

Lim, Guanie (2017) China's 'Going Out' Strategy in Southeast Asia: Case studies of the automobile and electronics sectors. *China: An International Journal*, 15(4): 157–178.

Liu, Hong and Guanie Lim (2019) The political economy of a rising China in Southeast Asia: Malaysia's response to the Belt and Road Initiative. *Journal of Contemporary China* 28(116): 216–231. Doi; 10.1080/10670564. 2018.1511393

Loh, Francis Kok Wah (2017) BRI, spike in Chinese investments in Malaysia: What are the implications to Malaysia', *Aliran*, 7 September. https://aliran.com/aliran-csi/aliran-csi-2017/bri-spike-chinese-investments-malaysia-implications-malaysias-politics-sovereignty/

Macaes, Bruno (2019) *Belt and Road: A Chinese World Order*. London: Hurst & Company.

Mahnubani, Kishore (2020) *Has China Won? The Chinese Challenge to American Primacy*, New York: Public Affairs.

Malaysiakini (2016) Dr M: Najib's China Deals May Threaten Malaysia's Sovereignty, 2 November.

Malaysiakini (2017) The Mystery Behind Kuantan's 'Great Wall of China', 9 October.

Marsh, Nick (2023) Forest City: Inside Malaysia's Chinese-built "ghost city." *BBC*, 5 December. https://www.bbc.com/news/business-67610677. Accessed 11 January 2025.

Matsumura, Masahiro (2019) A realist approach to Japan's Free and Open Indo-Pacific Strategy vs. China's Belt and Road Initiative: A propaganda rivalry, *International Journal of China Studies*, 10(2): 131–156.

Mohan, Giles and Ben Lampert (2013) Negotiating China: Reinserting African agency into China–Africa relations. *African Affairs*, 112(446): 92–110.

New Straits Times (2016) Mind the gap: ECRL can close east-west coast economic divide, says Najib. 28 November.

Rana, Renu (2019) Asian Infrastructure Investment Bank, New Development Bank and the reshaping of global economic order: Unfolding trends and perceptions in Sino-Indian economic relations. *International Journal of China Studies*, 10(2): 273–290.

Straits Times (2018) China accused of using Belt and Road Initiative for spying: Report. 16 August.

Tay, Chester (2016) ECRL deal signed by RM2 firm that was formed without parliament's approval. *The Edge Malaysia*, 8 November. https://theedgemalaysia.com/article/%20ecrl-deal-signed-rm2-firm-was-formed-without-parliament%20s-approval

The Economist (2020) The Pandemic is Hurting China's Belt and Road Initiative. 4 June. https://www.economist.com/china/2020/06/04/the-pandemic-is-hurting-chinas-belt-and-road-initiative

The Edge Malaysia Weekly (2016). The World's Costliest Railway. November 7–13.

The Star. (2019). ECRL to boost China investments. 19 April.

Tritto, Angela and Alvin Camba (2022) State-facilitated industrial parks in the Belt and Road Initiative: Towards a framework for understanding the localization of the Chinese development model. *World Development Perspectives*, 28: 100465.

Tritto, Angela and Alvin Camba (2023) The Belt and Road Initiative in Southeast Asia: A mixed methods examination. *Journal of Contemporary China*, 32(141): 436–454.

Wan, Ming (2015) *The Asian Infrastructure Investment Bank: The construction of power and the struggle for the East Asian international order*. London: Palgrave Macmillan.

Wang Yiwei (2016) *The Belt and Road Initiative: What will China Offer the World in its Rise*. Beijing: New World Press.

Wright, Tom and Bradley Hope (2018) *Billion Dollar Whale: The Man Who Fooled Wall Street, Hollywood, and the World*. New York: Hachette Books.

Xi, Jinping (2014) *The Governance of China*. Beijing: Foreign Languages Press

3 Reconceptualizing Mobile Infrastructures and Infrastructural Temporality in the Transnational Cattle Trade

Kengkij Kitirianglarp

Abstract

The transnational cattle trade in Southeast Asia long precedes the demarcated borders of the nation-state. In the first decades of the 21st century, China opened itself to increased trade with neighboring countries in the region, opening new trade routes and bringing new actors into the cattle trade. Chinese market forces have changed patterns, paths and fortunes of cross-border cattle traders, determining product quality, trade networks and routes.

My research conducted between 2019 and 2020 examines, in the context of the transnational cattle trade, value-creating processes by Thai cattle farmers, who are controlled indirectly by a brokerage system. Brokers act as middlemen who connect with other regional actors. My research findings show that, compared to brokers, Thai cattle farmers possess much less negotiating power. Against this backdrop, China's Belt and Road Initiative (BRI) is restructuring the cattle trade. The current study points out that although China has constructed fixed, material infrastructure to facilitate BRI projects in the region, informal infrastructure still determines the local level of the cattle production process. To understand how BRI impacts the transnational cattle trade, it is important to study the interrelationships between fixed-material and mobile-immaterial infrastructures to consider the transnational cattle industry not simply in terms of trade, but also as a production process.

Keywords

Chinese capitalism – transnational cattle trade – the Belt and Road Initiative – mobile infrastructure – infrastructural temporality

Introduction

> I went looking for a Chinese merchant who bought my cattle, but I couldn't find one. Wherever I go, I find only brokers, no real Chinese merchants. (Farmer from Tak province, interview December 2019)

In Tak province, Thailand, in 2019, I met a group of farmers who had given up raising cattle for export to China because it had bankrupted them. The debris generated and left behind by Chinese capitalism was evident in their villages. One of my questions was "Why was the situation this way?" Farmers in Sukhothai and Payao provinces were still producing cattle to sell to China, so I wondered how the Tak farmers ended up in that state. This became the starting point of my research. No farmers have ever met the Chinese merchants who buy their cattle. They have only met Thai brokers. The farmers negotiated prices and their demands with local brokers who represented the so-called Chinese merchants. One farmer told me that negotiating with the brokers was a challenge. All the brokers claimed they were unable to negotiate since they were acting on behalf of Chinese buyers. One day, this group of farmers went to the Laos-Thailand borders in Chiang Saen district, Chiang Rai province in search of the Chinese merchants, but there were none there, only brokers. As a researcher interested in the effects of the BRI on the cattle trade, I really wanted to interview Chinese merchants, but had to accept that I would never find one at the Chiang Rai border. It then dawned on me that if the farmers never had direct contact with Chinese merchants, it would be difficult to identify the direct effects of the BRI on the cattle farmers. Subsequently, I changed my research to focus on the relationship between the farmers and the brokers in Thailand. Since 2019, I have conducted several interviews and made observations in many provinces. As a result, I was able to map the brokerage system and networks of the transnational cattle trade (Kitirianglarp and Kantha 2020). I argued that due to its informality, the networks of brokers are centrally important.

From 2019 to 2020, I studied the cattle trade, but it was not until 2021 that I became aware of the BRI's influence on the organization of the cattle trade within the region. Since December 2021, I have revisited brokers and farmers in the networks that I had previously studied, although most of them have disappeared. One of my informants was arrested and incarcerated for smuggling cattle into China during the Covid-19 pandemic. Another informant, a farmer who had achieved great success in 2020, has since been bankrupted. He was in tears during our interview. This is an example of the uncertainty farmers face, which is a feature of transborder trade. Brokers, too, are subject to uncertainty and at high risk of bankruptcy. The wealth promised by the trade was not realized. Although the trade was driven by Chinese capital, the Chinese and the BRI megaprojects are invisible to the farmers, who interact only with Thai brokers. This ignited a new focus for my research: "How can we approach the BRI mega-infrastructure from below when it is invisible to the actors?"

To answer the question, I must reconceptualize my approach to the BRI. This paper aims to examine the BRI from below, from the vantage point of the actors involved at the very base of the cattle trade: the producers. This approach is essential to a fuller understanding of the BRI megaprojects and infrastructures. The paper is presented in three parts. First, it provides a brief description of the transnational cattle trade in the region. Second, it situates the BRI infrastructures within the capitalist political economy. In this context, the term "infrastructure" refers not only to the material built environment, but also to immaterial and mobile structures that are immanent to people's lives. This discussion draws on Marx's analysis of the living machine in late capitalism. Finally, based on the concept of the machine, I aim to conceptualize infrastructure as an apparatus of temporality, in which capital exploits labor power by controlling time. Perceiving infrastructure as temporality will help to understand how the BRI's mobile networks operate in the region. In sum, these conceptual tools will finally help me, as an anthropologist, make sense of the BRI from the perspective "below."

Background of the transnational cattle trade

The cross-border cattle trade in Southeast Asia long precedes the demarcated borders of the nation-state. It is characterized by long-distances that are traversed mainly on foot and the traders' reliance on middlemen. In the first decades of the 21st century, China has opened to trade with neighboring countries in the region, opening new trade routes and bringing new actors into the cattle trade. The arrival of China, with its much larger market, has dramatically changed the patterns, paths and fortunes of cross-border cattle traders, determining product quality, trade networks and routes. Local actors adapt to unpredictable fluctuations in the Chinese market. Thus, the various actors in the industry, whether brokers, farmers, or government officials, must remain flexible and stay abreast of the changing circumstances in China, which requires specific knowledge and skills. Based on my fieldwork observations, I propose that Chinese capitalism controls the cross-border cattle trade through highly flexible networks that have no fixed form.

Moreover, in lieu of direct institutional control, Chinese capitalism relies on numerous mechanisms and tools to absorb surplus value of labor and resources in the region. Hence, to understand the effects of the BRI from below, we must remain attuned to the fluidity and uncertainty of interactions between Chinese capital and local labor and resources, and not be lulled by the aggregate figures' illusions of fixed or stable trade patterns.

According to my 2019 study, the Chinese-influenced transnational cattle trade has four distinct characteristics. First, although China's demand for beef has grown exponentially over a decade, it has no official agreement to import live cattle from the Mekong region countries. Hence the cross-border cattle trade is "a semiformal trade," and fraught with uncertainty because it is unlawful in China (see Smith et al. 2015; Nkendah 2010). Therefore, to satisfy the demand for beef, cattle is covertly imported through informal channels from Myanmar, Laos, Vietnam, and Thailand. The export of live cattle from the Mekong countries faces significant risks in this process (see the issue of trust among Chinese capitalists in Jomo 2002: 325–353).

Second, farmers across numerous areas such as Tak, Sukhothai, Phayao, and the lower central and western regions of Thailand play a vital role in adding value to the cattle through the fattening process, which takes about three months.

Third, Thailand's "brokerage system" is essential for connecting the various actors including Myanmar cattle traders, livestock farmers, farmer's markets, and Chinese buyers. The brokerage system helps connect brokers with each other through both domestic and international networks. The more informal the trade, the more important the brokerage system. The Thai brokerage system has evolved over a long period of time into an essential link consolidating diverse economic activities from dispersed areas. It has expanded as a highly flexible network in a volatile and risky industry sector.

Fourth, comparing farmers and brokers reveals the brokerage system's high flexibility and power asymmetry. Brokers have greater bargaining power than farmers because semi-formal trade enables their networks to control the market systematically. Unlike farmers who are tied to fixed locations during the 3-month fattening period, brokers can move freely to distribute cattle across borders. This mobility combines with their role as intermediaries and claimed expertise in border situations to increase their leverage.

The brokerage system maintains power through low-risk operations while farmers bear most market volatility risks. Through control of credit and purchasing timelines, brokers can manipulate farmers into selling at reduced prices. After exhausting one village's resources, brokers simply move to new areas with the same false promises, creating a cycle where farmers risk bankruptcy while brokers maintain steady profits without assuming production risks. This systemic inequality is reinforced by farmers' limited understanding of the broader trade network they operate within.

In such semi-formal trade, which is legal in one area, while illegal in others, creating value for cattle is also through a semi-formal production process. Though Thailand has no direct border with China, it has a structural advantage in comparison over its neighbors, namely a standardized livestock system. In addition, there are key actors who have experience in cross-border trade, particularly experienced brokers both within the country and along borders. The brokers' network is the most important link between actors, both at the level of border connectivity, products, and actors. Brokers are the link between, first, cattle farmers, the main value creators in the process of moving cattle across borders; and, second, Chinese merchants who are buyers and govern-

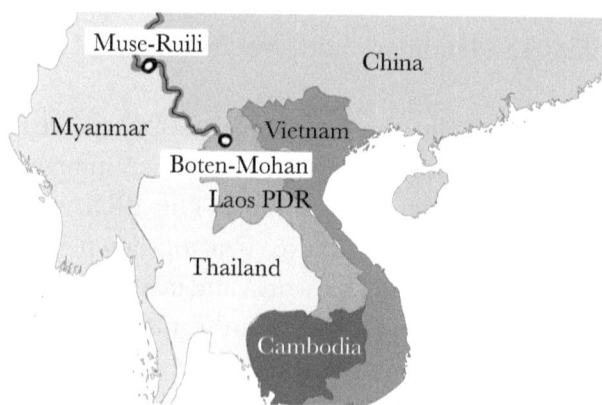

Figure 3.1 Muse-Ruili and Boten-Mohan: Principal gateways to China
Source: Created by the author's research team based on field research

ment agencies at various levels. Without the informal networks of brokers, the cattle trade would be impossible.

My more recent research, conducted in Thailand and Laos, examines the impact of the BRI infrastructure on the value-creating process of the cattle trade, the commodity-production part of the supply chain, with a particular focus on the interactions between the informal networks in the region and the material infrastructure of Chinese capitalism.

Since 2016, China has endeavored to formalize cattle trade in the region. The Chinese government has permitted five large state-owned enterprises to invest in the livestock industry in Muang Sing, Luang Namtha and has established export facilities on the Mohan-Boten border in Laos. This new infrastructure includes feedlots, slaughterhouses, quarantine stations, and veterinary systems, and was completed in mid-2021. The BRI strategy is three-pronged, seeking first, to dismantle the informal trade along the border, particularly the informal brokerage system; second, to shut down illicit trade routes by building a wall along the border and enforcing new policies to prevent the illegal flows of commodities; and finally, to build official and standard infrastructure both in Laos, Myanmar, and China.

Thus, compared to the situation in 2020, the regional cattle trade has been drastically transformed from an informal to a more formalized system imposed by China. The BRI, with its various forms and levels of infrastructure, is a top-down mechanism for China to disrupt the existing networks and institutionalize new ones. To this end, China has built the "Southern Great Wall" along the border between China and Myanmar to restrict the flow of people and products from Myanmar into China (Qi et al., 2022). The massive financial investment in the border-crossing infrastructure in Laos creates an additional formalized trade route, while the Myanmar crossing remains significant. The BRI project has forced Thailand and Myanmar to participate and cooperate with Laos and its Chinese-built infrastructure or be finally excluded from the opportunity of trading with China.

In short, the BRI project has greatly impacted the region, changed the power dynamics and relations among actors in the region. My aim is to understand how the BRI impacts on the value-creating process in the cattle trade through the networks and power relationships of people in Thailand, Myanmar, and Laos. Focusing on infrastructure, I lean on Karl Marx's theory of machines, and reconceptualize the BRI in terms of mobile infrastructure and apparatuses of temporal controls.

Mobile and immaterial infrastructures

In *Grundrisse*, Karl Marx portrayed *the machine* of late capitalism as a crystal or transformative form of the human labor force. The machine was both a fixed capital owned by capitalists and a productive force that expressed the labor force of humanity, which had been subsumed by capital. In other words, the machine is an apparatus that subsumes all living beings into the capital form. According to Marx, capital subsumption can be described as follows:

> Labour appears, rather, merely as a conscious organ, scattered among the individual living workers at numerous points of the mechanical system; subsumed under the total process of the machinery itself, as itself only a link of the system, whose unity exists not in the living workers, but rather in the living (active) machinery, which confronts his individual, insignificant doings as a mighty organism. (Marx 1973: 693)

Marx might have been the first to have conceptualized infrastructure as machines (see also Deleuze and Guattari 1983). In this context, Marx described roads as a kind of machine that helped facilitate the industrial revolution in Europe. Under capitalism, roads became an apparatus of control and dividing labor (see Harvey and Knox 2015). He perceived networks of infrastructure as the mega-machine that capital used to control and subsume the entire society. Borrowing Marx's insights into treating infrastructure as a machine allows me to combine the different living labor forces while crystallizing them into an apparatus of control separated from the living labor associated with it. In the end, when capital appears as a machinery form, it is not only as an apparatus of control, but ultimately as an apparatus which subsumes everything. According to Marx, subsumption means that capital will subordinate all kinds of social relations to the value-creating processes of capital (Marx 1973: 699).

Marx did not propose that machine domination was a permanent state of capitalism. In more advanced capitalism, he argued, the machine would withdraw itself from the production process, resulting in living labor fusing with the machine. In other words, living labor becomes a machine, and the machine, a crystallization of dead labor, becomes living labor. As a result, all social relations become centered totally on the production process, and the machine-as-dead labor becomes external to the value-creating process.

That is why, in *Grundrisse*, Marx rejected the classical political economy assumption that machine domination is a generalized phenomenon in capitalist society. It turns out that, in late capitalism, instead of machinic domination, living labor would become central to the production process (Lazzarato 2014). The machine, externalized from the process of production, becomes a parasite that is unnecessary to the creation of value. Instead, it taps into the living organs or networks of labor that produce value. Thus, the capitalist expropriation of value takes place outside the production process. While the production process is commonized and owned by the common, the apparatus of capturing surplus, which is privately owned by capital, remains outside the production process created by the commons. According to Marx, this is the condition of proletariat emancipation from capitalism. While labor builds the entirety of society by commonization of everything, the capitalist becomes an outsider who takes the surplus for free.

Accordingly, the machine – the infrastructure – is not only material, immobile, and permanent, but also immaterial, mobile, and temporal. As Marx predicted, in late capitalism, infrastructure is constitutive of the social relations of living people and their relationships with non-human things. To study infrastructure, we need to perceive it as a complex relationship of networks between humans, non-humans, and things. As Marx predicted more than a century ago, late capitalism is based on immaterial networks, which are central to the production of surplus.

In short, in my study of the cattle trade, I focus on immaterial social relations as a key to understanding the BRI. Based on my earlier

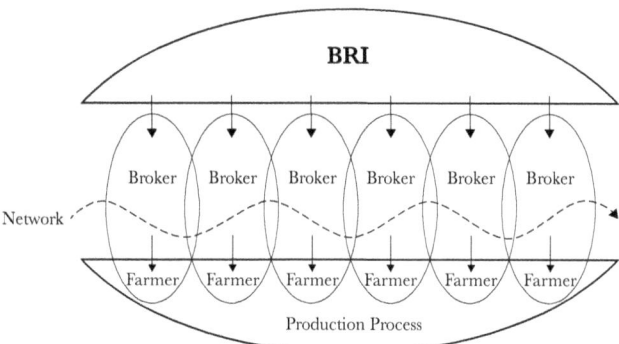

Figure 3.2 Map of actors and networks in the transnational cattle trade under the BRI

Source: Created by the author's research team based on field research

study, the transnational cattle trade in the region was conducted by semi-formal networks of people across and along borders and relied heavily on informal networks of people and things. Brokers played a key role in facilitating and connecting people, animals, and built infrastructure (Kitirianglarp and Kantha 2020) and are therefore important to understanding the relationships between immaterial and mobile infrastructure, as well as the material and fixed infrastructure created by the BRI.

The hypothesis of this paper is that rather than eradicating or destroying the informal networks in the region, the BRI infrastructure China built in Laos and along its borders with Myanmar facilitates a more thorough exploitation and extraction of surplus value from the transnational cattle trade. To perceive the BRI as a separate entity is useful for conceptualizing the complex relationship between the fixed and mobile infrastructure. This conception of mobile and immaterial networks is similar to the "cellular network infrastructure" proposed by Noam David et al. (2015), whose recognition of the importance of informal networks and power relations is quite rare in studies of infrastructure. Most researchers focus on the fixed, formal, material, and built infrastructure while treating immaterial networks of social relations as mere byproducts at best. In David et al.'s conceptualization, the mobility and cellularity of devices such as radios, weather-monitoring machines, and cybernetics – albeit being highlighted – lacked the characteristics of immateriality and power relations in the social relations and production process that are central to the operation of infrastructures in the BRI. Here, Brian Larkin offers a more fulsome view, proposing that "our study of infrastructure might ... center on built things, knowledge things, or people things" (2013: 329). His earlier *Signal and Noise* (2008) provided a brilliant example from colonial Nigeria of radio as an arena of the relationship between things.

In short, infrastructure is not merely about tangible objects like roads, buildings, electricity generation and distribution, or dams. Instead, infrastructure consists of three parts: 1) "built infrastructure;" 2) "social things" (culture), including knowledge, law, social relations, and language; and 3) "people things," which refer to the various ways people interact with each other and the built environment. Infrastructure, therefore, refers to the connection and movement of the three components that come together at a given time and place, and this coming together changes the power relationships of the buildings, social relationships, and the people who interact with each other (Larkin 2013). In this sense, infrastructure operates as an apparatus that controls and standardizes temporal processes – a key mechanism for capital accumulation.

I want to combine two main characteristics of infrastructure – mobility and immateriality – using Marx's notion of infrastructure as a machine. This framing is useful to research on the cattle trade in at least three ways: first, it emphasizes the complexity of different layers of infrastructure, mobile and immobile, permanent and temporal, as well as social and built environment; second, it helps introduce scholars of infrastructure to more flexible and informal forms, including networks of ordinary people, their cultural logics of trade, and their everyday relationship; and finally, focusing on the relationship of people and networks from below helps to elucidate the power relationships, embedded in time and space, between local, national, and transnational actors.

Subsequently, I intend to conceptualize the power relationship within complex infrastructures as social conflict by perceiving infrastructure as an apparatus of temporality. Hence, this will be helpful to achieve the main objective of the paper, which is to answer the question of how to study the BRI "from below."

Infrastructure as apparatus of temporality

As many scholars have observed, infrastructures are not only spatial but also temporal in nature (see Anand, Gupta, and Appel eds. 2018). Most infrastructure lasts longer than individual human beings. Even immaterial infrastructures, such as languages or social networks, are older than the human beings who live in them. Moreover, infrastructures "have long promised modernity, development, progress, and freedom to people all over the world" (Appel, Anand, and Gupta 2018: 3; cf. Hetherington 2017). According to Larkin, infrastructures are "building time and temporalities at the same time as they are building material forms that allow for the possibility of exchange over space" (2013: 327; cf. Appel 2018: 44). Therefore, "Focusing on time and temporality, in fact, helps us think of spatiality in new and interesting ways; it allows for a rethinking of spatialization as itself a temporal act and activity. Temporality is built into spatial expansion, contradiction, and scaling" (Appel et al. 2018: 16). In short, infrastructure, either material or immaterial, is in and of a certain space and time, and these two dimensions cannot be analyzed separately for we are always dealing with the spatial embeddedness of time and the temporal embeddedness of space. Space operates in a certain time, and time works in a certain space. And thus we must perceive infrastructure as processual, not a finished product (Appel et al. 2018: 18).

In a different vein, Marx perceived time as a form of power contestation and class conflict, rather than a neutral occurrence. David Harvey's *The Condition of Postmodernity* (1989) proposed that capital continuously transforms its apparatus of temporality to counter its own crisis. Changes in space and time are essential to capitalism and, for Marx, both space and time are non-neutral arenas for class struggle. Capital uses time to control labor power, and workers negotiate to free themselves from the capitalists' time (Alliez 1995). Bob Jessop (2006) further explains that capitalism does not operate only spatially but also temporally. The temporal-spatial fixes are tools of capital to overcome its inherent crisis. Spatial fixes help capital to encounter both inner and outer crises. According to Jessop:

> These attempts to resolve capital's contradictions through internal transformation reflect the inherent tension between the 'fixity' and 'mobility' of capital at any given moment and over time. This tension is evident within fixed capital itself (e.g., the mutual presupposition of fixed airports and mobile aircraft), circulating capital (raw materials, semifinished goods, finished products versus liquid money capital), and the relation between fixed and circulating capital (e.g., commercial centres and commodity flows). It also unfolds over time. For 'capital has to build a fixed space (or "landscape") necessary for its own functioning at a certain point in its history only to have to destroy that space (and devalue much of the capital invested therein) at a later point in order to make way for a new "spatial fix" (openings for fresh accumulation in new spaces and territories)'. (Jessop 2006: 148)

At the same time, temporal fixes are capital's strategy to control labor times. In Harry Braverman's classic analysis of the labor process (1974), controlling and measuring time is key to capital accumulation. Capital measures labor power by labor time: time used in the labor process. This abstraction is necessary for capital accumulation. In times of crisis, capitalism tendentially readjusts the measure of time and recombines multiple labor times into a new measure of temporality (see Hewitt 1993; Crary 2014; Stronge and Lewis 2021). Thus, capitalism tends to standardize space and time by fixing time and space to subsume multiplicities of labor time. This standardization of (space and) time is a function of the capitalist machinery, including clocks, factory machines, management techniques, and systems of division of labor.

In *Time for Revolution*, Antonio Negri advances Marx's analysis of machines in the stage of real subsumption, stating that "Real subsumption means the complete realization of the law of value... Labor is quality, time is quantity; in real subsumption, quality falls away, so all labor is reduced to mere quantity, to time" (2003: 27). So, time-as-quantity represents the capitalist command, commanding labor both within and outside the production process. Particularly in late capitalism, capital tends to command labor from outside the production process, or the process of value creation. Accordingly, capitalist infrastructure aims to command social labor times, reducing them to the singular quantity of temporality. To eradicate the multiplicities of time, capital has to transfer labor's power to command their own quality of time to the hands of the machines.

Drawing from the above literature, I choose to view infrastructure as an apparatus of temporality. By "apparatus," I follow Giorgio Agamben's definition, which includes:

> A) a heterogeneous set that includes virtually anything, linguistic and nonlinguistic under the same heading: discourses, institutions,

buildings, laws, police measures, philosophical propositions, and so on. The apparatus itself is the network that is established between these elements. B) The apparatus always has a concrete strategic function and is always located in a power relation. C) As such, it appears at the intersection of power relations and relations of knowledge. (Agamben 2009: 2–3)

So, a network of heterogeneous machines is an apparatus that seeks to combine different and multiple times into a mega-machine of temporality. Eradicating the obstacles presented by specificities of temporality helps the infrastructure to operate efficiently. As infrastructure operates in a network of heterogeneous temporalities, we can conceptualize it anthropologically from below. People and networks of people can negotiate with infrastructure temporarily, and capital also controls such people's and networks' temporality. In other words, temporality is an arena of class struggle between capital and labor. Capital uses temporal machines to control and exploit labor power. Here, the BRI infrastructure is perceived as an apparatus of temporality designed by Chinese capitalism to control and exploit labor power across the region.

In the transnational cattle trade, the BRI and informal infrastructures have cooperated in subsuming multiple labor times and standardizing them into parts of Chinese capitalism. In my earlier study, I proposed viewing the cattle trade as a semi-formal sector in which the brokerage system played a key role in connecting networks of people, commodities, capital, and governments. Without brokers' chains of networks, trade would be impossible. I identified three types of brokers in the chains of the transnational cattle trade: providers, creditors, and buyers (Kitirianglarp and Kantha 2020). In some cases, the same person might perform all three roles (see Figure 3.3).

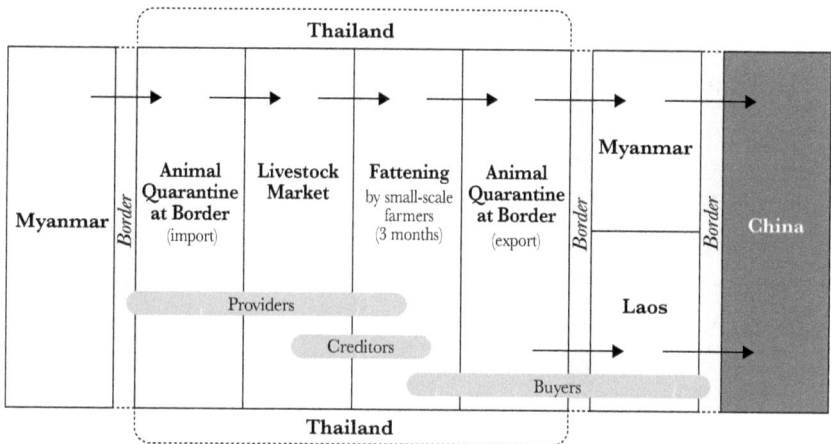

Figure 3.3 Roles and networks of brokers in the cattle trade
Source: Created by the author's research team based on field research

Providers provide cattle to the farmers. They buy a lot of cattle from the Mae-Sot border between Myanmar and Thailand, and sell them to small-scale farmers in the provinces. Farmers who buy the cattle feed them on their farms for at least three months until the cattle are robust enough to export. According to my informants, the small-scale farmers are often short of money for buying cattle, so they need credit. The *creditors* are local brokers who own large farms in the local area, who give short-term loans to poorer farmers. The expected repayment date is three months after the purchase, when the fattened cattle have been sold to the buyers. The creditors accumulate economic surplus by collecting interest from the indebted farmers. Late payment can be catastrophic for the farmers, so they must sell as soon as the cattle reach the standard weight. The *buyers* who represent Chinese merchants or Laotian brokers are the end of this value-adding chain. The buyer – who is frequently also the creditor – comes to the village to buy the fattened cows from the farmers, and negotiates the prices with the farmers. Any delay in the sale is a potential disaster for the farmers who must pay their debt on time. Although the local farmers are aware that they are trading with Chinese capital, they have neither seen nor understood where they are situated in the bigger picture. In short, although they are entangled in Chinese capitalism, they only see fragments of their situation. Their inability to see the bigger picture implies a higher risk.

As mentioned, Chinese capitalism does not directly control the cattle farmer's production process, but that does not mean that there is no control. Controlling labor power is necessary for all phases of capitalism. Accordingly, my argument here is that capital controls the labor power of farmers indirectly through the apparatus of temporality. It does so in two different, albeit interconnected, ways: first, by controlling *exchange time*; and second, by commanding *financial times*. These two apparatuses of temporality are operated locally by brokerage networks and systems.

Exchange time

According to Appel, "Infrastructure, metonymically the economy and development itself, becomes futurity and deferral at once" (2018: 53). As much as infrastructures can become a promise of the future, they can also be deferred. An economic anthropologist, Jane Guyer (2007: 410), refers to this deferral as the "fantasy futurism and enforced presentism" in which the hope projected on to the near future is infinitely deferred on behalf of the very distant future. To control time effectively means an ability to defer or delay the future or promise. And, as Shahram Klosravi argued, "Keeping people in prolonged waiting is a technique to delay them. Delaying is a technique of domination, making the other's time seem less worthy" (2021: 65).

Likewise, the brokerage system works on time control, especially in buying and selling times. In the transnational cattle trade in

Thailand, around half the cattle originate from Myanmar, where they are used as work animals before being sold for export. They are huge in physical structure, but extremely thin. Thus, they need to be fed before being exported to China. Thailand has long been a hub for feeding and quarantining the exported cattle in the region. Usually, the feeding duration is set within three months, and the duration of fattening is related to the cost. In late 2021, the cost of fattening one cow was 90 baht per day. If the broker postpones the purchase of cattle even by a couple of days after the cow has reached its maximum weight, the farmer incurs higher costs. It is not uncommon for brokers to use delaying tactics to prolong the period, using the farmers' anxieties about increasing costs to negotiate lower purchase prices. According to my findings, such deferrals increase the risks the farmers bear.

The cattle fattening industry works on the promise of a bright future; but, in fact, the farmers' future falls under someone else's control. The brokerage mechanism system gives the brokers' controlling power over purchasing time, with numerous excuses about the farmers' failure to deliver their cattle according to pre-determined standards. Sometimes, the brokers claim chaos at the border as an excuse for why the cattle cannot be exported. All these mechanisms of deferral intentionally reduce the farmers' bargaining power and, in the end, many farmers are forced to reduce the selling price of their cattle.

Financial time

As mentioned, the brokerage system works on the promise of a bright future and time control. In addition to buyers who regulate the purchasing time, creditors play a key role in controlling farmers' time. The creditor plays a role of lender to farmers from the very beginning, starting from the farmers adopting the cows from the providers to the fattening process. Most of the farmers I interviewed have relied on loans. Most of these loans consist of a three-month term corresponding to the fattening period prior to sale. The loan may cover the cost of cattle food, wages for farm workers, and other related expenses. Such loans are informal and bear high-interest rates, so late payments can mean the farmers losing their means of production and going bankrupt. During the three months of fattening, farmers must try to maintain their cows according to their standard weight, and protect their cattle from disease and predators. In short, they must ensure that their cattle reach the standard weight while staying healthy for the three months maturity period.

In this sense, farmers can find themselves squeezed between creditors and buyers. If the buyers delay buying cattle from the farmers, the farmers incur higher costs. Apart from the daily cost of feeding, the creditors continue to charge daily interest on their loans. In sum, the two mechanisms brokers use for controlling time are related, and result in reducing the farmers' negotiating powers. Meanwhile, the brokers' bargaining power increases in inverse proportion. The brokers' advantage derives from their role as intermediaries in dealing with buyers, as well as their understanding of the border situation. Ultimately, the farmers are exploited by these asymmetrical structures and are forced to sell their cows cheaply.

It is common that cattle trade farmers receive lower profit margins than they had expected. Many farmers have lost money, and many have been bankrupted from feeding cattle to sell to China. Having squeezed what they can from the farmers in one village, the brokers move on to another village and persuade the farmers there to buy cows for fattening with the same false promises and faux commitments. In my previous paper, I argued that China's cattle fattening business works through a "vicious cycle" that never ends.

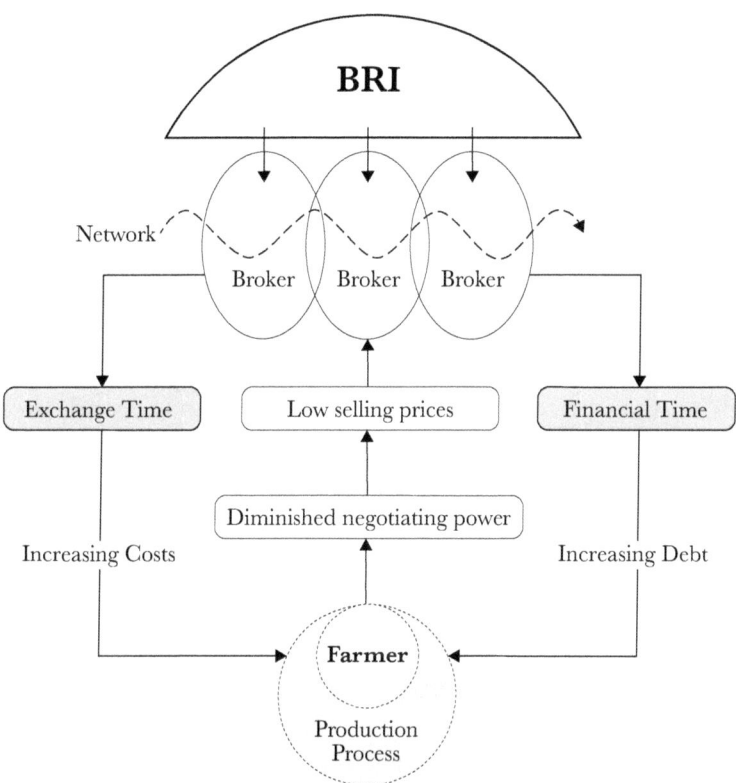

Figure 3.4 Apparatuses of temporality and vicious circle in the cattle trade
Source: Created by the author's research team based on field research

While farmers take risks and eventually collapse, the brokerage system continues to reap profits without bearing the risks of the production process (see Figure 3.4).

Such apparatuses of temporality and vicious circles are instruments of violence hidden in the processes through which the material and immaterial infrastructures act against the interests of the farmers. We unwittingly neglect the invisible mechanisms when we focus on tangible infrastructure. If we focus exclusively on the infrastructures intentionally created by the state, we remain oblivious to the social networks built on the relationships between local people. Furthermore, these social relationships are the real source of value creation; the BRI's infrastructures provide only mechanisms of capital subsumption and accumulation of surplus, which is itself "external" to the production process.

These temporal fixes have impacted local actors. First, due to China's monopoly of large-scale regional infrastructures such as railways, roads, ports, walls, checkpoints, slaughterhouses, and disease-controlling systems, as well as regulating "markets" (with its tremendous purchasing power), China determines the standards of goods and the prices for the cattle in the region. Second, brokers who control the informal networks of cattle trading can manipulate the production processes and their purchasing power by 1) delaying buyout time, and 2) shortening the time of shipping/sales, thus passing the burden of temporality to farmers. Finally, some huge Thai broker companies endeavor to coerce the Thai government to subsidize and facilitate the construction of infrastructure projects, such as the Thai Livestock & Meat Exporter's Chiang Rai Sandbox Market (*Chiangrai Focus* 2021), which intends to connect with China's BRI infrastructure in Laos while: 1) monopolizing trading with China and cutting out the retail brokers; and 2) negotiating power with China and Laos to extend the feeding time in Thailand as long as possible. However, no concrete scheme has been designed to support farmers.

Poignantly, the Chiang Rai Sandbox Market reflects an unbridgeable social gap in Thai society. On one hand, it reflects the hope that state support and large capital pledges can render assistance to farmers. Yet, on the other hand, these farmers are desperate, and oblivious to the changes imposed from above. Zooming out to the level of the BRI, the gap between knowledge and hope is much wider; I found it to be permanently unbridgeable. As I observed the informal meetings of small-scale farmers at the Sandbox conference, the farmers gathered in groups outside the meeting room to discuss their hopeless situation and I overheard that one of my informants, a broker, had been arrested and imprisoned in China. This contrasted sharply with the minister's hopeful speech about the Sandbox project inside the conference hall. Hope and desperation are two sides of the same coin. Keeping hope alive is key to the cattle trade. This violence of hopeless hope is what Guyer called "fantasy futurism and enforced presentism."

Conclusion

Even if local people go unnoticed within the mechanisms of the mega-infrastructure created by the state, their lives are greatly impacted by these infrastructures. Methodologically, we can identify local peoples' "ignorance" about infrastructure, which we know is an essential mechanism of said infrastructure. The mechanism of concealment and the creation of ignorance through infrastructure and apparatuses is the mechanism by which capital commands local people. It is this mechanism that offers local people hope and garners their consent to bear the risks of participating in the production of Chinese capital. In short, such ignorance is a cultural logic that shapes the behavior of local people and their reactions to regional variations.

This transnational cattle trade is not merely a trade, but also a value-creating process, in which the value of cattle is increased via mobile processes in which cattle farmers act as producers and brokers act as mobility-facilitators. The heart of this transnational cattle trade is a production process. This paper focuses on a producer – Thai cattle farmers – who are exploited by the brokerage system.

In conclusion, I argue that the BRI infrastructures initiated by Chinese capitalism aim to control cattle trade across the region by establishing formal and material infrastructure in Laos. At the same time, Chinese capitalism sustains the enduring informal infrastructure of the brokerage system, enabling local brokers to play a determinant role in the production process by commanding the apparatus of time, thus facilitating the transfer of surplus from local farmers to Chinese capital. In other words, Chinese capitalism operates outside the labor and production processes. It allows locals to create surplus freely, while passively accumulating the economic surplus produced by local farmers. As we have seen, there are two layers of infrastructures within the BRI: the immobile material infrastructures built by Chinese capital in Laos; and, mobile and immaterial networks locally interwoven through Thailand, Laos, and Myanmar. These two levels of infrastructural apparatuses work collaboratively in the region. Their practices are essential to Chinese capitalism subsuming surplus value from local production processes. Moreover, they give capital more flexibility while imposing uncertainty and risks on the local producers. Despite the close intertwinement of the material and immaterial infrastructures, they also work independently to some extent. Unlike production processes in industrial factories where producers are directly controlled by material infrastructure, the material infrastructure does not directly control the networked cattle brokers. Nor do the brokers directly control the cattle farmers' production processes; but they nevertheless exercise indirect control through 'apparatuses of temporality', which exist outside the production process. Thus, to clearly understand the impacts of BRI on the value-creating process within the cattle trade, it is essential to elucidate the complex relationship between these two kinds of infrastructure.

References

Agamben, Giorgio (2009) *"What is an Apparatus?" And Other Essays*. Trans. David Kishik and Stefan Pedatella. Stanford: Stanford University Press.

Alliez, Éric (1995) *Capital Times: Tales from the Conquest of Time*. Trans. Georges Van den Abbeele. Minneapolis and London: University of Minnesota Press.

Anand, Nikhil, Akhil Gupta and Hannah Appel (eds) (2018) *The Promise of Infrastructure*. Durham and London: Duke University Press.

Appel, Hannah (2018) Infrastructural Time. In Nikhil Anand, Akhil Gupta, and Hannah Appel (eds) *The Promise of Infrastructure*. Durham and London: Duke University Press, pp. 41–61.

Appel, Hannah, Nikhil Anand and Akhil Gupta (2018) Introduction: Temporality, Politics, and the Promise of Infrastructure. In Nikhil Anand, Akhil Gupta, and Hannah Appel (eds) *The Promise of Infrastructure*. Durham and London: Duke University Press, pp. 1–39.

Braverman, Harry (1974) *Labor and Monopoly Capital: The Degradation of Work in the Twentieth Century*. New York and London: Monthly Review Press.

Crary, John (2014) *24/7: Late Capitalism and the Ends of Sleep*. London and New York: Verso.

David, Noam, Omry Sendik, Hagit Messer and Pinhas Alpert (2015) Cellular Network Infrastructure: The future of fog monitoring? *Bulletin of the American Meteorological Society*, 96(10): 1687–1698.

Deleuze, Gilles and Félix Guattari (1983) *Anti-Oedipus: Capitalism and Schizophrenia*. Trans. Robert Hurley, Mark Seem, and Helen R. Lane. Minneapolis and London: University of Minnesota Press.

Guyer, Jane (2007) Prophecy and the near future: Thoughts on macroeconomics, evangelical and punctuated time. *American Ethnologist*, 34(3): 409–421.

Harvey, David (1989) *The Condition of Postmodernity: An Enquiry into the Origins of Cultural Change*. Oxford and Cambridge: Basil Blackwell.

Harvey, Penny and Hannah Knox (2015) *Roads: An Anthropology of Infrastructure and Expertise*. Ithaca and London: Cornell University Press.

Hetherington, Kregg (2017) Survey the future perfect: Anthropology, development and the promise of infrastructure. In Penny Harvey, Casper Bruun Jensen, and Atsuro Morita (eds) *Infrastructures and Social Complexity: A Companion*. London and New York: Routledge, pp. 40–50.

Hewitt, Patricia (1993) *About Time: The Revolution in Work and Family Life*. London: Rivers Oram Press.

Jessop, Bob (2006) Spatial fixes, temporal fixes and spatio-temporal fixes. In Noel Castree and Derek Gregory (eds) *David Harvey: A Critical Reader*. Oxford: Blackwell, pp. 142–166.

Jomo, Kwame Sundaram (2002) Chinese Capitalism in Southeast Asia. *Journal of Contemporary Asia*, 32(3), pp. 325–353.

Kitirianglarp, Kengkij and Pana Kantha (2020) Brokerage in the Transborder Cattle Trade: Semi-formal trade, risks, and inequality of power. *Political Science and Public Administration Journal*, 11(2): 141–160. (In Thai)

Klosravi, Shahram (2021) Prelude II Stolen Time. In Shahram Klosravi (ed.) *Waiting: A Project in Conversation*. Bielefeld: Transcript, pp. 65–70.

Larkin, Brian (2008) *Signal and Noise: Media, Infrastructure, and Urban Culture in Nigeria*. Durham and London: Duke University Press.

Larkin, Brian (2013) The Politics and Poetics of Infrastructure. *Annual Review of Anthropology*, 42: 327–343.

Lazzarato, Maurizio (2014) *Signs and Machines: Capitalism and the Production of Subjectivity*. Los Angeles: Semiotext(e).

Marx, Karl (1973) *Grundrisse*. Trans. Martin Nicolaus. London and New York: Penguin.

Negri, Antonio (2003) *Time for Revolution*. Trans. Matteo Mandarini. New York and London: Continuum.

Nkendah, Robert (2010) *The Informal Cross-Border Trade of agricultural commodities between Cameroon and its CEMAC's Neighbours*. NSF/AERC/IGC Conference, December 4, 2010. https://www.theigc.org/wp-content/uploads/2014/08/nkendah.pdf. Accessed 25 February 2020

Smith, Polly, Nancy Bourgeois Lüthi, Li Huachun, Kyaw Naing Oo, Aloun Phonvisay. Sith Premashthira, Ronello Abila, Phillip Widders, Karan Kukreja and Corissa Miller (2015) *Movement pathways and market chains of large ruminants in the Greater Mekong Sub-region*. World Organisation of Animal Health. https://rr-asia.oie.int/wp-content/uploads/2019/10/livestock_movement_pathways_and_markets_in_the_gms__final_.pdf. Accessed 18 October 2018.

Stronge, Will and Kyle Lewis (2021) *Overtime: Why We Need a Shorter Working Week*. London and New York: Verso.

4 Chinese Loans for Infrastructure Development? Narratives of Railways, Highways, and China's Belt and Road Initiative in Vietnam

Nguyễn Văn Chính and Đinh Thị Thanh Huyền

Abstract

Much has been written attributing Vietnam's concerns with China's Belt and Road Initiative to factors such as territorial disputes in the South China Sea, low quality infrastructure projects and expensive loans, etc. While these factors are undeniable, there is clear evidence that Vietnam is pursuing a hedging strategy, prioritising national security over borrowing capital for infrastructure development regardless of the costs. Vietnam's hedging strategy is to pursue a multilateral foreign economic policy and secure diverse sources of capital to fund its infrastructure projects to minimize its reliance on the BRI. This policy is driven by domestic politics in which groups of intellectuals, professionals and activists play key roles.

Keywords

The Belt and Road Initiative – hedging – domestic politics – transport infrastructure

Introduction

The Belt and Road Initiative is an ambitious strategy to expand China's influence around the world in the 21st century. The initiative seeks to expand trade by prioritizing infrastructure development and the integration of financial systems. China's BRI promoters claim that building and connecting infrastructure will be mutually beneficial, enabling better cooperation and common development, and promise high quality investment through BRI project finance, risk mitigation tools, and green finance (Ministry of Foreign Affairs, PRC 2020). BRI transport projects seem to offer great opportunities for developing countries to expand trade, increase foreign investment, and reduce poverty.

Studies of the effects of Chinese loans to poor countries for infrastructure development under the BRI framework, however, raise concerns about Chinese loans. Buchholz (2023), for example, based on World Bank data, demonstrates that the construction of China's New Silk Road infrastructure (ports, railways, and roads) has created a lot of debt for participating countries. As of 2020, China had officially lent about US$170 billion to low-and middle-income countries, up from around US$40 billion in 2010. According to Buchholz (2023), China's interest rates are higher than those from international institutions such as the International Monetary Fund or World Bank, or bilateral loans from Paris Club countries, and have shorter repayment terms. For Vietnam, the BRI's infrastructure development loan conditions are more like commercial loans "with unpredictable hidden risks" than other comparable sources of financing for general development purposes (Ministry of Finance 2022b).

The findings of these and related studies (Gelpern et al. 2021; Le Hong Hiep 2013, 2018), combined with its own early lessons about expensive Chinese loans, has prompted Vietnam to take measures to protect the economy, including adopting clear policies on foreign loans. In 2022, the Directive of Communist Party of Vietnam on Economic Diplomacy was issued. This policy aims, on the one hand, to create opportunities to borrow capital from numerous foreign partners for development purposes and, on the other hand, to ensure Vietnam's financial and economic security are not compromised by dependence on foreign financiers. This policy emphasizes three points: (1) Economic diplomacy is a central task, essential for mobilizing external resources to develop a non-aligned economy; (2) A multilateral foreign policy, seeking to intertwine economic interests, especially with neighboring countries and strategic partners will be continued; (3) Foreign economic cooperation must be associated with national security and defense, treating national interests and substantive efficiency as top criteria (Communist Party of Việt Nam (CPV) 2022).

In the past, Vietnam's foreign policy often prioritized domestic political interests and concerns. This new foreign policy seems more pragmatic, recognizing that national interests are best served through effective international economic cooperation with a diverse array of foreign partners. With this policy, Vietnam seems to have definitively prioritized national security above loans for infrastructure projects. On the one hand, it emphasizes national security as a prerequisite strategy and, on the other hand, tries to build a multilateral and balanced strategy in foreign relations. In this chapter, the questions under discussion are why Vietnam is so cautious – even wary – of loans from China? What factors influenced Vietnam's "hesitant" approach towards China and the BRI? This chapter examines Vietnam's needs for capital for transport infrastructure, the approach of Chinese partners and Vietnam's response to BRI loans for infrastructure projects to find answers to these problems.

Theoretical perspective and methology

The concept of "hedging" has become quite prominent in international relations discourse. As a familiar term for investors, hedging refers to the use of financial instruments to manage risks in financial commitments, including borrowings, investments and similar business activities. The term more recently has become an important theoretical concept in the study of foreign strategy. Kei Koga (2017) argues that hedging should be understood in terms of "balance of power" theory as located on a spectrum between "balancing" and "bandwagoning" as a state's third strategic choice. John Ciorciari and Jürgen Haacke (2019) observe that hedging normally refers in that context to a national security or alignment strategy, undertaken by one state towards another, featuring a mix of cooperative and confrontational tactics. The concept of hedging is posited in response to key questions about contemporary international relations theory and practice; for instance, how do states respond to rising powers that might challenge their security interests? Examining Middle Eastern countries' policies guiding economic relations with China, Salman and Geeraerts (2015) found that strategic hedging produces more-effective policies, improving the hedging states's capacity to strike a balance with the great powers while avoiding direct confrontation with the leading state.

In examining Vietnam's hedging strategy against China, Le Hong Hiep (2013: 333–368) identifies four characteristics: economic pragmatism, direct engagement, hard balancing and soft balancing. According to Le, these reflect the essence of the hedging strategy, providing Vietnam with opportunities to maintain a peaceful, stable, and cooperative relationship with China in the interests of its domestic development, while resisting undue pressure and deterring Chinese aggression. Liao and Ngoc-Tram (2020) point out that economic hedging is a strategy used by small states to create guardrails that protect them from veering into asymmetrical dependence on state powers that pose higher security risks than others. Economic hedging also reflects the nature of economic statecraft, specifically small states' recognition that great powers are always willing and able to use economic coercion in pursuit of their interests.

The economic security strategies outlined above have important implications for this research. In addition to economic factors, Vietnam's hedging strategy is influenced by territorial disputes in the East China Sea (Le Hong Hiep 2018; Thiện Nhân 2020). In the context of the BRI, hedging may also entail complex engagement policies including a constructive hedge against potential risks that may arise from doing business or economic cooperation with China. Hedging is a widely discussed concept in explaining the policies of small countries in the face of large countries. However, the research literature does not yet clarify the specific context and motivations of using hedging strategies, nor does it outline prudent calculations of the association between security risks and partnerships.

This chapter uses the concept of hedging to analyze Vietnam's new foreign economic policy in the context of its participation in the BRI. The study emphasizes two main points: (1) Controlling how much capital is borrowed from foreign countries, presumably focused on perceived risks from China. (2) Creating multilateral economic relations with foreign countries and diversifying sources for infrastructure development loans. In short, this foreign economic directive outlines Vietnam's hedging strategy, seeking on the one hand to balance commercial interests with strategic foreign policy by "making friends with all countries" and, on the other hand, promoting economic pragmatism, pushing a realist approach to foreign economic relations, and bolstering efforts to protect its national sovereignty from Chinese influence (Liao and Ngoc-Tram 2020).

The available literature indicates that among neighboring countries who have participated in China's BRI program, Vietnam has been the most reticent, despite its huge demand for infrastructure investment (Le 2018). Several reasons have been raised but not thoroughly studied. The most obvious reason for this reticence is a widespread lack of trust of the Chinese state's intentions among the Vietnamese which strongly shapes domestic politics and policies concerning economic relations with China. Among other things, Vietnam had a bitter experience with borrowing capital from China for infrastructure development between 2000 and 2015. The heavy consequences of these projects have not yet been overcome, even pushing some projects into debt and bankruptcy. A typical case is the Thai Nguyen Iron and Steel Plant project, with China Metallurgical Science and Technology and Commerce Corporation (MCC) as the EPC contractor, which has lasted for 15 years, from 2007 to 2024, used trillions of VND but is facing the risk of being abandoned (Tiền Phong 2024).[1] A report of the Ministry of Industry and Trade also indicated that among the 12 projects implemented by the Chinese EPC contractors with an investment capital of VND 63,610 billion (about US$ 2.5 billion), of which about 75% was borrowed from China, only two projects have been completed and put into production, the rest remain in dispute with the Chinese contractor (Vietstock Finance 2024). The reality of business losses with China has greatly affected Vietnam's internal politics and impacted its foreign economic policy.

---

1 This project named TISCO2 was started in September 2007 with a total investment of 3,843 billion VND, by a Chinese EPC contractor, expected to be completed in 2014. In May 2013, the TISCO2 project had to adjust the total investment to 8,104 billion VND (an increase of 4,261 billion VND, equal to 52% compared to the expected capital) but there was no progress. Up to now (2024), no solution has been found (Tiền Phong 2024). Note: the exchange rate of 1 US Dollar is equivalent to about 25,000 VN Đồng.

Competing development perspectives, the competing interests of various social groups, and public feedback in general, are impossible for the government to ignore. Therefore, this study also examines how Vietnam's internal politics affect its foreign economic diplomacy, particularly as concerns borowing for investment in transport infrastructure.

    To achieve our research objectives, this study uses a combination of qualitative and statistical data. We conducted eleven in-depth interviews with parliamentarians and experts in foreign economics and strategic research. Most of our interviewees have worked as members of the Prime Minister's Economic Advisory Group, taught at universities or done research at research institutions. Given that opinions on international relations and policy can be politically sensitive, our interviews took place primarily as open conversations rather than using questionnaires or pre-designed questions. The collected data extends our observations and informs the assumptions that we have been working with for years. We also conducted field observations during visits to key infrastructure projects, including the Ha Long-Mong Cai expressway project, the Hai Phong-Lao Cai railway, and the North-South expressway project. Using the ethnographic fieldwork approach, we listened to feedback from residents, professionals and managers working on the projects. This helps us understand the attitude of the people and policy makers towards the Belt and Road initiative "from within." Furthermore, we collected and analyzed opinions about China's infrastructure diplomacy expressed on various social media platforms. It is worth noting that comments posted on the facebook pages of intellectuals, including famous journalists, researchers, and influential social activists were also collected for reference as they reach large numbers, and seem to exert some pressure on the government's foreign policies. This chapter is developed mainly from qualitative information by ethnographies with the expectation of finding empirical evidence and insider perspectives.

The scarcity and questionable reliability of infrastructure-related statistical documents presents a significant challenge for this research, as both Vietnam and China consider such information to be classified state secrets. However, scattered sources of information from government agencies, AidData, Global Infrastructure Outlook and InfrasCompass provide valuable complements to the government's information gaps.

Vietnam's infrastructure investment needs

Policymakers in Vietnam believe that infrastructure plays a particularly important role in the socio-economic development of the country, and it is considered a key driver of economic growth and FDI (Nguyễn 2018). However, despite the government's efforts, so far, infrastructure in transportation and manufacturing has not improved much, many projects are behind schedule and promised high technology transfers have yet to be delivered at scale. In coming years, with the growth of free trade agreements (FTAs) and favorable investment policies, Vietnam's infrastructure is likely to improve significantly while presenting opportunities for investors. Vietnam currently spends nearly 6% of its GDP on infrastructure, compared to other countries in the region who spend an average 2.3%, making Vietnam the leading country in ASEAN for infrastructure investment. In Asia, Vietnam's infrastructure investment level is second only to China (6.8%), while Indonesia and the Philippines spend less than 3%, and Malaysia and Thailand spend less than 2% of GDP on infrastructure (*Tài Chính* 2017).

According to the Global Infrastructure Hub (2017), Vietnam needs on average US$25–30 billion annually for infrastructure to ensure its economic growth. However, the national budget can only provide US$15–18 billion (around 7% of GDP). Therefore, the country must source the remaining US$10–15 billion from investors. Table 4.1 presents GI Hub's data on Vietnam's infrastructure investment needs in relation to the strength of the economy. In terms of infrastructure investment to GDP ratio, Vietnam's infrastructure investment demand accounts for 6.28%, the highest in Southeast Asia and second in Asia after China. The country can however only meet around 83% of total infrastructure investment needs. Even so, there is still a gap between its current infrastructure and its aspirations which has negative impacts on the economy. As of September 2022, Vietnam was positioned 47th of 160 countries in infrastructure and 103rd in road quality in the World Economic Forum's rankings (Pham 2022). Although Vietnam allocates up to 6% of GDP for infrastructure annually, 90% of that spending comes from the public budget, placing a burden on the national debt and fiscal policy. The government therefore recently introduced public-private partnerships (PPP) to accelerate infrastructure upgrades with an expectation that 20% of investment in infrastructure will come from private funds in the coming years, compared to only 10% in the past.

To facilitate improvements in transport infrastructure, in 2021 the government issued Decision No. 1454/QD-TTg (Prime Minister 2021b) which promotes the development of the road system for the 2021–2030 period, as part of its vision to 2050. This ambitious plan aims to build a transport infrastructure system connecting local, regional, and international transport hubs. At the same time, this policy institutionalizes solutions and resource mobilization from all economic sectors. This plan emphasizes the importance of forming a highway system connecting economic and political centers, key economic zones, seaports, airports, and international gateways, connecting with neighboring countries within the Greater Mekong Subregion (GMS) and ASEAN. This

Table 4.1 Vietnam's total infrastructure investment need (2016–2040)

(USD billion)	Current trend	% of GDP	Need	% of GDP
Electricity	256	2.64	265	2.75
Telecom	99	1.02	99	1.02
Airport	3.8	0.01	5.2	0.06
Seaport	0.414	0.01	8.5	0.1
Rail	15	0.15	21	0.22
Road	79	0.81	134	1.38
Water	50	0.52	72	0.75
Total	503.214	5.16	604.7	6.28

Source: Global Infrastructure Hub 2017

decision also plans 41 expressways with a total length of about 9,014 km, including the 2,063 km long national arterial axis connecting the Mekong Delta with the northern border to support transportation throughout the country.

To realize these plans, Vietnam needs huge amounts of capital. However, for a small economy with a Real Gross National Product of about $231 billion (2018) and growth of 5–7% per annum (General Statistics Office 2024), infrastructure requirements are hard to realize. The inevitable solution is to borrow foreign capital and diversify domestic capital sources. Against this backdrop, how have Chinese lenders approached potential borrowers?

China's infrastructure diplomacy

China's Belt and Road Initiative is one of the largest infrastructure and investment projects in history, and China is willing to lend money to participating countries "to enhance regional connectivity and embrace a brighter future" (*Xinhua* 2015). Currently, China's infrastructure diplomacy towards Vietnam includes: (1) A meeting between the two countries' leaders and a propaganda campaign to promote cooperation; (2) Diversify lending methods for large infrastructure projects; (3) Create more opportunities for Chinese enterprises to bid on important projects.

The Belt and Road Forums held every two years provide the Chinese government leadership an opportunity to meet with the heads of participating countries. Official visits with heads of other countries typically discuss BRI issues and projects and conclude with joint statements that affirm the two states' commitments to the BRI.

China established the Asian Infrastructure Investment Bank (AIIB) in 2016 to help finance the construction of infrastructure in the region, and to share the burden of foreign loans with The Export-Import Bank of China (China Exim Bank), which was itself established in 1994 to provide financing to developing countries and promote the export of Chinese products and services. While EXIM Bank only lends through inter-government loan agreements, AIIB offers loans to a more diverse range of borrowers. At a meeting with General Secretary of the Communist Party of Vietnam, Nguyễn Phú Trọng, who was visiting China in January 2017, AIIB President Jin Liqun announced that the bank "wants to invest in infrastructure development, particularly railways, highways and seaports, in Vietnam" and "to work closer with the Vietnamese side in designing future projects and do its best to make co-operation in the field yield practical outcomes" (*Vietnam News* 2017). This was affirmed in a meeting with the Vietnamese government on 12 October 2018, when the head of the AIIB emphasized the bank's commitment "to meet infrastructure needs" and to be a reliable member of the Joint Development Bank, of which Vietnam is a founding member (Koushan Das 2018). In 2021 the AIIB was in negotiation with Vietnam regarding a loan of US$95 million for the 125 megawatts Dak Drinh plant in central Vietnam, which is majority owned by the state through PV Power (*Out-Law News* 2021).

Pursuing a balanced hedging strategy, Vietnam has reserved the Hekou-Hanoi-Hai Phong railway project for China and agreed to place the project within the BRI cooperation framework. China considers this a success in its infrastructure diplomacy efforts. China also paved the way for state-owned enterprises and economic groups to contact individuals in the political system and those charged with proposing infrastructure projects under Vietnam's Ministry of Transport. Local diplomacy is conducted intensely, aiming to enhance cooperation and exchanges between the two sides and to mobilize Chinese entities to participate in Vietnam's infrastructure projects (Government [of Vietnam] 2019; Hai Phong City 2019). These contacts between the two sides' leaders and businesses have produced concrete results. In 2019 China announced that a grant of 10 million Yuan (approx. US$1.5 million) was provided for surveying the 392 km long Hekou-Hanoi-Hai Phong railway (Ministry of Transport 2019).

According to Vietnam's Railway Department, for the period 2021–2030, Vietnam needs about 240,000 billion VND (approx. US$10 billion) in investment for national railways. The existing Hekou-Hanoi-Hai Phong railway, which was built during the French colonial period needs to be upgraded to increase transport capacity and connect with China. It is expected this railway will be rebuilt to international standards and connect with China's Hekou-Kunming railway system. Once completed, it will form a smooth railway connecting Hải Phòng with Kunming-Chengdu-Lanzhou and Horgos (the gateway to Europe).

However, Chinese support for this railway project was rejected by the public for several reasons. First, in terms of cost-benefit analyses, the economic efficiency of the route is not clear. People questioned whether Vietnam really needed to invest such a huge amount of money in this railway, and who would benefit. At present, the railway would not bring much profit to Vietnam although it would provide great benefits to China by connecting its southwestern region to the world through Hai Phong port. Second were concerns about repaying the debt. Borrowing the amount of money required for this railway project could create obstacles to building a North-South transnational railway, which is agreed to be of great importance to the country's development and needs a huge investment, estimated at $58 billion, which has not yet been secured. In the absence of investment capital for both projects, public opinion is concerned that the government spends a large amount of money on the railway project, which could leave behind a huge debt that cannot be repaid. Finally, the biggest concern is China's loan plan to build this railway. Until now, Vietnam has not made any specific decision on how to realize this railway, but the Chinese factor is believed to be the main cause of the delay. Vietnam seems to have a commitment from the state leadership to borrow Chinese capital to implement the project to ensure balanced relations with other superpowers. In 2023, Vietnam officially asked Japan to provide a new Official Development Assistance (ODA) to build the trans-Vietnam railway, estimated at US$68 billion (*Vietnamnet* 2023).

Vietnam's debts to China

The question of Vietnam's debts to China, and how those debts affect the relationship between the two countries, are of great interest to the Vietnamese public. Zachary Abuza and Phuong Vu (2021), citing AidData, reported that "Vietnam has borrowed (from China) $16,35 billion, second only to Indonesia in Southeast Asia. Vietnam was the 20th largest recipient of Chinese concessionary ODA, a mere $1,37 billion." However, it is unclear how reliable this data is because, by mutual agreement, Vietnam and China treat loans and aid arrangements as confidential, so these data cannot be confirmed by official figures. Since 2011, the *Public Debt Bulletin* (*Bản tin nợ công*) published by Vietnam's Ministry of Finance reports the total debt and types of debt but does not provide details such as debt owed per lending country. This makes it difficult to determine Vietnam's indebtedness to China. Before this change of practice, *Public Debt Bulletin* No.7 (Ministry of Finance 2011) reported that the government of Vietnam's total debt to China at the end of 2010 was $552 million and the government guaranteed a further $1.12 billion of the debt held by Vietnamese enterprises. Thus, Vietnam's total debt to China at the end of 2010 was about $1.64 billion. An analysis of Vietnamese borrowings from China between 2000 and 2013 to invest in 21 projects estimated the debt at about US$4.1 billion. Since 2013, after a string of enterprises experienced financial difficulties due to Chinese loans, Vietnam began to strictly control Chinese loans and no longer publicize these debts. According to Vu Quang Viet (2018), Vietnam's debt to China amounted to about US$6 billion in 2018.

China's share of Vietnam's total foreign debt remains unknown. According to the *Public Debt Bulletin*, in the period 2012–2021, Vietnam's external debt increased from $58 billion to $139 billion, of which, the government's direct external debt increased from $35 billion to $47 billion, while the foreign debt of enterprises increased from $23 billion to $93 billion (Ministry of Finance 2022a). This bulletin indicates that Japan is the country that lends the most to Vietnam, $14.6 billion in 2021. Specifically, Vietnam's major creditors are as indicated in Table 4.2.

While Vietnam's total debt to China is not high, investments by Chinese enterprises in Vietnam have increased significantly. According to data from the Ministry of Finance (2022), until November 2020, China invested US$2.1 billion in Vietnam,

Table 4.2. Vietnam's foreign creditors as of 2021

Lending country	Amount (billion US$)	International lending organization	Amount (billion US$)
Japan	14.6	World Bank	16.0
Korea	1.8	Asian Development Bank (ADB)	8.1
France	1.7	International Monetary Fund (IMF)	2.0
Russia	1.5	International Fund for Agricultural Development (IFAD)	0.2
Germany	1.5	European Investment Bank (EIB)	0.1
China	1.5	Fund for International Development (OFID)	0.1

Source: Bộ Tài chính (2022) Bản tin nợ công số 14 [The Ministry of Finance 2022. *Public Debt Bulletin* no. 14] 6 August 2022.

making it the third highest ranking foreign investor country in Vietnam. Accumulated to November 2020, Chinese enterprises have invested a total of US$18 billion in Vietnam across about 3,087 projects. Chinese FDI is present in most Vietnamese provinces and cities, but it is much more concentrated near border-crossings with China, which is convenient for the import and export of goods as well as travel between the two countries. However, there remains widespread concerns that these debts are being incurred to invest in development projects contracted to Chinese companies with terrible track records of delays, lack of transparency, cost overruns, environmental damage, poor construction quality, and high maintenance costs. And the Chinese loans are are more expensive than others, so why does Vietnam borrow from China at all? It appears that the decisions to borrow from China is not based on economic considerations alone, but also by political considerations. Vietnam and China are closely aligned with communist ideology and there is a perception that strengthening economic relations can help reduce political risk, and thus, borrowing from China is an important part of the hedging strategy to maintain balance in relations with other regional powers such as Japan.

Hedging against China: The North-South Expressway

Public investment and public-private partnership

According to the government's Road Network Plan for 2021–2030, vision to 2050 (Prime Minister 2021b), Vietnam plans to build more than 5,000 km of expressways from 2021 to 2030, with an estimated capital investment of more than 900 trillion VND (approx. US$36 billion). This is an ambitious plan with great challenges in terms of capital investment. The original plan was for the state to provide about 40% from its budget, and seek the rest from other sources, including international financial institutions, ODAs, and public-private partnerships (PPP).

In September 2021, the government approved the detailed planning of the North-South Expressway with a total length of 2,063 km, starting from the Hữu Nghị border crossing (to Guangxi province, China) in the north and running to Vietnam's southernmost city, Cà Mau. As planned, the North-South Expressway will pass through 32 provinces and cities and affect more than 60% of the country's population, connecting to 74% of seaports and most key economic zones. According to estimates of the Ministry of Transport, the total investment in the period 2021–2030 for 729 km of this four-lane highway is 146,990 billion VND (approx. US$6.3 billion), for an average investment rate of about 115.8 billion VND (approx. US$5.1 million) per km. The government initially planned to fund the expressway via public-private partnership (PPP), but ultimately decided on public investment using government funding (National Assembly 2022;

Ministry of Transport 2020). The reasons for this change have not been made public. Our respondents suggest it could be a sign of policy failure, ultimately decided by its reticence to borrow. However, behind that reticence may be a concern that PPP agreements could open a path for foreign businesses and banks to take ownership of Vietnam's essential transport infrastructure, which would in turn make it more difficult for the state to control foreign debt. Public investment with state capital or ODA loans, in contrast, gives the state greater control, reducing risks of financial dependence.

International bidding and the domination of Chinese enterprises

The North-South expressway project is divided into eleven sections. Initially, the government proposed using public-private partnerships to finance and international tenders to build the expressway. In March 2019, Mr. Yan Jiehe, PCG's founder and chairman China Pacific Construction Group (PCG), visited Vietnam and met with Deputy Minister of Transport Nguyễn Văn Công to introduce the PCG and outline its vast experience investing in and constructing road and highway infrastructure in China and expressed his desire to participate in the construction of the North-South expressway. Mr. Yan also advised that, for important arterial roads such as this one, the government should not be looking for investment from small private capital but should partner with a company capable of financing the whole project. Vietnam could invest in the form of EPC (Engineering, Procurement and Construction) or BTO (Build, Transfer, Operate), he said, because "this is a model that is highly appreciated and applied successfully in China and can be complete model of public-private partnership investment." He suggested that the best approach is for private enterprises to fully finance the project, and the government will later buy back the whole or partial project, and he declared that PCG was prepared to finance and complete the entire project, from design, construction, labor, construction materials, etc., to ensure the quality and timely progress of the project.

Vietnam's Ministry of Transport listened attentively to Mr. Yan Jiehe's proposal. Then Deputy Minister Nguyễn Văn Công restated that the North-South expressway project would be awarded through an open and transparent bidding process, and the government would not be appointing contractors. Pointing out that "PPP investment form is still very new to Vietnam," he said "the Ministry of Transport will carefully study the PCG's proposal, consider whether it can be applied to Vietnam" and invited PCG to bid for the component projects of the expressway (*Vietnamnet* 2019). As planned, in April 2019, the Ministry of Transport released an international invitation to tender to find the best contractors. The Minister of Transport declared he was determined "resolutely not to appoint a contractor but organize an international bidding, if the first bid cannot find a good contractor, then bid again!" (*Vietnamnet* 2019).

By September 2019, the Project Management Board of the Ministry of Transport had received 60 submissions. Among the bidders were two investors from France (VINCI Highway and Horizon Invest) and three Korean contractors (Daewoo Engineering and Construction Co., Ltd., Lotte, and Hyundai). Two joint venture consortiums (Vietnamese and Chinese) and four Vietnamese investors submitted bids. The vast majority of bids, though, were from big Chinese enterprises, including famous Chinese corporations such as China Railway Construction Investment Group, China Railway 21st Group Co, China Railway 6th Bureau Group, China National Machinery Import and Export Corporation, China Road and Bridge Corporation, Metallurgical Corporation of China, China Harbor Engineering, China

Gezhouba Group, etc. These enterprises bid for all components of the North-South expressway (Thanh Niên 2019b).

The number of Chinese enterprises bidding for all projects raised concerns that Chinese construction corporations would gain the upper hand, take the right to build Vietnam's strategic highways and put Vietnam in a vulnerable position. Because of such concerns, after reviewing the international submissions, the Ministry of Transport officially announced that it would not invite select contractors to bid for the North-South expressway as originally planned but would instead directly appoint domestic contractors for finance and construction.

The Ministry offered three reasons for cancelling international bidding: (1) The competition among contractors was not high. (2) The North-South expressway is a key national project that has a great role to play in the country's socio-economic development, it is necessary to carefully review legal procedures to ensure compliance with the provisions of the Law on Bidding; (3) As the world becomes more complex, the project needs to ensure national security, promote internal resources, and create conditions for domestic enterprises to benefit (Tiền Phong 2019).

Among the reasons given, there was no mention of the Chinese contractors. However, news that there was a strong possibility of Chinese contractors winning contracts to build the North-South expressway aroused suspicion. Anger over the dozens of EPC projects worth trillions of VN *đồng*, conducted by Chinese contractors, that racked up huge debts flared up again (*VnExpress* 2020). Vietnam has learned three major lessons from previous EPC projects: (1) Its domestic governance capacity is weak, lacks transparency, is prone to corruption, and is easily manipulated by Chinese contractors; (2) Contractors often offer low prices to win bids, then build slowly, deliberately delaying progress to increase project costs to two or three times the original price; (3) Construction quality by Chinese enterprises is poor and the technology provided is typically outdated. These issues are frequently canvassed in the public media, which puts pressure on government decisions. Below, I will summarize different opinions on the topic of Chinese loans for infrastructure development and how these views affected the government's foreign economic policy.

Social feedback and the voice of intellectuals

Vietnam is a totalitarian society with a one-party state which does not tolerate political opposition. Civil society and non-government organizations are constrained while mass organizations are created to carry out the CPV's agenda. However, since the mid 1990s, various forms of disapproval and resistance have emerged, becoming a common feature of Vietnam's political landscape. Nationwide protests about the government's perceived dependence on China and its provocative behavior in the East Sea have become more frequent (Kerkvliet 2019: 2).

Although "voices from below" are not as powerful as the party authorities, these protests show that citizens are deeply aware of their role in the country's well-being, and that the authorities cannot simply ignore the opinions of the masses. Citizens' modes of communication are very diverse; they can be direct, verbal, organized but also indirect, nonverbal, unorganized. The latter, especially, are difficult to analyze, but the views expressed through various social media networks that create two-way communication and influence between citizens and authorities can be collated and analyzed. While studying social commentary on Vietnam borrowing Chinese capital to develop transportation infrastructure, we found that certain experts, researchers, intellectuals, journalists, and social activists have very strong voices which are often able to arouse social discord and sometimes contribute to changing state policy.

Based on the view that such social actors can influence government decision making, we collected the opinions of intellectuals, social activists, politicians, and experts who are often involved in policy-making processes. Their opinions may not necessarily reflect public sentiments but nevertheless create certain pressures on the government's decision-making. The foreign economic policy of the state reflects the concerns of these social groups (Baviera 2012).

The Vietnamese experts and politicians we interviewed can be divided into two groups based on their opposing views on Chinese business involvement in developing Vietnam's infrastructure. One group – we will call them "economic pragmatists" – is generally "in favor of Chinese loans." They believe that the mass social movement to ban Chinese investors is misguided. Although not as large as the opposing group, members of this group have strong social and professional positions. Their argument has three main points: (1) The losses and generally bad experience of the EPC projects undertaken by Chinese firms were at least in part due to Vietnam's poor management skills (which, in turn, were attributed to lack of experience in doing business with foreign enterprises). (2) The decision to finance the North-South expressway project via a public-private partnership (PPP) was in accordance with the Investment Law, which stipulates an open international bidding process. It should be left to the competent authority to decide if the project has an impact on national security or sovereignty, not public opinion. (3) Chinese contractors have great financial resources backed by the Chinese government's Belt and Road Initiative, so it is very convenient. Chinese investors are not only knowledgeable about Vietnam's economy but are also prepared to make risky investments in Vietnam's infrastructure. Unlike Western investors, the Chinese do not demand revenue guarantees, nor exchange rate guarantees, and are prepared to accept payment in Vietnamese Đồng.

The "pro-Chinese investment" group includes development economist Nguyễn Trí Hiếu and politician Nguyễn Đức Kiên, Deputy Chairman of the National Assembly's Economic Committee and Head of the Prime Minister's economic advisory group. Mr. Nguyễn Đức Kiên frankly expressed his views in public as follows:

> When I went to meet with businesses of the Federal Republic of Germany in April, many German experts told me that in the last eight years Germany has not had any new railway or high-speed road projects. Therefore, if we require experience in building new highways of the same scale in the last three years, German enterprises cannot meet requirements for taking part in the bidding. With such criteria, only Chinese enterprises can meet them. (Dân Trí 2019)

Mr. Nguyễn criticized the press and social media for pushing the China issue too far, misconstruing the true nature of the problem. He is convinced that Vietnam should take advantage of China's huge capital to develop its infrastructure rather than unethically discriminating against them due to ungrounded fears. At the same time, he stresses that it is necessary to ensure that contracts set out clear conditions and gaurdrails, adding: "We need to have constraints so that if they violate, we can sanction."

The other group comprises intellectuals, activists, and senior government advisers who oppose doing business with Chinese enterprises. We can call this group "economic ethicists." Their four main arguments are: (1) It is unclear what benefits Vietnam will derive from proposals to build roads and high-speed railways connecting to China, but such projects would incur huge debts for future generations to pay, making development unsustainable. (2) Vietnam must learn important lessons from its history of doing business with Chinese enterprises. Almost all EPC projects undertaken with Chinese firms have failed, leaving Vietnam's economy in debt and in some cases financially and technically dependent on China. (3) The people will not accept an economy that is deeply dependent on China or threatens the country's sovereignty, and they will not accept China's reassurances as long as Vietnam's maritime territory continues to be occupied, disputed, and threatened by China. (4) The North-South expressway is the national arterial road and cannot be arbitrarily assigned to foreigners. It is necessary to be more cautious in foreign policy, limiting any compromise to territorial integrity, national security, and sovereignty. An overriding question for this group is: If Chinese debt leads to economic and political dependence, will it be possible to sue for territory later?

This group iincludes experts and social activities such as Mr. Phạm Sỹ Liêm (Vice Chairman of Vietnam Construction General Association), Mr. Lê Thanh Vân (standing member of the Finance and Budget Committee of the National Assembly). Mr. Lê Đăng Doanh (former director of the Institute of Strategic Economics), Ms. Phạm Chi Lan (economist, member of the Prime Minister's economic advisory group), Mr. Trương Trọng Nghĩa (lawyer, Delegate of the National Assembly), Mr. Nguyễn Ngọc Chu (mathematician), etc.

In our conversation, Mr. Phạm Sỹ Liêm shared his opinion: "People don't always lend money to us, and we quickly agree without thinking. We can't always nod our heads; we must know how to shake our heads." Mr. Lê Thanh Vân concurred:

> We cannot mobilize capital at any cost, regardless of national security and without carefully considering the quality of contrac-

tors. We have had too many lessons. So, I suggest the government be very careful about this expressway project. Personally, I do not agree to let the Chinese contractors do the North-South highway.

This group emphasizes the important connection between economics and ethics, combining nationalist sentiments with their recognition of the need for international cooperation. They advocate developing multiple strategic partnerships that provide benefits to the nation's economic interests and well-being. They do not condone pursuing economic benefits regardless of the costs, but instead seek respect, sharing, and win-win cooperation. The data presented in Table 4.3 document Vietnam's success in pursuing multiple foreign relationships and developing diverse sources for financing its expressways without Chinese capital.

Conclusion

In a sense, Vietnam has been engaged with the Belt and Road Initiative since before its present incarnation. Previous initiatives to develop corridors connecting China's eastern and southwestern economic centers with Southeast Asia through Vietnam were discussed and agreed to by the two countries' leaders. However, so far, the Hai Phong–Lào Cai railway project connecting to China's Hekou-Kunming railway is the only project that has been officially approved under the BRI, and apart from the aid for a planning survey, no infrastructure loan agreement has been signed between Vietnam and China.

As we have seen, Vietnam has put national security first, being wary of the costs of borrowing to develop infrastructure and limiting the amount of investment from China, even though the country has a great need for improved infrastructure.

Table 4.3 Foreign loans for expressway construction in Vietnam (2009–2022)

	Name of highway	Length	Year of construction	Total investment	Foreign loans
1	Hà Nội–Hải Phòng	105 km, maximum speed 120 km/h	2009–2015 Korean contractors, Chinese Vietnam	45.500 billion VND	KB Bank, Česká republika
2	Nội Bài–Lào Cai	264 km, maximum speed 100 km/h	2009–2014 Korean contractor (6/8 bidding packages), Guangxi (China) & Việt Nam	US$1.5 billion	The Asian Development Bank (ADB)
3	Hạ Long–Móng Cái	176 km, maximum speed 100 km/h.	2014–2022 Sun Group (Vietnam)	14.000 billion VND	Public Private Partnership
4	Cao tốc Bắc–Nam phía Đông	2,063 km, maximum speed 100 km/h	2021–2025 Vietnam contractors	148.492 billion VND	PPP and government budget
5	Hà Giang–Lào Cai	83.3 km, maximum speed 100 km/h	2022–2027 Vietnam contractors	8.737 billion VND	ODA Korea, (Keximbank)
6	Lai Châu–Lào Cai	147 km, maximum speed 80 km/h	2022–2025 Vietnam contractors (Transport Ministry)	5.300 billion VND	ADB and Australian Government:
7	Trung Lương–Mỹ Thuận	51 km, maximum speed 80 km/h	2009–2013 Vietnam contractor (Đèo Cả group)	12.668 billion VND.	PPP (BOT contract)
8	Bến Lức–Long Thành	57.8 km, maximum speed 100 km/h.	2015–2025 Vietnam contractors (VEC)	31.320 billion VND	ADB and JICA (Japan)

Source: Department of Roads (2023)

Vietnam's hedging strategy seeks to balance its relations with China by maintaining strong relations with other ODA-providing countries, thus avoiding dependence on any one country. The success of this strategy can be seen in the data that shows that none of the eight most recently built highway projects in Vietnam involve Chinese financing. This is not to say that Vietnam will completely ban Chinese investments, merely that any borrowing from the BRI will be limited in the interests of national security.

Previous research has tended towards concluding that Vietnam has avoided Chinese loans for transport infrastructure because it increases public debt while the quality of Chinese-built infrastructure is poor and the cost is high. However, insights derived from interviews with influential social groups indicate that domestic politics plays a great tole in shaping Vietnam's foreign diplomacy. The views of elite social groups play an important role in the government's policy making processes, influencing macroeconomic policy, and driving Vietnam towards more pragmatic international integration, while respecting the public's demands to maintain internal peace and avoid social conflicts. Understanding the impact of domestic politics in relations with China, the BRI, and its prospects in Southeast Asian countries needs to be deepened.

References

Abuza, Zachary and Phuong Vu (2021) Vietnams hidden debts to China expose its political risks. *The Diplomat*, 8 October.

Baviera, Aileen (2012) The Influence of Domestic Politics on Philippine Foreign Policy: The case of Philippines-China relations since 2004. RSIS Working Paper No.241 S. Rajaratnam School of International Studies Singapore.

Buchholz, Katharina (2023) International Loans: The countries most in debt to China. *Statista* https://www.statista.com/chart/19642/external-loan-debt-to-china-by-country/ Accessed 2 October 2024.

Ciorciari, John D. and Jürgen Haacke (2019) Hedging in international relations: An introduction. *International Relations of the Asia-Pacific*, 19(3): 367–374. https://doi.org/10.1093/irap/lcz017

Communist Party of Vietnam (Đảng Cộng sản Việt Nam) (2017) Thông cáo chung Việt Nam – Trung Quốc, 14 January 2017 (Vietnam-China Joint Communiqué). https://dangcongsan.vn/thoi-su/thong-cao-chung-viet-nam--trung-quoc-423692.html

Communist Party of Vietnam (Đảng Cộng sản Việt Nam) (2022) Chỉ thị của Ban Bí thư (số 15-CT/TW, ngày 10/8/2022) về công tác ngoại giao kinh tế phục vụ phát triển đất nước đến năm 2030 (Directive No. 15-CT/TW on economic diplomacy in service of national development until 2030). https://tulieuvankien.dangcongsan.vn/he-thong-van-ban/van-ban-cua-dang/chi-thi-so-15-cttw-ngay-1082022

Dân Trí (2019) Nhà thầu Trung Quốc quan tâm dự án cao tốc Bắc–Nam: Đại biểu nói "hoàn toàn bình thường" (National Assembly member said "completely normal"). *Báo Dân Trí*, 25 May.

Department of Roads (2023) Hệ thống đường cao tốc Việt Nam. Phòng Lưu trữ Bộ Giao thông Vận tải (Vietnam Expressway System. Unpublished report, Ministry of Transport Archives).

Finance (Tài Chính) (2017) Việt Nam chi đầu tư hạ tầng thuộc hàng cao nhất châu Á. (Vietnam spending on infrastructure investment among the highest in Asia). *Financial Magazine*, 23 March.

Gelpern, Anna, Sebastian Horn, Scott Morris, Brad Parks and Christoph Trebesch (2021) *How China Lends: A Rare Look into 100 Debt Contracts with Foreign Governments*. Peterson Institute for International Economics, Kiel Institute for the World Economy, Center for Global Development and AidData at William & Mary.

General Statistics Office (Tổng cục Thống kê) (2021) Tăng trưởng kinh tế Việt Nam từ 2016 đến nay (Vietnam's economic growth from 2016 to present) https://vietnambiz.vn/gdp-viet-nam-nam-2021-tang-258-20211229093517812.htm

General Statistics Office (Tổng cục Thống kê) (2024) Bức tranh tăng trưởng năm 2023 và triển vọng phát triển kinh tế năm 2024 (The growth picture in 2023 and the economic development outlook in 2024) https://www.gso.gov.vn/du-lieu-va-so-lieu-thong-ke/2024

Gezgin, Ulaş Başar (2020) Reception of Chinese Belt and Road Initiative in Vietnam: Between Security Concerns and Infrastructure Financing Needs. *Asya Araştırmaları Dergisi* (International social science journal of Asian studies), 1(4): 115–124. ISSN: 2667-6419

Global Infrastructure Hub (2017) Forecasting the significant changes that drive infrastructure need. https://cdn.gihub.org/umbraco/media/1530/global-infrastructure-outlook-factsheet-24-july-2017.pdf

Government [of Vietnam] (Chính phủ) (2019) Thủ tướng tiếp tỉnh trưởng Vân Nam, Trung Quốc. Báo *Chính phủ*, (Prime Minister receives the governor of Yunnan province, China). *Government* Newspaper, 30 May.

Hai Phong City (Thành phố Hải Phòng) (2019) Lãnh đạo thành phố tiếp, làm việc với Phó Bí thư tỉnh Vân Nam (City leaders receive and work with Deputy Party Secretary of Yunnan province). https://thanhphohaiphong.gov.vn/lanh-dao-thanh-pho-tiep-lam-viec-voi-doan-pho-bi-thu-tinh-van-nam-2.html

Hu, Zhihua (2019) Vietnam's Connectivity and Embeddedness in the Maritime Silk Road and Global Maritime Network. IEEE *Access*, 7: 1–1. DOI:10.1109/ACCESS.2019.2923528

Kerkvliet, Benedict J. Tria (2019) *Speaking Out in Vietnam: Public Political Criticism in a Communist Party-Ruled Nation*. Cornell University Press.

Koga, Kei (2017) The Concept of 'Hedging' Revisited: The case of Japan's foreign policy strategy in East Asia's power shift. *International Studies Review*, 20(4): 633–660. DOI: 10.1093/isr/vix059

Koushan Das (2018) Vietnam and AIIB: Meetings infrastructure needs. *Vietnam Briefing*, 12 October.

Le Hong Hiep (2013) Vietnam's hedging strategy against China since normalization. *Contemporary Southeast Asia*, 35(3): 333–368.

Le Hong Hiep (2018) The Belt and Road Initiative in Vietnam: Challenges and prospects. *ISEAS Perspective*, 18. https://www.iseas.edu.sg/wp-content/uploads/pdfs/ISEAS_Perspective_2018_18@50.pdf, Accessed 2 Oct 2024.

Liao, Jessica C. and Dang Ngoc-Tram (2020) The nexus of security and economic hedging: Vietnam's strategic response to Japan-China infrastructure financing competition. *The Pacific Review*, 33(3–4): 669–696. https://doi.org/10.1080/09512748.2019.1599997

Minh Quang (2023) Việt Nam nợ nước ngoài 139 tỷ USD: Cao hay thấp so với nước khác? (Vietnam's foreign debt of USD 139 billion: High or low compared to other countries?) 15 January. https://vietnambiz.vn/viet-nam-no-nuoc-ngoai-139-ty-usd-cao-hay-thap-so-voi-nuoc-khac-2023112114825638.htm.

Ministry of Finance (Bộ Tài Chính) (2011) *Bản tin nợ công* số 7 (Public Debt Bulletin no.7). https://qln.mof.gov.vn/ban-tin-no-cong/ban-tin-no-cong-so-7.htm

Ministry of Finance (Bộ Tài Chính) (2022a) *Bản tin nợ công* số 14, ngày 6 tháng 8 năm 2022 (*Public Debt Bulletin* no. 14). https://qln.mof.gov.vn/ban-tin-no-cong/ban-tin-no-cong-so-14.htm

Ministry of Finance (Bộ Tài Chính) (2022b) Vốn FDI từ Trung Quốc vào Việt Nam: Tiềm ẩn không ít rủi ro khó lường (FDI from China to Vietnam: There are many hidden risks that are unpredictable). https://nfsc.gov.vn/vi/nghien-cuu-trao-doi/von-fdi-tu-trung-quoc-vao-viet-nam-tiem-an-khong-it-rui-ro-kho-luong/

Ministry of Foreign Affairs, PRC (2020) *The Belt and Road Initiative: Progress, Contributions and Prospects*; https://www.mfa.gov.cn/ce/cegv/eng/zywjyjh/t1675564.htm

Ministry of Transport (Bộ Giao thông Vận tải) (2019) Thông cáo báo chí về việc nghiên cứu, lập quy hoạch tuyến đường sắt mới khổ tiêu chuẩn Lào Cai-Hà Nội-Hải Phòng (Press release on the study and planning of a new railway line of standard gauge Lao Cai-Hanoi-Hai Phong). *Giao Thông*, 20 August.

Ministry of Transport (Bộ Giao thông Vận tải) (2020) Suất vốn đầu tư cao tốc Bắc-Nam được tính thế nào? (How is the investment cost of the North-South expressway calculated?) http://cucqlxd.gov.vn/suat-von-dau-tu-cao-toc-bac-nam-duoc-tinh-the-nao-3204.html, 06 June.

National Assembly (Quốc hội) (2022) Nghị quyết số 44/2022/QH15 về chủ trương đầu tư dự án xây dựng công trình đường cao tốc Bắc Nam phía Đông, giai đoạn 2021–2025 (Resolution No. 44/2022/QH15 on investment policy on the construction project of the East North-South Expressway, period 2021–2025) https://luatvietnam.vn/dau-tu/nghi-quyet-44-2022-qh15-quoc-hoi-216139-d1.html. Accessed 11 January 2022.

Nguyễn, Văn Thể (2018) Tầm quan trọng của việc đầu tư cơ sở hạ tầng đối với phát triển kinh tế. Phát biểu tại Hội nghị Thượng đỉnh hợp tác vùng Mekong, 29–31 March 2018, (Minister of Transport Nguyễn Văn Thể: The importance of infrastructure investment for economic development (Speaking at the Mekong Regional Cooperation Summit, 29–31 March 2018), Hà Nội. https://ngkt.mofa.gov.vn/phat-trien-co-so-ha-tang-dong-vai-tro-then-chot-doi-voi-tang-truong-kinh-te/ 2 April.

Out-Law News (2021) AIIB plans refinancing of Vietnamese hydropower plant. 16 September.

Pham, Celina (2022) Why Vietnam's infrastructure is crucial for economic growth. *Vietnam Briefing*. 9 September. https://www.vietnam-briefing.com/news/why-vietnams-infrastructure-crucial-for-economic-growth.html/

Prime Minister (Thủ tướng Chính phủ) (2021a) Quyết định số 1769/QĐ-TTg phê duyệt quy hoạch mạng lưới đường sắt thời kỳ 2021–2030, tầm nhìn đến năm 2050, ngày 9 tháng 10 năm 2021. (Decision No. 1769/QD-TTg approving the railway network planning for the 2021–2030 period, with a vision to 2050, dated October 9, 2021).

Prime Minister (Thủ tướng Chính phủ) (2021b) Quyết định số 1454/QĐ-TTg ngày 1 tháng 9 năm 2021 phê duyệt quy hoạch mạng lưới đường bộ thời kỳ 2021–2030, tầm nhìn đến năm 2050 (Decision No. 1454/QD-TTg dated 1 September 2021 approving the road network planning period 2021–2030, vision to 2050).

Salman, Mohammad and Gustaaf Geeraerts (2015) Strategic hedging and China's economic policy in the Middle East. *China Report*, 51(2): 87–101. https://doi.org/10.1177/0009445515570440

Thanh Niên (2019a) Trung Quốc viện trợ 10 triệu NDT lập dự án đường sắt Lào Cai–Hà Nội–Hải Phòng (Thanh Niên: China donated 10 million yuan to establish the Lao Cai-Hanoi-Hai Phong railway project). Báo *Thanh Niên*, 25 November.

Thanh Niên (2019b) Dự thầu cao tốc Bắc-Nam: Nhà đầu tư Trung Quốc áp đảo (North-South expressway bid: Chinese investors dominated) *Báo Thanh Niên*, 17 July.

Thiện Nhân (2020) Sáng kiến "siêu bẫy nợ" BRI: Các nước hạ lưu sông Mekong phải trả chi phí nào cho cơ sở hạ tầng? Người tiêu dùng Việt Nam (BRI 'super debt trap' initiative: What costs do lower Mekong countries have to pay for infrastructure?). *Vietnamese Consumers*, 18 December.

Tiền Phong (2019) Hủy đấu thầu quốc tế cao tốc Bắc–Nam (Cancellation of international bidding for North-South Expressway) *Báo Tiền Phong*, 25 Sept.

Tiền Phong (2024) Dự án nghìn tỷ thua lỗ Gang thép Thái Nguyên giai đoạn 2: Trình phương án giải quyết (Thai Nguyen Iron and Steel Project Phase 2 lost thousands of billions: Presenting a solution). 10 July.

Vietnam News (2017) AIIB eyes infrastructure development in Vietnam. 13 January. https://vietnamnews.vn/economy/349672/aiib-eyes-infrastructure-development-in-viet-nam.html

Vietnamnet (2019) Làm cao tốc Bắc-Nam: Trung quốc dễ thắng thầu (Building the North-South Expressway: China easily wins the bid). 16 March.

Vietnamnet (2023) Thủ tướng đề nghị Nhật cho vay ODA thế hệ mới làm đường sắt tốc độ cao Bắc–Nam. (Prime Minister requested Japan to lend new ODA to build the North-South high-speed railway). 16 December.

Vietstock Finance (2024) Dự án Gang thép Thái Nguyên thua lỗ ngàn tỷ đồng: Tìm phương án giải quyết (Thai Nguyen Iron and Steel project lost trillions of VND: Finding a Solution). 10 July.

VnExpress (2020) 12 projects at a loss to the industry and trade owed VND 63,300 billion. 10 October. https://vnexpress.net/12-du-an-thua-lo-nganh-cong-thuong-no-hon-63-300-ty-dong-4174546.html.

Vu Quang Viet (2018) How much does Vietnam borrow from China? 4 September. https://nhadautu.vn/viet-nam-muon-cua-trung-quoc-bao-nhieu-d12995.html

Xinhua (2015) China unveils action plan on Belt and Road Initiative. 28 March. https://english.www.gov.cn/news/top_news/2015/03/28/content_281475079055789.htm. Accessed 25 April 2022.

Zaara Zain Hussain (2011) The effect of domestic politics on foreign decision making. *E-International Relations*. 7 February. https://www.e-ir.info/2011/02/07/the-effect-of-domestic-politics-on-foreign-policy-decision-making/

5 | Constructing the Field: Anthropological Infrastructure Studies on Transnational Railways in Laos and Thailand[1]

Panitda Saiyarod

Abstract

This paper presents methodological considerations for researching China's transnational railways in Southeast Asia as part of the Belt and Road Initiative (BRI), using case studies in Laos and Thailand. It is part of a larger study examining the infrastructures that support transnational railway operations and how they are adapted by host countries and integrated into the social lives of local people. The railway is understood as both material infrastructure and as an abstract concept to explore its impact on local communities. The paper argues that the "ethnography of infrastructure" is well suited to study the dynamics, contingencies, and messy outcomes that characterise current BRI practices. By applying a dynamic ethnographic lens to examine infrastructures, my research field is constructed through collaboration and intervention that requires constant reflexivity from the researcher. The railway project is perceived as a platform where multiple actors compete for political power, negotiate agendas, influence each other, and strive to achieve their goals.

---

1 This research is part of the project *China's Transnational Railway: A Comparative Study of the Railway's Impact on Local Communities in Thailand and Laos* was funded by The Office of National Higher Education Science Research and Innovation Policy Council (NXPO), Thailand (2021–2024).

Keywords

BRI projects – railway – infrastructure – ethnography – communities

In January 2022, I began my first field trip with a simple question guiding my brief visit to Khorat and Nong Khai provinces in Thailand: how do people living near the proposed railway construction sites perceive and react to the railway, and how might these projects affect nearby communities? This field trip commenced about a month after the official opening of the Laos-China Railway (LCR). Nong Khai, a border city just across the Mekong River from Vientiane, the capital city of Laos, was my starting point for observing changes that followed the LCR's opening in early December 2021.

Near the Nong Khai Railway Station, we saw many freight trucks with the words "China Railway" and "中国铁路" painted on their trailers, awaiting reloading before crossing over to the Lao station. Along the Mittraphap Highway, in front of the Thai-Laos Friendship Bridge, a continuous line of freight trucks stretched from dawn until dusk, ready to cross the border. Plans were in place in Nong Khai for a new international passenger station and a dry port to enhance connectivity with Laos. However, construction had not yet begun, and there were very few visible physical effects around the Nong Khai station.

In contrast, the high-speed train station in Khorat was to be located in the city centre. At the time of my fieldwork, the China-Thai railway project was being constructed as an extension of the earlier section connecting Bangkok to Khorat. Many Thai subcontractors laid the foundation work for the high-speed railroad project, each working on different sections of the railway. For example, one company was responsible for a 37.45-kilometre stretch that includes building ramps and elevated tracks and preparing the foundations for roads, water systems, and other relevant infrastructures, beginning in January 2021. The Thai contractor primarily provided the labor, while China Railway provided the technical expertise and supervision, with Chinese engineers and translators present on site.

Within the city area of Khorat, approximately 166 households have lived in informal settlements along the existing track, residing in poorly constructed houses on land owned by the State Railway of Thailand (SRT) for decades. These communities were forcbly relocated to make way for the China-Thai railway construction. Seven communities were negotiating with the SRT to lease alternative land. Beyond exploring their resettlement issues, the residents of these settlements provided insights into migration issues and urban poverty. Listening to their life histories, we learned that despite being labeled "intruders" by the SRT, they had made significant contributions to Khorat city. Many were hard-working, with well-developed entrepreneurial skills.

I observed that the sense of urgency among those affected by the construction varied across the sites. My preliminary findings indicate that socioeconomic background significantly influences responses to railway construction. For example, concerns arose that ramps and track design at Khorat station might affect several housing estates (gated communities) and surrounding communities in three townships. A working group formed, including local politicians, entrepreneurs, teachers, and other residents who demanded changing the track design from ramps to elevated tracks. They took a wide range of actions to change the railway design, including writing letters to official authorities and politicians, erecting protest signs, and organizing demonstrations. After several attempts, they finally received a positive response and, at the time of writing, were awaiting official confirmation of the track's redesign.

Whether directly affected by the construction or not, during our conversations with various groups along the route from Nong Khai to Khorat, we consistently heard development discussed in terms of *Kwam Charoen*, which implies progress, civilization, modernity, national benefits, and improved transportation for the country. The variety of feelings, perceptions, expectations, imaginations, and responses towards the railway project captured our attention. Particularly notable were the different strategies employed to address concerns about resettlement and other impacts.

This working paper discusses a methodology for studying the Belt and Road Initiative (BRI) by focusing on China's transnational railways in Southeast Asia, using case studies in Laos and Thailand. It aims to highlight the role of ethnography in infrastructure studies and sketch out the contours of this methodology in light of the transnational railway development. I adopt an ethnography of infrastructure methodology to examine how China's railways transform the social fabric of communities along the tracks. Furthermore, this research focuses on infrastructures that facilitate and support transnational railway construction and operations, including ideas, knowledge, policies, practices, and technologies. I ask how they are interwoven, transformed, translated, improvised, assembled, and disassembled in the host countries and local communities. While this paper represents my analysis, it draws on fieldwork conducted collaboratively. My colleagues in Vientiane provided significant contributions to site-specific observations in Laos, while a research assistant in Thailand offered valuable insights, particularly in Khorat.

Except for the Laos-China Railway (LCR), other BRI railway projects in Southeast Asia have been postponed or delayed. For instance, Malaysia, Indonesia, and Thailand have revised their construction plans many times in the face of domestic political difficulties. The BRI, launched in 2013, offers a lucrative vision of regional economic growth through large-scale infrastructure projects. According to Chinese representatives, the BRI projects will improve connectivity between member countries and thus facilitate inclusive economic development. Since its launch, the massive infrastructure investments under the BRI have received substantial academic attention, particularly analyses from geo-economic and geopolitical perspectives.

However, a growing body of literature has revealed a need for more grounded approaches to studying the BRI and Chinese transnational infrastructures (Klinger and Muldavin 2019; Lu 2021; Oakes 2021a; Oliveira et al. 2020; Sidaway et al. 2020; Sidaway and Woon 2017; Yeh 2018). For example, a project-based approach has been employed to study the financialisation mechanisms of China's railway projects in Laos (Chen 2020). Additionally, some works scrutinise the geo-economic win-win argument, emphasizing how such projects often create development enclaves that reinforce inequalities across state lines (Rowedder 2020; Sidaway et al. 2020).

Therefore, this research adopts a project-based approach, exploring the cases of the Laos-China railway (LCR) and the Thailand-China railway (TCR) project. The ultimate goal of this research is to understand the transnational railway development process in terms of collaboration, negotiation, mitigation, and implementation across levels of government and their effects at the local level. Furthermore, as a part of the BRI, I aim to assess the railway's contribution to "inclusive infrastructure"[2] development in both countries. In particular, this working paper presents concepts and methodologies for navigating both theoretical and empirical aspects of the research.

---

2 Inclusive infrastructure is defined as any infrastructure development that enhances positive outcomes in social inclusivity and ensures no individual, community, or social group is left behind or prevented from benefiting from improved infrastructure (Global Infrastructure Hub 2019).

This working paper has two objectives. First, I hope to contribute to the BRI literature by examining case studies of railway infrastructure in Thailand and Laos from fieldwork at sites of development. Second, the paper seeks to contribute to methodological discussions about how to research highly complex regional infrastructures. For instance, I explore the challenge of identifying effective empirical scales and units of analysis for studying transnational infrastructures, as their impacts often transcend specific locations. How can we engage with voices and practices operating at different scales and across various sites? And how are they integrated, translated, improvised, reconciled, and (dis)connected?

In addition, I review the literature on infrastructuring ethnography for its valuable suggestions and building blocks. It appears that ethnography is well suited to study these dynamics, contingencies, and messy outcomes that characterise current BRI practices. The paper is divided into three parts: the first introduces China's transnational railway projects and the social life of railways for further exploration; the second presents the relevant anthropological approaches and concepts, including railway ethnography, the politics of infrastructure and the technology of imagination; the third discusses the merits of studying infrastructure using ethnographic research tools. I then conclude by reflecting on the methodology and my intervention in the field.

The BRI: China's transnational railway in Southeast Asia

Since the BRI was launched in 2013, it has been widely portrayed as a proactive effort to strengthen connections between China, Europe, Asia, and beyond. The land-based "Silk Road Economic Belt" comprises six development corridors connecting China to

Central Asia, Russia, and Europe; while the "Maritime Silk Road of the 21st century" connects China with Southeast Asia, India, the Arabian Peninsula, Somalia, Egypt, and Europe. Southeast Asia has been a priority area since the beginning, and several countries in the region have made arrangements with China on various projects, including industrial parks, pipelines, highways, and digital infrastructure (Kuik 2021b; Chirathivat et al. 2022: 223).

The BRI identifies five major cooperation priorities: policy coordination, infrastructure connectivity, trade facilitation, financial integration, and people-to-people ties (State Council of the People's Republic of China 2015). Railway development stands out as vital to the BRI in Southeast Asia. Many countries, including Malaysia, Singapore, Laos, and Thailand, have agreed to participate in China's Pan-Asia Railway network. The Thailand-Laos-China railway routes play an important role in overland connectivity between China and its neighbours. Although the Laos-China Railway (LCR) and Thailand-China Railway (TCR) are separate projects in different countries, they form part of China's broader vision to connect Kunming to Bangkok via Vientiane. However, while the Laos-China railway had opened and was running at the time of my fieldwork, little progress has been made on the Thailand-China high-speed train link, at least in terms of physical infrastructure. Track construction of the Thailand-China high-speed railway had only reached the Khorat province, while the land had not yet been acquired in other areas.

Other Southeast Asian cases reveal how financial coalitions navigate complex challenges. In Malaysia, China's coalition with Najib Razak's government was disrupted by a corruption scandal and a change in leadership. Under Mahathir Mohamad, the East Coast Rail Link was renegotiated to reduce costs and increase the role of Malaysian state-owned enterprises (Lokman 2019). Despite the change of government that threatened the project's continuance, coalitions swiftly aligned with the new regime (Camba 2020b: 3). Similarly, the Philippines' inclusion of regional-local elites in the Bicol South Rail Project (BSRP) exemplifies strategic adaptation to local demands. Initially, some elites sought to delay the project by lobbying for additional train station stops in their provinces. Duterte's administration countered opposition by allowing Chinese online gambling, generating profits for oligarchs and securing their consent. The financial coalition later addressed regional-local elites' concerns, enabling the project to proceed. These cases indicate that the success of Chinese railway projects relies on more than initial agreements; it depends on a coalition's ability to adapt and form strategic alliances in continually shifting economic and political landscapes (ibid).

Furthermore, Indonesia's handling of the Jakarta-Bandung HSR project is an example of Southeast Asian agency in leveraging the US-China rivalry. Like Thailand approaching Japan for potential railway investments, Indonesia has crafted a foreign policy involving Japan, China, and the US, an approach which has been aptly described as a "beauty contest," wherein Indonesia competes for the major powers' attention, leveraging their interest to secure advantageous deals and promote economic integration for Jakarta (Tritto et al. 2022: 236).

Having explored the broader tapestry of the BRI's railway ventures across Southeast Asia, I now zoom in on two specific cases: the Laos-China Railway and the Thailand High-Speed Rail Project. By delving deeper into their historical contexts, logistical intricacies, and ongoing challenges, I aim to unveil the nuanced effects of the BRI's implementation at the micro level. This allows us to move beyond generalizations and dissect the complexities inherent in each project, offering a richer understanding of the BRI's potential and pitfalls within the region.

Laos-China Railway

China has designated the LCR as one of six international BRI economic corridors and a key pathway to the Southeast Asia market (Suhardiman et al, 2021: 79). Accordingly, it has intensively promoted the project as mutually beneficial for both countries. The Lao government embraced the LCR as an opportunity to transform the landlocked country into a land-linked one. Initial reports claimed that the railway had created new opportunities for Laos' development, boosting the economy throughout the country by providing fast and convenient transportation. "It is time-saving and convenient, which will drive the Lao economy to a higher level," said the Vice President of the Lao National Assembly, Sommad Pholsena (*Global Times* 2022).

Construction began on the Laos-China Railway in December 2015 and it opened for operations on 3 December 2021. The railway stretches 414 km from Vientiane station to Boten station at the border with China on a 1,435 mm wide track, passing through 167 villages in 13 districts and five provinces. It features 167 bridges, 75 tunnels, and 32 stations and was designed for speeds of up to 160 km/h for passenger trains and 120 km/h for freight services (DiCarlo 2021; Suhardiman et al. 2021; Wei 2021). In addition, a new Law on Railways was issued in 2018 to guide railway development and establish measures to monitor the construction process (Open Development Cambodia 2018).

The Lao central government institutionalized its decision-making authority to facilitate the LCR projects, in accordance with relevant laws and regulations, including a requirement to conduct a feasibility study, rehabilitation and repair plan, resettlement and compensation guidelines (Suhardiman et al. 2021: 82). The LCR management structure comprises several steering committees at central, provincial, and district levels, tasked with coordination, providing guidance, monitoring the impact of resettlement, and managing compensation (ibid.). This institutionalized network structure for the LCR project reflects the central government's strategy to secure the national interests and centralised power while addressing local concerns (ibid.).

Suhardiman et al. (2021) examine how Lao state power is exercised across different levels of government through land compensation and the local effects of construction, examining land compensation in Naxang village in Luang Prabang Province as a case study. The study reveals how the central government uses compensation rules to extend its spatial power throughout the country and how these power relationships between central and provincial district governments have reshaped the LCR project's implementation. Although the state claimed that land compensation would eliminate poverty, this was not the experience of the affected households (ibid.). This grounded research indicates how multiple actors are involved in creating, translating, and mistranslating LCR projects at many levels. It also provides insight into the project's structure, facilitating comparison of the affects of the projects in Thailand and Laos.

Thailand-China Railway (TCR)

Although the State Railway of Thailand (SRT) has a history of more than 122 years, its heyday has passed. The arrival of the BRI has played a crucial role in reviving railway development in Thailand. Initially, the Thai government agreed to a collaborative railway project under the BRI that included a rice and rubber trade deal. Negotiations for a high-speed railway project began in 2012 but were suspended due to political instability in Thailand. Negotiations resumed in 2014, with several meetings between government agencies, resulting in an agreement on a framework of cooperation covering the development of railways nationwide, extending from the capital, Bangkok, to Nong Khai. Under this framework, the first phase would build the railway from Bangkok to Nakhon Ratchasima (Khorat), and the second phase would complete the route from Khorat to Nong Khai.

The entire SRT railway project will feature dual 1.435-metre gauge tracks and span 837 kilometres. The first phase would be a 256 km high-speed railway from Bangkok to Nakhon Ratchasima, with six stations along the route from Bangkok to Khorat. The second phase, to be completed later, would run through Khorat, Khon Khan, and Udon Thani and end at Nong Khai. The system was designed for a maximum speed of 250 km/h. Thai enterprises would build the railway, including the supply of locally sourced raw materials and construction labor.

The Thai government has agreed to finance construction primarily through domestic loans, with minor contributions from foreign sources. Thailand retains full ownership and construction management, while collaborating with China on technical systems and project design. The Chinese and Thai governments constantly promote their grand vision of the economic advantages and benefits of cross-border trade along this important international route connecting Thailand, Laos, and China which is envisaged to one day be extended south to Kuala Lumpur and Singapore.

This background to China's involvement in the Laos and Thai railways helps to shape my general understanding of how partner countries have responded to the Belt and Road Initiative (BRI) and its associated projects. Specifically, the contrast between rapid completion of the Laos-China Railway (LCR) and slow-to-get-started Thailand-China Railway (TCR) vividly illustrates the different outcomes of collaboration and negotiation between governments. It has been well documented that Chinese railway projects often do not materialise as originally planned and frequently struggle to manage the expectations and perceptions of the people they affect. In the following sections, I review studies of railway construction sites to reveal the social life of Chinese railways in Southeast Asia.

A grounded approach to the social life of China's railways

The BRI is huge and complex and escapes definition or understanding as a static form or fixed policy. The railway network alone extends far beyond logistics and tracks, reshaping both the physical landscape and the social fabric along its path. The construction of new stations and the increased movement of passengers and goods are catalysts for change, and fuel expectations of prosperity. Southeast Asian responses to the BRI railway projects have varied significantly by country, influenced by their unique historical, economic, and political landscapes. And within each of the countries involved, diverse and multi-layered reactions are found both across and within all societal strata, from political elites to local communities.

Tim Oakes (2021) thus suggests viewing the BRI as a form of "development theatre" that presents an aspirational evolutionary discourse produced by China. Rather than a policy, he sees it as an exercise in imagining a possible future through illusory maps of lines and corridors across the globe. From this perspective, studies of the BRI should consider its flexibility, responsiveness and adaptability to specific conditions encountered along the way (Oakes 2021b). To this end, many recent project-based studies have adopted a grounded approach for examining the social life of infrastructure. It is important to question how infrastructure interacts with and affects both humans and non-humans, how it shapes the physical and social environments of communities, how it is integrated into daily life, and how it is shaped in turn.

Many works have explored the geo-economic and geopolitical implications and political forces of contestation regarding the Thai-China high-speed railway (Chirathivat et al. 2022; Wu and Chong 2018). For example, Trin Aiyara (2019) argues that domestic political circumstances – conflict between parties, bureaucratic procedures, and judiciary intervention – delayed the Thai-China railway project. Other scholars have examined how economic statecraft has driven the Sino-Thai rail project (Lauridsen 2020). However, like most studies of the Thailand-China railroad, these researchers focused on state-centric and institutional or structural perspectives, while neglecting local agencies, transnational actors, and community responses. Without locally conducted qualitative research, a deep understanding of China's transnational infrastructure remains out of reach.

My preliminary findings in Laos reveal a broad range of responses to the railway development. Despite concerns that Laos might have incurred significant debt to China, many locals appreciated the convenience of the railway for both long and short trips, as well as the opportunities presented by the travelers it brings. But there is also much discontent in the community, especially among those who express disappointment in what they perceive to be low rates for land compensation, and those whose village graveyards have been desecrated for station construction.

Others, however, appreciate the new houses they were provided as compensation, viewing them as valuable family assets. Many were hopeful for job opportunities and other benefits from the industrial zones developing near the railway stations. We learned of some locals who were learning Chinese to enhance their employment prospects with the railway company.

Meanwhile, in Thailand, especially in communities that might be impacted by track construction, residents were banding together to voice their concerns. Their demands varied, including calls for track redesigns to address flooding concerns and minimize impacts on their way of living, requests for housing rights through land rental provisions, and appeals for fair compensation for resettlement and displacement.

As we have discussed, the study of railways should extend beyond merely examining materials and technologies. It should encompass the dynamic relationship between railways and their surrounding environments, highlighting how they both shape and are shaped by local ways of living. This interplay can entail cultural values, urban accommodation issues, bureaucratic challenges, and deficiencies in inclusive design, among other things, thus underscoring the complex and reciprocal effects of infrastructure and society.

Recent works on China's influence on infrastructure development worldwide have added new layers of analysis to the study of BRI. Ethnographic fieldwork has revealed the connection between techno-politics and power, the hegemonic narratives of state projects, and local practices in response to the effects of infrastructure development (Goodfellow and Huang 2021; Harris 2013; Oakes 2021a; Rippa 2020; Saxer 2016). For example, in the Thai railway project, the dynamics between government, rail operators, private investors, NGOs, and local communities have impacted the design, financial structures, regulations and standards, as well as the construction timeline.

My research investigates social relations and practices in response to the railway project in different communities along the tracks. I am fully aware that these communities are not homogenous or unchanging, but rather are constantly adapting to dynamic social and political contexts. Communities are formed by diverse identities, values, and ways of life, resulting in a variety of differences in social capital and economic power that can lead to conflict or cooperation. Hence, I also interrogate the social structures within those communities, especially social hierarchy, power constraints, and conflicts. Throughout, I consider the sociality of communities to understand how individuals and groups interact during infrastructure transitions.

Anthropology of infrastructure and railway studies

Anthropologists have contributed to the study of infrastructures by using the ethnographic approach to examine the "dense social, material, aesthetics and political formations" of infrastructures (Anand et al. 2018; Carse 2012; Elyachar 2010; Harvey et al. 2017; Simone 2004). They have sought to pluralise the analytical frame to analyse the complexity of social relations entangled in infrastructure systems. From this perspective, infrastructure is not just material (roads, railways, sewers) but also social (institutions, economic systems, media forms) and philosophical (intellectual trajectories) (Howe et al. 2016: 549).

The study of railroads in anthropology is typically framed in terms of modernity, ruination, affect, and state governance (Schweitzer and Povoroznyuk 2020: Swanson 2020). The journal *Transfers* (vol. 10) presents a collection of research papers on railroads in Europe and Asia, using anthropological perspectives to analyse infrastructure and reach a more comprehensive understanding of its benefits and challenges. Railroads, as symbols of modernity, have different meanings for different actors and play out differently depending on local circumstances. For example, they may represent the state's ambition and the interests of investors and private companies. They can also symbolise mobility and hope for socioeconomic development while paradoxically creating isolation and immobility (Ponsavady 2020).

Swanson (2020) suggests that studying the lives and afterlives of railways and other large-scale infrastructure through an ethnographic and historical lens is ideal for cross-site comparison of translation and contradistinction, while also also analyzing urgent political issues such as governance, wealth, inequality, and ecology.

Drawing on these works, I use the broad definition of infrastructure, studying the railway as both hard (material assemblages) and soft (abstractions) infrastructure to explore its impact on local communities (Anand et al. 2018). The vast majority of scholarly research on the BRI has focused on visible (hard) infrastructure. The invisible (soft) infrastructure needs to be explored much further, particularly abstractions such as ideas, imagination, aspiration, and institutions. My research focuses particularly on ideas, hope, and imaginaries associated with the railway. I also examine the infrastructure work of China's transnational railways as a collection of organisational techniques, comprising administrative and technical support, and bureaucratic mechanisms that regulate or maintain the railway operation (Bowker 1994).

These abstractions are not merely theoretical but are actively shaped and reinforced through cultural expressions and promotional efforts. To illustrate these concepts, I explore how railway promotions in Laos materialise both physically and ideologically. Cultural exchanges, such as the song *Yidaiyilu* by Vilayphone Vongphachanh, celebrate themes of 'mutual benefits' and 'enhanced connectivity,' marking the 55th anniversary of China-Laos diplomatic ties. Similarly, the bilingual song 'Take the Train to China' (ຂີ່ລົດໄຟໄປທ່ຽວຈີນ/坐着火车去中国), officially produced by Vientiane 93.0 Radio and China Media Group, reinforces these narratives, encapsulating the aspirations of Laos and China for deeper connectivity as a hallmark of progress.

Promises of China's railway: Futurity, temporality and imaginaries

As Gupta (2018) observes, drawing on Appadurai's framework, infrastructural projects are tangible manifestations of future visions, an embodiment of the future, so to speak. Infrastructures represent aspirations, anticipations, and imaginings of the future: people envisioning the kind of society they hope to live in (Gupta 2018). The collective volume *The Promise of Infrastructure* (2018) edited by Anand, Gupta and Appel, illustrates the forms of power and the indefinite future generated by infrastructure. They treat infrastructure as a conceptual tool to explore the social future and its effects on everyday sociality in a series of case studies. Many cases demonstrate that infrastructure often carries promises of progress, development and a surreal future, bringing together diverse and disparate actors – including governments, state-owned enterprises, private companies, banks, engineers, and experts – in the name of a utopian future.

A high-speed railway project is certainly future-oriented; it often promises improved transportation conditions such as comfort, speed, and even reduced carbon emissions. Nevertheless, despite the great optimism and expectations surrounding such projects, they also create new uncertainties, and thus new infrastructure proposals can spark both hopes for a better future and fears of unintended consequences (Swanson 2020).

Infrastructure is often constructed to respond to crises or meet present needs, but it is also a plan and anticipation of a future that has not yet arrived (Howe et al. 2016). Infrastructure projects exemplify how the future shapes the present. For instance, new railway stations were being constructed in Thailand in anticipation of the China-Laos-Thai railway. The transnational railway's development foreshadows numerous socioeconomic changes. Tools such as city plans, railway maps, and station designs not

Photo 5.1 Billboard in front of railway station in Vientiane, 2 June 2023. Photo by author

only prepare for these changes but also envision the "desired" future cityscape.

Additionally, the extensive promotion of the railway across online platforms, social media, and various art forms like poems, songs, and photographs, in my view, serves to render the infrastructure both more tangible and more desirable in the daily lives of the local population. The circulation of such information and ideas helps to make infrastructure imaginable and attractive for the population (Schwenkel 2018: 114). Nevertheless, such imaginings trigger mixed feelings and actions, including fears of displacement, expectations of fair compensation for land, hopes for employment or business opportunities, and environmental concerns.

Scholars suggest that infrastructure can be seen as a concrete metaphor. For instance, it is a physical presence in the landscape that facilitates the circulation of information, goods, and people. It is also a bio-political project that aims to foster the health and well-being of the population while promoting discipline and control. It can also be seen as an aspiration, a symbol of progress and a better future (Harvey 2018: 80). The Lao-China Railway crosses a river and passes through tunnels and mountains, demonstrating China's mastery of modern technology and innovation in the railway industry. Apart from circulating goods and passenger circulation, it symbolizes a particular Chinese future.

Of course, Thailand and Laos both had special economic zones, new communities with modern buildings and infrastructure, roads and highways, and dispersed Chinese communities long before the railway projects began. However, these pre-existing characteristics set the stage for the patterns of land speculation observed in anticipation of the railway projects. Such speculation often begins long before the infrastructure is committed to, driven by expectations of future development. Bear (2020) proposes embracing speculation as a research method for exploring real estate markets and infrastructure financing; she argues that we often speculate by using various technologies of imagination, such as promotional brochures, branding, international agency reports, political visions, government inquiries, risk analyses, ethical investment measures, and government guarantees. In short, these technologies promise to predict, stimulate, imagine and control the uncertain future.

The notion of technologies of imagination helps to broaden my source of analysis and introduce ways to compare the tools, measures, and actions used in different contexts to handle uncertain futures. Viewing the railway as a future-oriented project raises questions such as: How have the surrounding communities responded to uncertainty? What is the role of railways in imagining the future of a nation, province, community, family, or individual?

The high-speed railway may evoke a sense of progress and modern futurity; but like all infrastructures it is always already on the way to becoming ruins (Gupta 2018). Akhil Gupta (2018) views infrastructure as an open-ended process that is ephemeral, elusive, temporal, and perpetually decaying. Furthermore, committing to an infrastructure project does not mean it will be completed; it can be suspended, delayed, redesigned, retrofitted, repaired, or abandoned due to financial failures, social and political struggles, technical errors, and material shortages. By acknowledging the temporality of infrastructure, we can recognise that high-speed railway projects can generate very different social outcomes than what was intended or planned.

The politics of infrastructure: Planning and implementation of the railway projects

Infrastructure is not only material, but also an aspirational terrain for negotiating promises and ethical norms of political authority (Appel et al. 2018: 20). Infrastructures distribute vital resources such as energy, water, and information. Thus, infrastructures are sites for political performance where government officials, engineers, and construction companies are engaged in designing effective systems to serve a specific population, typically elites, ruling classes, and capitalist investors. It is thus not uncommon for infrastructure planning to become negotiations of power between state agencies and populations that are unfairly governed.

Infrastructure both connects people and divides people. The benefits of infrastructure are rarely shared equitably to all people. It can facilitate full access to a particular resource for some groups while preventing others from sharing equal access (Reeves 2017). Not only are marginalised groups often excluded, but new groups are marginalised. Infrastructure can politically divide a community by defining membership levels that determine ways of living (Anand 2011; Carse 2012). In my fieldwork, I found evidence of this in a resettlement issue in Khorat.

According to Boholm (2011), planners aim to manage the relationships between the state, citizens, and other parties involved in the project. As such, the practices, discourses, and technologies produced by the planners provide rich data for ethnographic examination. In this research, the master plan of the transnational railway was ideal material for studying the interactions among planners, non-governmental organisations, government officials and local citizens. The power relationships between stakeholders, reflected in the hierarchical structures of the master plan, highlight the dominance of certain actors, such as government agencies and corporate interests, in implementing infrastructure projects.

Using the anthropological lens to study planning provides insight into how planners and other stakeholders envisage their desirable future and reveals how planning organises local populations to align with that vision. I analyse the power of words in ritual performances, such as the speeches at the project's launch, comments in public hearings and social media, rumors, and scale models to better understand the kinds of social, spatial and technological relations such performances entail and how people deal with them (Abram and Weszkalnys 2011).

However, as Schwenkel (2018) observes that even though they are designed for particular populations, other populations often repurpose infrastructures through political claims and material practices, the view similarly argued by Braun and Whatmore (2010). This repurposing highlights the divergence between the intended benefits envisioned by designers and the future imagined by the populations impacted. In many cases, marginalised people have made themselves visible to the state and public by demanding that the infrastructure proposals take their views and needs into account. In this way, infrastructural negotiations can reveal a lot about the ethics and morals of political leaders.

Building infrastructure is promoted as an effective method of serving the "public good" which is both inclusive and essential to the functioning of society (Batt 1984; Beeferman cited in Di Nunzio 2018). However, ethnographers and geographers have observed that building infrastructure is not a neutral undertaking (Gupta 2018: 66). In fact, while pipelines, highways, and electric power lines symbolise social progress, their purpose is often to serve vested interests, enforce regimes of control, and create geographies of discrimination. This does not, however, simply mean we should consider pipelines, highways or railways to be consequences of politics; on the contrary, it requires rethinking the nature of politics itself (Barry 2001).

Infrastructure and technical knowledge influence government decisions and political processes (Bennett 2010; Collier 2011; Foucault 2010; Mitchell cited in Di Nunzio 2018). Infrastructure also shapes ideas about the public good and understandings of citizenship, such as the ability to access infrastructure (Anand 2012; Appel et al. 2015; Humphrey 2020). In other words, although infrastructure might serve powerful interests and create segregated geographies, it can also provoke claims and demands from below (Barry 2013; Das 2011; Holston 2021)

During our first and following visits with the affected communities in Khorat, it was clear that they were having difficulties dealing with relevant authorities and subcontractors. As mentioned, conflicts between SRT and local communities at the construction site were palpable. I noticed that the negotiation process and measures taken to raise their voices vary between different groups. In the informal settlement communities, we found that many households have had to leave because of floods caused by excavation during the railway construction. We were told there had been a few confrontations between the Thai subcontractor, Chinese engineers, the SRT officers and families that refused to move. Drawing on the politics of infrastructure concepts, I expect to more deeply explore the construction plans, conflicts, dealings and various responses from the affected communities. Furthermore, I search for innovative methods that individuals, families, communities, and groups have improvised to handle undesired struggles caused by unequal access to those infrastructures.

Ethnography of infrastructure

My fieldwork commenced in January 2021 and continued until early 2024, across diverse locations in Laos and Thailand, specifically Nong Khai, Khorat, Luang Nam Tha, Vientiane, and Boten with support from local collaborators and research assistants. These sites were chosen to explore and compare the impacts of diverse socio-cultural and political contexts on the BRI at different stages of railway construction. In Khorat, Thailand, I collaborated with staff at the the Four Region Network[3] to support local communities grappling with resettlement challenges. Meanwhile, in Laos, we formed a partnership with a Vientiane-based researcher, who periodically visited Boten and a village in Luang Nam Tha, broadening my research scope.

We conducted semi-structured interviews, focus groups, participant observations, mobile interviews, and applied the snapshot methodology. We engaged with a wide array of stakeholders, including officials from the State Railway of Thailand (SRT) and China Supervision Consultant (CSC), as well as district and

---

3 The Four Regions Slum Network (FRSN) is a Thai non-profit organization founded in 1998, dedicated to advocating for the rights of the urban poor (Thaitrakulpanich and Duggleby 2022).

sub-district officers, engineers, construction firm personnel, and local inhabitants directly affected by the railway projects. This comprehensive engagement allowed us to develop a multifaceted understanding of the BRI's impact across communities.

To directly observe the railway's impact, I travelled from Vientiane to Kunming via the China-Laos railway and undertook road and rail trips along the tracks in Thailand, from Nong Khai to Khorat. We conducted interviews in situ, traversing construction and resettlement sites on foot, as well as travelling by motorcycles and cars to observe physical transformations in commercial and residential areas at each field site. We created community maps as necessary to help understand how towns were changed.

To cope with the challenges of studying complex phenomena such as railway projects, I am guided by Star's (1999) concept of an "ethnography of infrastructure." According to Star, infrastructures are relational; their existence, function, and value depend on specific users and contexts. This perspective focuses on the processes through which infrastructure emerges and elements become infrastructure, rather than on defining what infrastructure inherently is. Guided by this approach, this research seeks to understand how affected communities perceive railway construction projects and to evaluate the myriad impacts on diverse groups, paying particular attention to how equitably the benefits are distributed.

My approach was also informed by Karasti and Blomberg's (2017) methodology for studying infrastructure ethnographically. They argue that a new approach is needed to follow connections and embrace the varying nature of infrastructure, which can encompass not just physical things but also the relationships between them. "Nailing down" the sampling criteria too tightly in advance, they observe, risks limiting the researcher's ability to engage with the phenomenon at hand (ibid.). Rather than treating this research field as a singular "place," this research remains open to the surprises and serendipity that the field will bring. Especially because those who engage with the railway – whether planners, engineers, contractors or resettled communities – do not perceive its effects and meaning the same way researchers do; their experiences and perspectives offer us insights to more deeply understand infrastructure (ibid.).

This research also follows Marcus's (1995) proposal of multi-sited ethnography as a means to re-envision ethnography as a relevant strategy for investigating phenomena dispersed over a wide range of places while maintaining ethnography's greatest strength, its ability to generate empirical data. According to Marcus (1995), a multi-site approach enables the researcher to formulate the ethnographic object in various ways without assuming its totality or unity. His "tracking" approach includes the following critical entities: person, thing, metaphor, story, biography, or conflict across various sites (Marcus 1995: 105–110). In short, Marcus suggested the researchers examine the circulation of cultural meanings, objects, and identities in diffuse time-space via multi-sited ethnography (ibid.: 96). On this basis, I identified the main stations, at Khorat, Nong Khai, Vientiane and Boten as initial sites for our fieldwork. However, rather than viewing them as geographically bounded "field sites," I treated them as entry points for my studies of infrastructure.

These approaches have guided me in exploring impacts, tracking phenomena, and examining the relational dynamics of transnational railway projects. Throughout my journey in Laos, especially in a small village in Luang Nam Tha, I investigated compensation issues and found that residents' experiences are marked by complex power dynamics and varied reactions to railway construction and compensation. On both sides of the border I found that the views and voices of smaller and marginalized groups – encompassing their hopes, desires, and perspectives – are often ignored.

In a similar vein, Jensen and Winthereik characterised technology infrastructures in development aid as "fractal landscapes," where complexity is reproduced, and stability and connectivity are difficult to predict (2013: 12). They argue that both theoretical and methodological flexibility is required to follow connections and identify disconnects, which are key to conceptualising the field. During fieldwork, I must assess the strategic relevance of each location, which requires sensitivity and openness (as per Marcus 1995). Using this methodology, the field emerges from the researcher's interactions with phenomenon during the research process.

For, Jensen and Winthereik ethnographic research must treat infrastructures as emerging, "based on a fractal, recursive imagery of infrastructure" (2013: 9). In this sense, multi-sited, connective, seamful and fractal approaches do not require ethnography to present a comprehensive picture of infrastructures; instead, they emphasize viewing infrastructures as in-the-making, emerging, and recursive (Jensen and Winthereik 2013: 9; Karasti and Blomberg 2017: 257). Similarly, Hine argues that field boundaries emerge through investigation rather than being predefined, making determining the scope of a field a continuous process that adapts to evolving empirical landscapes (Hine 2009: 4; Karasti and Blomberg 2017: 249).

The notion of "infrastructuring ethnographically" sheds light on studying the large-scale transnational railroad by focusing on connections and emergent phenomena, reflexively determining the scope of inquiry, and embracing the partiality of understanding such complex projects. Particularly, the researcher's agency plays a significant role in determining the focus of the study (Karasti and Blomberg 2017). I repeatedly observed issues around compensation, resettlement, as well as the complex power dynamics that emerged through negotiation among various actors. For instance, in Laos, the compensation process involves multiple layers of decision-making, often excluding affected homeowners. In Thailand, issues around resettlements in Khorat have revealed the power dynamics between the SRT bureaucracy, local politicians, and organisations of marginalised urban citizens. Identifying these complex and multilayered relationships have, in turn, gradually reshaped my field of study.

Inverting infrastructural relations: Polymorphous engagement

Abstract infrastructure encompasses its often unseen aspects, crucial for smooth operation, such as maintenance and repair (Bowker 1994; Star 1999). These elements, while visible to those directly involved in performing them, remain unnoticed by the broader public. Ethnographic methods address this invisibility, examining phenomena from multiple angles. Infrastructure inversion, for example, reveals overlooked operational processes and tasks vital for sustained functionality (Karasti and Blomberg 2017). Rather than focusing solely on the visible or end results of infrastructure, this method examines the behind-the-scenes activities and day-to-day operations that are often neglected.

By applying this approach, I was able to uncover the intricate interplay between technical, socio-organisational, and institutional elements in infrastructure development. Institutions like government agencies, funding bodies, and standards organisations are not just involved in the process but actively shape and are shaped by the operational tasks. For example, in Khorat, I examined the coordination between Thai subcontractors and Chinese engineers, revealing how budget constraints, time pressures, and Thailand's bureaucratic processes played a pivotal role in shaping construction decisions and localizing "the Chinese standard." While initial interviews with stakeholders from various spheres provided insight into their roles, infrastructure inversion allowed me to go beyond surface-level understanding, showing how these institutions directly influence operational outcomes, often in ways not immediately visible in formal discussions.

Of course, in studying a transnational project of this scale, there are many obstacles to accessing key-players, especially high-level administrators and foreign agencies in Laos and Thailand. Hence, I adopted a revised "studying up" method of "polymorphous engagement" to enhance my analysis. This term, coined by Hugh Gusterson (1997: 116), refers to the methodological approach of interacting with informants across several dispersed sites, including virtual ones, and collecting data from a wide array of sources in various ways. Thus, this research included informal interviews, extensive reading of newspapers, official documents, posts on social media, web material, blogs, online newsletters, Zoom meetings, observations, and popular culture sources such as songs, poems, animation, and YouTube videos. While multi-sited ethnography focuses on physical movement between sites, polymorphous engagement incorporates virtual platforms, expanding the range of actors and data sources, which is essential for studying transnational infrastructure projects.

Another potential obstacle to developing a fuller understanding of the impact of these projects can be the reluctance of villagers and other potential informants of expressing any views that might be perceived as critical of the project and, by extension, the government. Under these circumstances, gathering information from online platforms offers access to public perceptions that are difficult to discuss openly. In Laos, for example, where sensitivity around criticising China's railway project or expressing views opposing the government in face-to-face conversations might pose risks for villagers, comments on social media can shed light on how Laotians perceive the project. Similarly, in Thailand, online comments are a rich source of general perceptions, which can be compared with both the views of those directly affected by the projects and the views that are more publicly acceptable to express.

We also collected life histories to study affected communities in Khorat. Life histories provide insight into individual experiences and perceptions over time, revealing human dilemmas, struggles, and achievements, and shedding light on values, beliefs, and social norms (Kothari and Hulme 2004). We conducted extended interviews, asking respondents to describe life events and experiences in their own words. Respondents were encouraged to focus on their memories of settling down in the informal settlement, their occupations, and their way of living before the railway construction began. Via this method, we recorded the projects' impact on families, personal lives, and emotions, which are seldom considered in analyses of development (Kothari and Hulme 2004: 13).

Although life histories are by definition individual stories, their subjects invariably locate themselves within the broader social and cultural context in which their life unfolded. In analysing the accounts of marginalised individuals, I attempt to highlight their agency and how their personal history intersected with broader sociocultural contexts (Kothari and Hulme 2004: 13). The life histories from marginalised communities in Khorat revealed their active role in urban development as laborers and highlighted their expectations for alternative affordable housing and new employment opportunities post-resettlement.

Conclusions

From the outset, I adopted a polymorphous ethnographic approach, allowing me to navigate the multifaceted realities and capture the contingent nature of China's railway projects. Through this examination of projects in Laos and Thailand, I shed light on the complexities of transnational infrastructure, highlighting both the promise and politics of such endeavors. These projects are exemplars of the promise of infrastructure to enhance economic growth through improved connectivity in the region. However, they also reflect the politics of infrastructure, involving negotiations, power dynamics, and local impacts.

This paper highlights the critical need to examine how railway infrastructures become platforms for politics of redistribution and collective responsibility (Beauregard 2015; Young 2011). Viewing China's railway projects as complex networks of relationships reveals their potential for oppression. Ethnography greatly enriches railway studies by uncovering the lived experiences and hidden power dynamics involved. Therefore, I interpret railways as evolving processes, exploring the complex relationships and cultural impacts throughout construction. This approach amplifies marginalised voices, emphasising the cultural significance and community values overshadowed by physical infrastructure. In doing so, it offers a deep understanding of the social world surrounding railways, revealing human stories, power dynamics, and cultural nuances. Such insights are essential for developing equitable, inclusive, and adaptive infrastructure.

In summary, this paper proposes to view railway projects as platforms where multiple actors negotiate agendas, influence one another, and compete with rival ideas in order to achieve their goals. The ethnographic approach provides opportunities to interact and engage with the field; intervention is inevitable (Pors et al. 2002: 4). Thus, the field is not a predetermined place or object of inquiry that can be simply entered. Through interactions between researchers and phenomena, our field emerges. Through collaboration and intervention, our field is constructed (Estalella and Criado 2018). Ultimately, I hope that it will lead to the silenced voices being heard over the loud noise of railway construction.

References

Abram, Simone and Gisa Weszkalnys (2011) Introduction. Anthropologies of planning: Temporality, imagination, and ethnography. *Focaal*, 2011(61): 3–18. https://doi.org/10.3167/fcl.2011.610101

Aiyara, Trin (2019) The Long and Winding Railway: Domestic politics and the realization of China-initiated high-speed railway projects in Thailand. *Chinese Political Science Review*, 4(3): 327–348. https://doi.org/10.1007/s41111-019-00124-2

Anand, Nikhil (2011) PRESSURE: The PoliTechnics of Water Supply in Mumbai. *Cultural Anthropology*, 26(4): 542–564. https://doi.org/10.1111/j.1548-1360.2011.01111.x

Anand, Nikhil (2012) Municipal disconnect: On abject water and its urban infrastructures. *Ethnography*, 13(4): 487–509. https://doi.org/10.1177/1466138111435743

Anand, Nikhil, Akhil Gupta and Hannah Appel (eds) (2018) *The Promise of Infrastructure*. Durham and London: Duke University Press.

Appadurai, Arjun (ed.) (2013) *The Future as Cultural Fact: Essays on the global condition*. New York : Verso Books.

Appel, Hannah, Nikhil Anand and Akhil Gupta (2015) Introduction: The Infrastructure Toolbox. Theorizing the Contemporary, *Fieldsights*, September 24. https://culanth.org/fieldsights/introduction-the-infrastructure-toolbox

Barry, Andrew (2001) *Political Machines: Governing a technological society*. London: Athlone Press.

Barry, Andrew (2013) *Material Politics: Disputes along the pipeline*. Hoboken: Wiley-Blackwell.

Batt, William H. (1984) Infrastructure: Etymology and import. *Journal of Professional Issues in Engineering*, 110(1): 1–6. https://doi.org/10.1061/(ASCE)1052-3928(1984)110:1(1)

Bear, Laura (2020) Speculations on Infrastructure: From colonial public works to a post-colonial global asset class on the Indian railways 1840–2017. *Economy and Society*, 49(1): 45–70. https://doi.org/10.1080/03085147.2020.1702416

Beauregard, Robert A. (2015) *Planning Matter: Acting with things*. Chicago: University of Chicago Press. https://doi.org/10.7208/chicago/9780226297422.001.0001

Bennett, Jane (2010) *Vibrant Matter: A political ecology of things*. Durham: Duke University Press.

Boholm, Asa (ed.) (2011) *New Perspectives on Risk Communication Uncertainty in a complex society*. Oxfordshire: Routledge.

Bowker, Geoffrey C. (1994) *Science on the Run: Information management and industrial geophysics at Schlumberger, 1920–1940*. Cambridge: MIT Press.

Braun, Bruce and Sarah J. Whatmore (eds) (2010) *Political Matter: Technoscience, democracy and public life*. Minneapolis: University of Minnesota Press.

Camba, Alvin (2020) *Deraling Development: China's railway projects and financing coalitions in Indonesia, Malaysia, and the Philippines*. GCI Working Paper 008, Global Development Policy Center, Boston University. https://www.bu.edu/gdp/files/2020/02/WP8-Camba-Deraling-Development.pdf

Carse, Ashley (2012) Nature as Infrastructure: Making and managing the Panama Canal watershed. *Social Studies of Science*, 42(4): 539–563. https://doi.org/10.1177/0306312712440166

Chen, Wanjing Kelly (2020) Sovereign Debt in the Making: Financial entanglements and labor politics along the Belt and Road in Laos. *Economic Geography*, 96(4): 295–314. https://doi.org/10.1080/00130095.2020.1810011

Chirathivat, Suthiphand, Phutthakān **Ratchathōn** and Devendrakumar, A. (eds) (2022) *China's Belt and Road Initiative in ASEAN: Growing presence, recent progress and future challenges*. Singapore, London, Hackensack: World Scientific.

Collier, Stephen J. (2011) *Post-Soviet Social: Neoliberalism, social modernity, biopolitics*. Princeton: Princeton University Press.

Das, Veena (2011) State, citizenship, and the urban poor. *Citizenship Studies*, 15(3–4): 319–333. https://doi.org/10.1080/13621025.2011.564781

Di Nunzio, Marco (2018) Anthropology of Infrastructure. *LSE Cities Research Note 1*. London.

DiCarlo, Jessica (2021) *Lost in Translation: Environmental and social safeguards for the Laos-China Railway*. Global Development Policy Center. https://www.bu.edu/gdp/2021/02/11/lost-in-translation-environmental-and-social-safeguards-for-the-laos-china-railway/

Elyachar, Julia (2010) Phatic labor, infrastructure, and the question of empowerment in Cairo. *American Ethnologist*, 37(3): 452–464. JSTOR. http://www.jstor.org/stable/40784608

Estalella, Adolfo and Tomás Sánchez Criado (eds) (2018) *Experimental collaborations: Ethnography through fieldwork devices*. New York: EASA Series, Berghahn Books.

Foucault, Michel (2010) *The Birth of Biopolitics: Lectures at the Collège de France, 1978–79*. Edited by Michel Senellart. Translated by Graham Burchell. London: Palgrave Macmillan.

Global Infrastructure Hub (2019) *Inclusive Infrastructure and Social Equity*. https://inclusiveinfra.gihub.org/

Global Times (2022) China-Laos Railway exceeds expectations, defies critics, injecting momentum into regional prosperity as part of the BRI. 7 September. https://www.globaltimes.cn/page/202209/1274899.shtml

Goodfellow, Tom and Zhengli Huang (2021) Contingent infrastructure and the dilution of 'Chineseness': Reframing roads and rail in Kampala and Addis Ababa. *Environment and Planning A: Economy and Space*, 53(4): 655–674. https://doi.org/10.1177/0308518X20967962

Gupta, Akhil (2018) The Future in Ruins: Thoughts on the Temporality of Infrastructure. In Nikhil Anand, Akhil Gupta and Hannah Appel (eds) *The Promise of Infrastructure*. Durham: Duke University Press, pp. 62–79. https://doi.org/10.1215/9781478002031-003

Gusterson, Hugh (1997) Studying Up Revisited. *PoLAR: Political and Legal Anthropology Review*, 20(1): 114–119. https://doi.org/10.1525/pol.1997.20.1.114

Harris, Tina (2013) Trading places: New economic geographies across Himalayan borderlands. *Political Geography*, 35: 60–68. https://doi.org/10.1016/j.polgeo.2012.12.002

Harvey, Penny (2018) Infrastructures in and out of Time: The Promise of Roads in Contemporary Peru. In Nikhil Anand, Akhil Gupta and Hannah Appel (eds), *The Promise of Infrastructure*. Durham: Duke University Press, pp. 80–101.

Harvey, Penelope, Casper Bruun Jensen and Atsuro Morita (eds) (2017) *Infrastructures and social complexity: A companion*. London and New York: Routledge.

Hine, Christine (2009) How Can qualitative internet researchers define the boundaries of their projects? In Annette N. Markham and Nancy K. Baym (eds) *Internet Inquiry: Conversations About Method*. London: Sage, pp. 1–20. https://doi.org/10.4135/9781483329086.n1

Holston, James (2021) *Insurgent Citizenship: Disjunctions of Democracy and Modernity in Brazil*. Princeton: Princeton University Press. https://doi.org/10.2307/j.ctv1hw3xwv

Howe, Cymene, Jessica Lockrem, Hannah Appel, Edward Hackett, Dominic Boyer, Randall Hall, Matthew Schneider-Mayerson, Albert Pope, Akhil Gupta, Elizabeth Rodwell, Andrea Ballestero, Trevor Durbin, Farès el-Dahdah, Elizabeth Long and Cyrus Mody (2016) Paradoxical Infrastructures: Ruins, retrofit, and risk. *Science, Technology, and Human Values*, 41(3): 547–565. https://doi.org/10.1177/0162243915620017

Humphrey, Caroline (2020) *Rethinking Infrastructure: Siberian Cities and the Great Freeze of January 2001*. London and New York: Routledge.

Jensen, Caspar Bruun, and Brit Ross Winthereik (2013) *Monitoring movements in development aid: Recursive partnerships and infrastructures*. Cambridge: The MIT Press.

Karasti, Helena and Jeanette Blomberg (2017) Studying Infrastructuring Ethnographically. *Computer Supported Cooperative Work (CSCW)*, 27(2): 233–265. https://doi.org/10.1007/s10606-017-9296-7

Klinger, Julie M. and Joshua S. S. Muldavin (2019) New geographies of development: Grounding China's global integration. *Territory, Politics, Governance*, 7(1): 1–21. https://doi.org/10.1080/21622671.2018.1559757

Kothari, Uma and David Hulme (2004) Narratives, stories and tales: Understanding poverty dynamics through life histories. Economics Series Working Paper GPRG-WPS-011, University of Oxford.

Kuik, Cheng-Chwee (2021) Asymmetry and Authority: Theorizing Southeast Asian responses to China's Belt and Road Initiative. *Asian Perspective*, 45(2): 255–276. https://doi.org/10.1353/apr.2021.0000

Lauridsen, Laurids S. (2020) Drivers of China's Regional Infrastructure Diplomacy: The case of the Sino-Thai railway project. *Journal of Contemporary Asia*, 50(3): 380–406. https://doi.org/10.1080/00472336.2019.1603318

Lokman, Tasnim (2019) Improved ECRL deal: Costs reduced by RM21.5 billion. *New Strait Times Online.* https://www.nst.com.my/news/nation/2019/04/478754/improved-ecrl-deal-costs-reduced-rm215-billion.

Lu, Juliet (2021) Grounding Chinese investment: Encounters between Chinese capital and local land politics in Laos. *Globalizations*, 18(3): 422–440. https://doi.org/10.1080/14747731.2020.1796159

Marcus, George E. (1995) Ethnography in/of the World System: The emergence of multi-sited ethnography. *Annual Review of Anthropology*, 24: 95–117.

Oakes, Tim (2021a) The Belt and Road as method: Geopolitics, technopolitics and power through an infrastructure lens. *Asia Pacific Viewpoint*, 62(3): 281–285. DOI:10.1111/apv.12319.

Oakes, Tim (2021b) *The BRI as an Exercise in Infrastructural Thinking.* Toronto: Belt and Road in Global Perspective. https://munkschool.utoronto.ca/belt-road/research/bri-exercise-infrastructural-thinking

Oliveira, Gustavo de L. T., Galen Murton, Alessandro Rippa, Tyler Harlan and Yang Yang (2020) China's Belt and Road Initiative: Views from the ground. *Political Geography*, 82: 102225. https://doi.org/10.1016/j.polgeo.2020.102225

Ponsavady, Stéphanie (2020) Editorial. *Transfers*, 10(2–3): 1–3. https://doi.org/10.3167/TRANS.2020.1002301

Pors, Jens Kaaber, Dixi Louise Henriksen, Brit Ross Einthereik and Marc Berg (2002) Challenging divisions: Exploring the intersections of ethnography and interventions in IS research. *Scandinavian Journal of Information Systems*, 14(2): 3-7.

Reeves, Madeleine (2017) Infrastructural Hope: Anticipating 'independent roads' and territorial integrity in Southern Kyrgyzstan. *Ethnos*, 82(4): 711–737. https://doi.org/10.1080/00141844.2015.1119176

Rippa, Alessandro (2020) *Borderland Infrastructures: Trade, development, and control in western China*. Amsterdam: Amsterdam University Press.

Rowedder, Simon (2020) Railroading land-linked Laos: China's regional profits, Laos' domestic costs? *Eurasian Geography and Economics*, 61(2): 152–161. https://doi.org/10.1080/15387216.2019.1704813

Saxer, Martin (2016) Pathways: A concept, field site and methodological approach to study remoteness and connectivity. *HIMALAYA*, 36(2): Article 15. https://digitalcommons.macalester.edu/himalaya/vol36/iss2/15

Schweitzer, Peter and Olga Povoroznyuk (2020) Introduction. Precarious connections: On the promise and menace of railroad projects. *Transfers*, 10(2–3): 137–151. https://doi.org/10.3167/TRANS.2020.1002311

Schwenkel, Christina (2018) The Current Never Stops: Intimacies of energy infrastructure in Vietnam. In Nikhil Anand, Akhil Gupta and Hannah Appel (eds) *The Promise of Infrastructure*. Durham: Duke University Press, pp. 102–129. https://doi.org/10.1215/9781478002031-005

Sidaway, James D., Simon C. Rowedder, Chih Yuan Woon, Weiqiang Lin and Vatthana Pholsena (2020) Introduction: Research agendas raised by the Belt and Road Initiative. *Environment and Planning C: Politics and Space*, 38(5): 795–802. https://doi.org/10.1177/2399654420911410

Sidaway, James D. and Chih Yuan Woon (2017) Chinese Narratives on 'One Belt, One Road' (一带一路) in Geopolitical and Imperial Contexts. *The Professional Geographer*, 69(4): 591–603. https://doi.org/10.1080/00330124.2017.1288576

Simone, AbdouMaliq (2004). People as Infrastructure: Intersecting fragments in Johannesburg. *Public Culture*, 16(3): 407–429. https://doi.org/10.1215/08992363-16-3-407

Star, Susan Leigh (1999) The Ethnography of Infrastructure. *American Behavioral Scientist*, 43(3): 377–391. https://doi.org/10.1177/00027649921955326

State Council of the People's Republic of China (2015) *Action Plan on the Belt and Road Initiative*. http://english.www.gov.cn/archive/publications/2015/03/30/content_281475080249035.htm

Suhardiman, Diana, Jessica DiCarlo, Oulavanh Keovilignavong, Jonathan Rigg and Alan Nicol (2021) (Re)constructing state power and livelihoods through the Laos-China Railway project. *Geoforum*, 124: 79–88. https://doi.org/10.1016/j.geoforum.2021.06.003

Swanson, Heather Anne (2020) Why Railroads Now? Anthropology of infrastructure and debates around 'green' transit. *Transfers*, 10(2–3): 270–282. https://doi.org/10.3167/TRANS.2020.1002318

Tritto, Angela, Mary Silaban and Alvin Camba (2022) Indonesia's 'Beauty Contest': China, Japan, the US, and Jakarta's spatial objectives. In Seth Schindler and Jessica DiCarlo (eds) *The Rise of the Infrastructure State: How US-China Rivalry Shapes Politics and Place Worldwide*. Bristol: Policy Press, pp. 227–240.

Wei, Siyuan (2021) *The effect of the development of China-Laos Railway on Thailand's export trade to China*. Ph.D. Dissertation, Naresuan University. http://nuir.lib.nu.ac.th/dspace/handle/123456789/4452

Wu, Shang-Su and Alan Chong (2018) Developmental Railpolitics: The political economy of China's high-speed rail projects in Thailand and Indonesia. *Contemporary Southeast Asia*, 40(3): 503–526. https://www.rsis.edu.sg/staff-publication/developmental-railpolitics-the-political-economy-of-chinas-high-speed-rail-projects-in-thailand-and-indonesia/

Yeh, Emily T. (2018) *The Geoeconomics and Geopolitics of Chinese Development and Investment in Asia*. Oxfordshire: Routledge.

Young, Iris Marion (2011) *Responsibility for Justice*. Oxford: Oxford University Press. https://doi.org/10.1093/acprof:oso/9780195392388.001.0001

6 | Shadow Zones: Fraudulent Infrastructure, the Alchemy of Sovereignty, and Destructive Economies in Shwe Kokko SEZ/KK Park and Thailand's EEC

Pinkaew Laungaramsri

Abstract

Special economic zones play a key role in China's Belt and Road Initiative. The massive connective infrastructure – including highways, fiber optic cables, railroads, oil pipelines, ports, and airports – being developed with Chinese funding throughout Eurasia and Africa has created new nodes of control in the form of special economic zones (SEZs). Although these SEZs are nodes of political and economic power that serve China's strategic purpose in the region, they are at the same time more than that, sometimes becoming "shadow zones" – economic frontiers where obscure regulatory regimes deliberately disrupt established ecologies and social orders to facilitate new forms of unruly resource extraction and capital accumulation. Using case studies of Shwe Kokko SEZ and KK Park in Myanmar's borderlands and the recycling industry in the hinterland of Thailand's Eastern Economic Corridor (EEC), this paper argues that the proliferation of illegal and unhealthy economic activities in special economic zones created by Chinese capital are not aberrations and are inseparable from China's economic expansion in the region. Shadow zones emerge in response to changing regional and global geopolitics in which the Chinese state is the key actor. These emerging zones can be characterized by the following features. First, the deployment of infrastructure's allure to induce mobilities of capital, people, and socio-economic networks in the creation of the zone. Second, the alchemy by which various forms of frontier sovereignty are at play to bend and suspend the rule of law while blurring the boundary between legality and illegality. And third, a "destructive economy" that benefits the developers and their alliance networks while causing severe health, environmental, and economic damage, and frequently creating new hubs of organized crime.

Keywords

shadow zones – infrastructure urbanism – transnational crime – EEC – recycling industry – flexible sovereignty

Introduction

On 20 September 2023, Fifa (pseudonym) a young Thai man who had been duped into taking a sketchy job in Myanmar was rescued at the border by the Thai military. Fifa said that he had been recruited by a Thai woman who promised him an online administrator position for a 17,000 baht salary ($US 491). The company arranged transportation to take him across the Moei River in Mae Sot, a Thai border town near the so-called New City project of KK Park near the village of Maw Hto Talay, Myawaddy, an area controlled by the Karen National Union's (KNU) 6th Brigade. Upon arriving at the address in KK Park, Fifa's passport was confiscated. He was put to work right away and was allowed to use his mobile phone only briefly after work. The person who gave him a contract to sign told him that he would be working on a "slaughtering website." Fifa immediately realized that he had been lured into an online fraud job. He was told to create a fake profile as an investment expert in order to seduce victims into fake investment schemes. His monthly target was 50,000 baht while working 12–14 hours per day. Fifa was rescued after six days with the help of the KNU and the Thai military in Mae Sot through his family's connection (Interview with Fifa, 20 September 2023). Fifa was fortunate to escape the criminal hub unharmed; other people from various parts of the world who fail to meet their targets were often subjected to torture inside the prison-like park. Some people were transferred to work in other large-scale Chinese-run industries, especially online casinos in the Shwe Kokko special economic zone, situated some 40 kms north of KK Park (Interview with former worker, 25 August 2022).

Meanwhile, in eastern Thailand, more than 200 local villagers from Bo Thong district, Chonburi province (150 kilometers southeast of Bangkok) protested against a plastic production and recycling plant operated by a Chinese-Thai-Japanese joint venture in Ken United Thailand Free Zone Industrial Park under the EEC Development Plan. Villagers were concerned that the pollution from the plant would affect their agricultural crops and local environment. Ken United is reportedly only one of 12 recycling factories planned to be built in the area. Although company representatives assured local villagers that there would be no environmental impact from the operation of their plant, the locals complain of the smell of toxic fumes emitted from the plastic and metal waste recycling plant. The Bo Thong case is one among many other rural communities in the EEC area that have suffered disastrous impacts from the emissions of Chinese-owned recycling industries. In some of these communities such as Nong Pawa in Rayong province, villagers are no longer able to cultivate their land, as their water and soil have been severely contaminated by the pollution allegedly caused by recycling factories.

Shwe Kokko special economic zone, KK Park and EEC, despite their different origins and characteristics have several things in common. All zone developers, a Chinese private company and the

Thai government, position their projects within the grand strategy of the Belt and Road Initiative. All three zones promise to boost economic growth and sustain long term economic development through massive infrastructure investment, by building new cities with digital technology. And development in these zones has gone astray, gradually becoming channels for large-scale human trafficking, refuges for cyber-criminals, and sources of toxic pollution from disastrous industries.

How are we to understand this phenomenon, especially in relation to China and the BRI? Proponents of special economic zone studies tend to treat this kind of zone as an anomaly unrelated to other developments. For example, Thibault Serlet, director of Adrianople Group, a research and business advisory firm concentrating on SEZs, describes "a corrupt zone that has a large and disproportionate impact on the reputation of the industry as a whole" (Serlet 2019). Serlet calls for international SEZ organizations to publicly condemn the Golden Triangle SEZ in northern Laos so that "bad SEZ[s]" that "fall below the required standards of decency" would not damage the credibility of the SEZ trade associations (Serlet 2022). Serlet's approach to illegal activities is rather common among social scientists, who typically neglect illegal economy or treat it as separate from the processes of capitalist production.

My argument is that the proliferation of illegal and unhealthy activities in economic zones operated by Chinese capital must not be viewed as isolated aberrations disconnected or unrelated to the growing economy in the region, but rather as a response to changing regional and global geopolitics in which the Chinese state is the key actor. By Chinese capital, this chapter refers to a particular type of private Chinese transnational capital – capital which is mobile, fluid, and convertible, exists outside state control and/or conceals illegal activities. I follow Lee Ching Kwan's suggestion of "varieties of capital" which highlights the multiple forms of Chinese capital that operate in the Global South[1] and Alvin Camba's notion of Chinese flexible capital – the capital that originates from the accumulated private savings of Chinese investors and aims to extricate itself from the Chinese state's jurisdictional reach[2] (Lee 2018; Camba 2020). Similar to Camba's flexible capital, the illicit Chinese capital that is currently active at the border of Thailand and Myanmar and the hinterland of EEC has mostly moved/ fled from the Chinese state's control and regulation. This kind of capital has relocated into the sphere of what I call "the shadow zone" – the economic frontier where an obscure regulatory regime is at play in which existing ecologies and social orders are deliberately dissolved to pave the way for a new form of unruly resource extraction and capital accumulation.

---

1 In her study of Chinese investment in copper mines and construction sites in Zambia, Ching Kwang Lee suggests that Chinese capital should not be viewed as a monolithic phenomenon but processes and relations of power that are embedded in the society where capital activities are operating (Lee 2018). Lee develops the notion of "varieties of capital" where Chinese state capital varies according to circumstances and is structured toward the long-term interest of the Chinese state which differs from the global private capital that is deployed with the short-term purpose of maximizing shareholder value (ibid.).

2 Based on case studies of the Kaliwa Dam project and online gambling in the Philippines, Camba demonstrates how China's overaccumulation crisis has resulted in the movement of two types of capital to the Global South. The first type is state-backed capital that aims to impose the model of development and render recipient states legible to improve China's inter-state disputes and manage potential disagreements. The second type is flexible capital, private capital with the primary aim to extricate itself from the restraints placed by the Chinese state (Camba 2020a). Although these two types of capital have different logics, they can also coincide. As Camba explains, flexible capital, before extricating itself from the state's regulation, can attend to the overarching goals of the Chinese state (Camba 2020a: 3).

These emerging zones are characterized by the following features. First, the deployment of infrastructure's allure to induce mobilities of capital, people, and socio-economic networks in the creation of the zone. Second, the alchemy whereby various forms of frontier sovereignty bend, obscure, and even suspend the rule of law while blurring the boundary between legality and illegality to allow illicit practices to persist. Third, a destructive economy that benefits originators and their alliance networks while causing drastic health, environmental, economic damage, or turning the area into a hub of organized crime.

Using the case studies of Shwe Kokko SEZ, KK Park and the recycling industry in the EEC's hinterland, this chapter will first discuss the development of shadow zones in Myanmar's borderland and recycling businesses in the industrial margins of eastern Thailand. It demonstrates that the shadow zones of special economic development flourish in the interstices and are not isolated aberrations, but are in fact intrinsic to China's engagement with globalization and regional economies, wielding its economic might to change the rules and norms to its advantage, in collaboration with the weaker and quasi-states in the region who hope for a share of the benefits such engagement promises. The chapter then examines the politics of infrastructural practices in which technopolitics of "new cities" and "recycling infrastructure" are deployed both to project a vision of the economy of the future and to obscure the fraudulent aspects of economics generated by such infrastructures. The chapter also investigates the ways in which different kinds of sovereignty are exercised in the Shwe Kokko SEZ, KK Park and in the EEC to facilitate the state-evading movement of capital and people and economic practices that breach the law. Local as well as (inter)national responses to the politics of shadow zones will also be discussed to gain insight into how divergent interests, interventions, and negotiations turn these areas into multiply contested zones of entangled risks.

More importantly, investors in these zones are interconnected and highly mobile. For example, the network of online casinos (AKA Crown Cash Network) rotated its headquarters between Myanmar's Kokang Administrative Zone and Sihanoukville, Cambodia, before settling in Sihanoukville after military conflict increased in the Kokang area (Farrerly et al, 2022). The Chinese investor, Shé Zhijiang, who runs the Yatai International Holding Group (Yatai IHG), the main developer of the Shwe Kokko SEZ, was also involved in a casino and other business in Cambodia before the joint Cambodia-China law enforcement crack down on criminal activities in Cambodia in late 2018 which prompted the relocation of online gambling and other illegal activities from Sihanoukville to the border between Myanmar and Thailand. The Golden Triangle SEZ's investor, Zhao Wei, was also a former casino tycoon in Mong La, Myanmar before moving to northwestern Laos to evade Chinese authorities who were investigating reports of official state funds being used for gambling in his casinos.

Despite the shady aspect of these shadow zones, developers of the zones often position themselves and their businesses as patriotic overseas Chinese, loyal to Communist Party initiatives, while attempting to connect their businesses to China's BRI (Tower, cited in Kennedy and Southern 2022). In some cases such as the Golden Triangle SEZ, the Chinese government tends to turn a blind eye to its illegal activities while acknowledging the zone's contribution to the BRI (ibid.). But in the case of the Shwe Kokko SEZ, despite persistent claims by investors that the zone is part of the Belt and Road Initiative, the Chinese government explicitly distanced itself through its embassy in Myanmar which, in August 2020, publicly announced that Shwe Kokko "is a third-country investment and has nothing to do with the Belt and Road Initiative" (Naing 2022) –

a denial offered in the context of mounting allegations of human trafficking and other crimes in the area.

The rise of shadow zones

Since 2006, when China announced the Overseas Economic Cooperation Zones program aimed at supporting SEZs overseas through state-funded joint ventures between Chinese companies and local counterparts, there has been a considerable increase in Chinese FDI in the region (Figiaconi and Lodetti 2020). Southeast Asia's SEZs rapidly increased in number, with approximately 500 zones at last count, mostly concentrated in Vietnam, Thailand, Myanmar, Laos, and Cambodia. Following an economic downturn in China in the early 2020s, with dwindling consumer demand and rising unemployment rates, Beijing has increasingly relied on SEZs under the BRI framework to enhance its economic presence abroad (ibid.). China's expansion of SEZs, however, is not a singular or unidimensional success story of investment. On the contrary, SEZs are built by land grabbing, forceful relocation of communities, destruction of local livelihoods and environmental pollution – the disastrous aspects of development which have often been cast as byproducts rather than integral to SEZs.

Several SEZs are hubs of criminal activity, where legitimate development schemes and entertainment businesses co-exist with illegal activities such as gambling, sex, drugs, environmental crime, money laundering, online fraud and human trafficking. The coexistence of legal and illegal economic activities can be seen from two interrelating bases. First, the development of shadow zones depends on the availability of a combination of structural factors, including the zone's specific infrastructure, an existing consumer market and its demand for unauthorized commodities, labor force segmentation, and the regional and global networks of the capitalist economy. Second, these factors are largely determined by the historically developed structure and activities of the state, including flexible attitudes towards legal enforcement. Sihanoukville SEZ in Cambodia is a case where development of the zone has been a product of the influx of Chinese private and state-backed investment into the country, increasing demand for timber in China, increasing demand for ivory-smuggling, and the advantages of coastal and hinterland locations that are favorable for transporting illicit goods (Farrelly, Dawkins, and Deegan 2022).

As Manuel Castells (2010: 168) pointed out, development of communications networks facilitates not only the circulation of legal commodities, but also various forms of criminal trades where the illicit and the licit are intertwined. To understand the organizational strength of global crime, then, we need to examine the interplay between flexible networking at the local and global levels (Castells 2010: 186). Of course, illegal timber harvesting, wildlife trafficking, and gambling were already common in the areas around the Golden Triangle SEZ and Sihanoukville long before the BRI. But the BRI opened new avenues for these activities to be refashioned under a new developmental trope of smart/new city with advanced digital technology. China's ban on online gambling resulted in a massive flight of Chinese gamblers and gambling businesses to other parts of the region. In the case of recycling enterprises in Thailand's EEC, China's ban on imports of foreign waste to combat domestic pollution prompted the country's recycling industry – notorious for being poorly regulated and for destroying the living environment of local populations – to move their operations to places with weak regulatory regimes, such as Thailand. From this perspective, it is clear that shadow zones are not static manifestations of an underground economy, but rather dynamic and volatile responses to the fluctuating global demand for commodities, regional development, and China's changing policies towards various industries and enterprises.

From Shwe Kokko SEZ to KK Park

Shwe Kokko special economic zone is a planned new urban area and casino city located in the Shwe Kokko township near the Moei River, which forms the border between Myanmar and Thailand. The Shwe Kokko area used to be a stronghold of the Karen National Liberation Army (KNLA) before being taken over by the Myanmar army (*Tatmadaw*) following in-fighting among the Karen groups. A former local KNLA officer, Saw Chit Thu, who later became head of the Border Guard Forces (BGF) – a branch of the *Tatmadaw* – was granted the authority to control the border area between Karen state and Thailand as a reward for assisting the *Tatmadaw* in combating the KNLA. Covering an area of 120 square kilometers (12,140 hectares) with an estimated value of $US15 billion, Shwe Kokko New City was built by the Hong Kong-registered developer Yatai International Holding Group (Yatai IHG), headquartered in Bangkok, in partnership with Chit Lin Myaing Company, owned by the Karen State Border Guard Force. Although the project has often been refered to as the Myanmar Shwe Kokko Special Economic Zone, the Myanmar government officially recognizes only three SEZs: the Thilawa, Dawei and Kyaukphyu SEZs. According to Myanmar's SEZ Law, investors can be granted a land use permit of 50 years, extendable for another 25 years. Yet, the Karen Peace Support Network reports that the lease for Shwe Kokko was for 70 years, extendable to 99 years. The overlapping sovereignty or what Andrew Ong calls "disaggregated sovereignty" (Ong 2020) has allowed the Chinese investor to negotiate with both the central Myanmar government and the Karen BGF group to maximize profits.

The Shwe Kokko casino town project was marketed as an international integrated resort (IR), branding the destination as a world city complete with modern housing, condominiums, entertainment complexes, hotels, shopping centers, a golf course, casinos, an industrial zone with a cargo depot, and an airport. According to Yatai IHG, the first phase of the project, covering 214 acres, was in progress with US$500 million already invested. A video advertisement from Yatai International promoted the project to potential investors as the "only area in Shwe Kokko that is authorized to operate casinos," while highlighting the casinos as a lucrative source of revenue (see King 2020). The company expected revenues from the casino to reach US$11.4 billion within ten years. The Yatai company website claimed that the project was part of China's ambitious Belt and Road Initiative (BRI). As of 2020, there were an estimated 17 casinos operating along the Moei River, but the Myanmar government rejected these figures, declaring that no official permission for a casino business had been granted to the developer (Kyaw Ye Lynn 2020).

About 40 kilometers north (but downstream) of the Shwe Kokko SEZ lies the gigantic KK Park, a notorious scam city operated by Tran-Asia International Holding Group – a subsidiary of Huanya Holding Group and Troth Star Company. The area of KK Park, however, is under the administration of the Karen National Union (KNU) who has leased the land to the Huanya International Holding Group. The United States Institute of Peace (USIP) reported that some of the investors are connected to gambling businesses and cryptocurrency ventures in Sihanoukville (Tower and Clapp 2020). USIP also indicated that the KK Park project, the Saixigang Industrial Zone project and the Shwe Kokko new city project have all been connected to the network of Chinese criminal syndicates which include the 14k Triad crime group leader Wan Kuok-koi – a long-time gangster and criminal and now the chair of the Dongmei Group investment company (ibid.). Unlike the Shwe Kokko New City Project, which was widely publicized in both Chinese and international media, the KK Park is a rather low-key operation. There has been scant media coverage of activities in this zone. A former worker at KK Park who had also worked for an online gambling business at Shwe Kokko New City commented that whereas Shwe Kokko is an open city that welcomes tourists and gambling customers, KK Park is a closed city with high levels of security (Interview with Ms. A, 20 September 2023). No one is allowed to enter KK Park without permission. But like Shwe Kokko, KK Park is protected by the Karen ethnic armed group who assisted the Chinese investor from the initial land grabbing, although the Karen National Union (2023) has officially denied any involvement with the infamous KK Park and its illegal activities.

Shwe Kokko New City Project and the KK Park have both been under close scrutiny by the US government. On 9 December 2020, Wan Kuok Koi and his Dong Mei Group were sanctioned by the US Treasury Department which identified him as as a leader of the 14K Triad "who engages in drug trafficking, illegal gambling, racketeering" as well as "bribery, corruption and graft" (US Department of the Treasury 2020). The Treasury Department also claimed that the Chinese enterprises behind the BRI projects "have several things in common: their leadership has links to criminal networks or actors involved in illicit activities in other parts of Southeast Asia, as well as China; they have pre-existing organizations engaged in casinos and crypto currencies; they advertise themselves online to be associated with Beijing's BRI and flaunt connections with key Chinese government agencies; and all of them have established associations that actively seek to assist Chinese nationals" (ibid.).

The US Institute of Peace documented the complex transnational connections of Chinese investors who were forced out of Cambodia's Sihanoukville and elsewhere in Southeast Asia for illegal gambling activities, and relocated to Karen State to build three megacities as a hub for casinos (Shwe Kokko, Huanya and Saixigang). It reported that the chair of Yatai International Holding, Shé Zhìjiāng – also known as Shélúnkǎi (佘伦凯), Dylan She and Tang Kriang Kai – has Cambodian citizenship and is involved with the massive Long Bay casino project in Cambodia's Koh Kong province (Frontier 2022). On 13 August 2022, Shé was detained by the Thai police in Bangkok on an Interpol red notice published in May 2020, and was waiting to be extradited to China (Chen 2023). Shé's arrest had no impact on business operations at Shwe Kokko, though, as other stakeholders immediately replaced him.

The relocation of casino businesses from China, Cambodia, and the Phillipines to the ethnic Karen controlled area in Myanmar's borderlands is believed to be an attempt to elude the Chinese government. Andrew Ong calls the casino city at Shwe Kokko a "third-generation online gambling enterprise" which emerged due to China's steady suppression of the online gambling industry. For Ong, the first-generation online casinos were mostly located near China's borders, such as in Myanmar's Kokang region, Wa region, Mong La, and Boten in northern Laos which were within easy reach of Chinese government sanctions. The second-generation online casino industry developed mainly in Cambodia and the Philippines beginning in the early 2010s before they, too, were forced to close down. Shwe Kokko, the third-generation, is geographically distant from China and is relatively autonomous from the national government. Although the Myanmar government began investigating Shwe Kokko in early 2020, the investigation was suspended following the coup in 2021.

During the Covid-19 pandemic, border crossing from Thailand into the casino city was suspended, but construction of the new city continued. Most of the agricultural farmland was confiscated and an entertainment complex was built. Interviews with villagers by Karen Human Rights Group and Karen Peace Support Network reported that the forced resettlement took place in 2017–2018. Villagers' were compensated between 30,000 and 50,000 baht (US$960–1,600) or with land in other areas. The houses that were destroyed by the project were compensated based on the quality of the houses, for example, a high quality or large house was compensated for 100,000 baht to 150,000 baht (US$3,200–4,800). It is not known how many villagers were employed to work in the zone. According to a local Thai official, development in the zone had been accelerating.

> Residential buildings, hotels, a hospital, entertainment complex, including a shopping mall have been built. Chinese products are shipped to container facilities via Laem Chabang port in Chonburi province to Mae Sot and transferred to Shwe Kokko via Pier no. 34. Schools in Shwe Kokko are taught in Chinese. They hire Karen people to be security personnel in the outer area with a salary of 10,000 baht. In the inner part Chinese soldiers in plain clothes are hired to guard the area. (Interview, 2 July 2022)

In February 2025, Thailand strategically cut electricity to the Myawaddy border region, effectively targeting the notorious scam centers operating across the border. This decisive action forced the Border Guard Force (BGF) to finally crack down on criminal enterprises flourishing in Shwe Kokko and KK Park. In the aftermath, hundreds of Chinese victims and lower-level criminals were handed over to Chinese authorities, while the kingpins behind these fraudulent operations managed to escape. To what extent this incident will have any impact on the zone remains to be seen. However, online fraud operations are characterized by flexible and malleable networks of criminal coalitions. The reassembly and relocation of these criminal networks elsewhere is likely to occur.

The politics of waste-to-energy industry in the EEC's hinterland

Thailand's Eastern Economic Corridor has been positioned as part of China's BRI. A memorandum of understanding with China was signed in 2019 to facilitate Chinese investment in EEC projects. Somkid Jatusripitak, a senior economic advisor to the Thai military government at the time, was the key figure in negotiating the China-Thailand partnership in the EEC. Under the Thai military government, city and town planning laws and regulations in Special Economic Zones were overridden and Chinese investment in the EEC increased exponentially. Although there have been extensive studies about the environmental impacts of industrial estates in eastern Thailand, little attention has been paid to the connection between BRI, transnational Chinese capital, and the destruction of the everyday lives of the local people.

The politics of the waste-to-energy industry in the EEC highlights some highly contentious dimensions of the BRI. Recycling waste industries have mushroomed in the EEC, especially after China banned the import of solid waste in 2017. As a result, a number of Chinese recycling industries sought opportunities in Southeast Asian countries. Thailand with its weak enforcement of environmental regulations has become one of the favored sites. While the EEC is promoted as a megaproject that the government hopes will accelerate the development of a high-tech economy, the creation of the mega infrastructure space in EEC destroyed the local infrastructure vital to agricultural livelihoods. A local resident in Bo Thong district, Chonburi Province, complained that the factories had been built in a predominantly agricultural zone without consulting local villagers. A small meeting had been held in the village, but only a few villagers attended. Over the past decade, villagers in Chon Buri, Rayong, and Chachaengsao have filed numerous complaints against the toxic impact of the recycling plants. Some have initiated legal action against the companies, seeking compensation for the loss of agricultural products and livelihood as well as for rehabilitation of the ecosystem.

Nevertheless, the recycling of imported waste continued to increase at an alarming rate. Director of the 13th Regional Environment Office – responsible for Chonburi, Rayong, Chanthaburi, Trad, Chachoengsao, and Samut Prakan – reported that an inspection of 95 plastic and recycling factories in the area between mid-December 2020 and January 2021 found that more than 70% were owned by Chinese companies. Some companies, however, had moved their equipment out of their factories upon learning about the legal charges against their business. Local villagers expressed concerns that the polluters had run away from their cleanup responsibilities. Local people were also concerned that there would be a dozen similar plants being established in the vicinity in the near future which would worsen the environmental situation. As one local resident complained:

> Information from EARTH Foundation shows that stake holders of Ken United Thailand are relating to the waste recycling business in other areas of Chachoengsao and Samut Sakorn. Villagers and some organizations made an inquiry to the relevant authority. But they denied such connection. After the establishment of the [Ken United] plant and the operation of its machines, people began to be affected by noise and toxic fumes from the factory. This is a plastic recycling plant which

is located near my house. Not only the smell of plastic melting that people have experienced, but also some other smells of waste including metal substance. Local villagers suspect that there are other kinds of recycling substances being [processed] apart from plastic. Other concerning environmental impacts include water shortages and water pollution. The plant is located near a national park and public water resources. They divert water from these water resources into their plant. When it rains, waste water from the plant also seeps into the public water resource. (Interview, 5 July 2022).

For China, SEZs are nodes of connective infrastructure and key to the success of the BRI. BRI SEZs take many forms ranging from an industrial park to a new city. In mainland Southeast Asia, infrastructure connectivity is the key driver of China's "sphere of influence" in the region (Raymond 2021). While transport connectivity such as roads, rails, and internal waterways serve as "lines of access" to Southeast Asia, SEZs across the region provide "nodes of control" that serve China's geo-economic goals of regional integration.

But special economic zones, especially those funded by the Chinese government and investors, comprise more than nodes of political and economic power that serve China's strategic purposes in the region. These infrastructure spaces are media of what Easterling (2014) calls "extrastatecraft," a highly contagious and globalized urban form and a vivid vessel built in international zones that is both outside and in addition to statecraft, combining multiple forces such as state, non-state, military, market, and non-market so as to bypass legal, ethical, political and financial requirements that could impede market forces. For Easterling, zones are technologies of "extrastatecraft" and "spaces of exception," segregated from national laws or regulations, where diverse forms of sovereignty and extraterritoriality are concurrently at play. Buildings, fences, and other facilities within the zone are therefore material existence that are site of authorities which becomes the basis of self-governing power of zone developers beyond the reach of the state. Many shadow zones have their own armed "security guards" who police the zone, while national police authorities must seek permission to enter the zone.[3]

It has become increasingly common for infrastructure space developments to situate their industrial and trading infrastructure in a broader "world city template" (Easterling 2014). Zone infrastructures have become the key engine driving the development of cities, what Tim Oakes calls "infrastructural urbanism" (Oakes 2021). In many areas, especially on the frontiers of nation-states in Southeast Asia, infrastructural urbanism and the creation of new cities have been promoted as the most promising way to increase foreign direct investment, boost local economies, and end poverty.

Urban infrastructures built in Chinese funded SEZs, however, do not necessarily deliver transformative benefits to the local economy. Outside the states' jurisdiction, some zones have become strategic venues for shadow economies. Studies of BRI overwhelmingly focus on formal economic exchange among nation states and have paid little attention to the informal and unauthorized economies facilitated by the BRI. The advent of BRI as one form of globalization involves not only state actors, but an assemblage of supranational, quasi-state, and non-state actors from multilateral institutions, private enterprises, business groups, and criminal syndicates collaborate and compete with

---

3   In the case of GT SEZ, the Lao police advised victims from human trafficking inside the zone who called to ask for help that they must escape by getting out of the fence themselves. The Lao police could rescue these victims only after they were out of the property of the zone as the police were not able to enter the zone without permission from the company.

formal state actors to create rules and rework norms (Rosenau 2003). At the same time, the zones created for this informal economy are often characterized by mega-infrastructure built in humongous, geographically isolated spaces. Following Marc Auge (1995), these space might be called "non-places;" transitory places where human actors pass through as anonymous individuals without relating/identifying in any intimate sense; desolate places where the poetics of dwelling does not thrive. Such non-place spaces, however, are not built from nothing. On the contrary, the emerging new cities of zonal infrastructures are typically made by replacing or eradicating pre-existing places, destroying the living infrastructure and livelihood of rural spaces, and rendering entire communities abject.

The EEC's shadow zone is characterized by weak enforcement of environmental regulations and a zoning system that disregards adverse industrial impacts on local environment. Global discourses of a "circular economy" and "recycling" have, ironically, greenwashed the recycling industry as "environmentally friendly." The discourse of recycling evokes images of conserving resources and protecting the environment by reducing the amount of waste sent to landfill and combustion facilities. It conceals the ugly fact that the unregulated recycling of plastic and solid waste is a hazardous enterprise that transformed many of China's agricultural areas into heavily polluted "dead zones" with severe health problems (Minter 2014). In the US, although proponents of the recycling industry claim that new technologies make it possible to handle mixed and harder to recycle plastic with little environmental impacts, critics counterargue that the technology remains unproven particularly with regards to toxic emissions (Gribkoff 2022). The environmental impact caused by the recycling industry in the EEC largely reproduces the environmental disaster that plagued the area when it was called the Eastern Seaboard, with serious air pollution, industrial waste and untreated toxic wastewater. In the shadow zone of the EEC, local livelihoods and the environment are now facing similar threats presented under the guise of a better environment.

Fraudulent infrastructure and the allure of infrastructure

Studies of infrastructure especially in the field of Science and Technology Studies (STS) although emphasizing infrastructure-in-use, in practice, and in power and social relations, tend to pay scant attention to the ways in which infrastructures can be in flux, in disguise, or are in fact fraudulent. In many shadow zones, notions of infrastructure "use" and "user" are not necessarily associated with the material feature and function of the infrastructure itself but is employed to serve other disguised purposes such as money laundering and scam activities. Impressive modern buildings constructed in these "new cities" are frequently "non-places" in Marc Auge's sense that have nothing to do with creating the advertised future. These are spaces and artifacts that assist criminal activities to generate substantial profits by diverting their criminal funds into infrastructure investment without attracting attention to the underlying activity or the persons involved. Zone infrastructures such as roads, buildings, and airports thus help to disguise the sources by changing the form of capital and transforming illegal funds into legal infrastructure which is used for further illegal activities.

Advertised as a luxurious casino and entertainment complex, the premises of the KK Park housed the architecture of cybercrime and human trafficking. Several victims have described it as a place where tens of thousands of vulnerable young people from various places were coerced to labor. They were lured into the buildings by various subterfuges, and then trained, tricked or tortured to work as scammers defrauding people from their home countries over the phone. Physical infrastructure and online infrastructure are both significant components of extra-statecraft that serve as technologies that not only bypass state regulations in an accumulation of illegal capital but also challenge the efficacy of international institutions and regional collaboration in controlling such illegal networks.

Infrastructure's allure also represents a mechanism by which the recycling industry creates a green imagery of environmental sustainability. As recycling has been defined as a futuristic and sound infrastructure, it is automatically associated with waste reduction, redesign, reuse, composting and clean infrastructure. Similar to fraudulent infrastructure, infrastructure's allure functions to disguise or obscure the destructive aspect of the infrastructure of recycling businesses. This is because the discourse of recycling infrastructure tends to conflate the end product with the making process, leaving the process of transforming waste into a usable product illegible and unimportant. As a result, in many countries, the treatment of materials such as plastic waste in facilities that emit unhealthy toxicants are excluded forms of recycling infrastructure. The most tragic aspect of infrastructure's allure is that environmentally unsound recycling infrastructure always comes at a cost: the destruction of the everyday life infrastructure of the people that the recycling claims to conserve.

The alchemy of sovereignty

Some degree of sovereignty and the ability to use it are prerequisites to the emergence of shadow zones and their self-governing regimes. Indeed, the impact of SEZs on state sovereignty have prompted numerous social scientists to rethink their theories of sovereignty, especially the state's claim to exclusive control of a definite or bounded territory. Sovereignty has increasingly come to be understood as divisible and reconfigurable (Pauly and Grande 2005), while state territory can also be unbundled (Ruggie 1993) and infrastructural power can be exercised across networks and beyond the territory of the state. These processes both de-territorialize nation-states and re-territorialize citizenship around cities and hinterlands, regions, and continental-level political entities (Agnew cited in Holden 2017: 4). As a result, we are beginning to witness increasingly complex, multiple, and overlapping hierarchies of sovereignty in which political authority has been reconfigured across different functional dimensions and spatial scales (Pauly and Grande 2005).

Yet, flexible sovereignty is also historically contingent and contextually specific, involving not only the state but also the interactions between state and non-state actors. In the case of the EEC, the special economic zone policy was suspended during the brief period of democratic government (2004–2014) in response to the strong civil protest against the idea of leasing land to foreign investors on a long-term basis. The military government following the 2014 coup d'état reinstated this special economic zone. The EEC project started in 2017 as one type of SEZ and an extension of the notorious Eastern Seaboard project. The military government not only resurrected the idea of SEZs but made sure that the projects spread through ten provinces in various attempts to connect with the BRI. At least 19 laws which protected the rights of people in the zone were overruled.

Different historical contingencies were at play in the creation of the Shwe Kokko SEZ. Driven by the Chinese state's continuing effort to eradicate offshore gambling, Chinese casino investors sought a frontier area beyond the reach of both China and the local nation-state. In the borderlands between Myanmar and Thailand which were controlled by the Karen Border Guard Force and not directly governed by the Myanmar state, Shwe Kokko offered an ideal place for fugitive investors to both evade the Chinese state's intervention and to rebrand their illegal business. The *Tatmadaw* has denied having any stake in the Shwe Kokko new city project but the Myanmar Investment Commission officially approved the first phase of the project. Distancing itself from the notorious project would allow the *Tatmadaw* to both profit from the undisclosed deal and exert its power on the ethnic armed forces in the area. A similar position was taken by the Chinese state. While the project was temporarily suspended by the Myanmar government in 2020, another military coup renewed the agreement with the BGF as reward for the border army's assistance to the junta. It is clear that in this frontier area, overlapping deal-driven sovereignty, although constantly in flux, benefits numerous parties. In these shadow zones, the freedom to play in the lacuna of the not-yet space of sovereignty is key to the politics of frontier capitalism. This alchemy of sovereignty gives life to the illicit movement and collaboration of the shadow economy propelled by numerous and diverse actors in the assemblage of illicit capital.

The assemblage of shadow zones

Among the key characteristics of the assemblage of shadow zones are mobility and the ability to deterritorialize and reterritorialize as necessary to maximize capital accumulation. Following Deleuze and Guattari who argue that things generally defined as discrete subjects or objects such as humans, artworks, crimes, and institutions, can be conceptualized as assemblages which are reasonably mobile configurations of acts, affects, emotions, utterances, things, practices and concepts that produce effects based on their shifting configurations and connections, Phil Crockett Thomas (2020) suggests that crime should be viewed as an assemblage. Thomas contends that crime is characterized by its multiplicity: it is both a designation for an event, and a category of diverse acts and practices which are historically and geographically contingent (Thomas 2020: 72). Connectivity and mobility are thus important principles of the assemblage (Deleuze and Guattari 2004a). Organizing flows of power, including and excluding, collaborating with both similar and different kinds of networks are how the assemblage reproduces itself. In doing so, an assemblage of crime might generate a certain kind of territory in order to hide other ways of assembling crime which engenders different effects (Thomas 2020: 73). This act of mobility entails deterritorializations which Bogard calls "lines of flight" (Bogard 2006: 108).

The mobile characteristics of crime assemblages can be found in the shadow zones of the Shwe Kokko SEZ in south eastern Myanmar and the Golden Triangle SEZ in northern Laos. I argue that the movement of the shadow economy around the borderlands of Myanmar, Thailand, and Laos represents not only a line of flight to evade authorities and conceal the emerging assembling crime, but also the possibility of capital accumulation. As shown in various cases, the transfer of capital and labor in criminal activities from one shadow zone to the other has been part of the circulating networks of goods generally practiced in the internet scam industry. Some victims of the online scamming industry are sold to other sites when they fail to generate income. A parent of an 18-year-old Laotian from Luang Namtha told Radio Free Asia about the plight of his son:

> What happened to him was like what happened to many other Lao workers: he first worked as an online chatter at the Kings Romans Casino in [Laos'] Bokeo province, but when he couldn't do the work, he was traded to the casino in Myanmar. (Radio Free Asia 2023)

These trafficking victims are of various nationalities including Chinese. In early March 2023, 14 Chinese casino workers were intercepted by the Thai police while being illegally transported from the Kings Roman casino to Myawaddy via Thailand (ASEAN Now 2023). While it is unclear which company was responsible for the trafficking of these workers, the Thai truck drivers who were arrested for transporting the Chinese workers confessed that they were paid 7,000 baht per head to transport the Chinese from Laos into Myanmar (ibid.). Two other Chinese cyber-scam workers who were trafficked from the Golden Triangle SEZ to KK park in Shwe Kokko reported that they were lured by an agent who had offered well-paying jobs in a company in northern Laos but were forced to commit cyber-fraud once they arrived at the Laos border (Interview, 19 March 2023). When they asked the agent to send them back home, they were instead sold and transported by boat to KK Park via Tachileik. At KK Park, they were forced to engage in a romance scam, seducing overseas Chinese victims into romantic relationships before encouraging them to invest money in fraudulent schemes. For the first couple of months, the company paid them 4,000–5,000 yuan each per month for salaries. But subsequently they were paid a commission of 4–5% of the money that they cheated from the victims, and when they failed to find enough victims they were brutally punished. As a result, the two workers decided to escape on foot and were eventually rescued by KNLA soldiers at the border.[4] For trafficking victims

---

4   These two Chinese were the first known cases of human trafficking from China into the Shwe Kokko area. There were also four cases of Chinese students from a local vocational school in East China's Anhui Province who were lured to Myanmar for work in a telecom fraud outfit but were rescued and sent home safely (*Global Times* 2023). These cases have prompted the Chinese government to call on the government of Myanmar to seriously increase efforts to crack down on internet scam activities, especially those operating at the border (ibid.).

who could not escape, paying a ransom seemed to be the only way to regain their freedom. The father of a young Lao man held at a casino at the Myawaddy border reported that there were at least ten Lao victims who were released by the Chinese scam companies after their parents paid ransoms ranging 10,000 to 200,000 Thai baht (US$300 to $5,850) (Radio Free Asia 2023). A young male Thai victim who was tricked into the crypto-scam at KK Park was freed after his family paid his captors 150,000 baht ($US 4,300) (Interview with V., 25 August 2022). Transnational ransoms in the internet scam industry have not only called into question the existence/efficacy of national territory and its sovereignty, but also points to the mobility of the crime assemblage of the shadow zones in which capital is accumulated through regulating the flow that transcends national boundaries.

Conclusion

This chapter has explored the connections between the rise of shadow zones in the interstices of state power in Southeast Asia and the development of regional and global economies of various trades and industries in which China plays a pivotal role. Comparing case studies of Shwe Kokko SEZ, KK Park and the recycling industry in the EEC's hinterland, this chapter has demonstrated certain characteristics these shadow zones share with each other and with numerous other zones in the region. These include: infrastructure couched in futuristic idioms of modern cities and green technologies which conceal scam activities and hazardous manufacturing practices; the manipulation of sovereignty to negotiate selective deterriorialization and facilitate the maximization of illicit profits; and destructive economies in which a few enjoy tremendous benefits at the expense of people's livelihoods and living-environments. Although these zones have different aims and types of operations, they share the evasive characteristic of fleeing state regulation while seeking to maximize their fluid capital in a weak regulatory regime.

Shadow zones have developed as unruly economic frontiers under the influence of the BRI and in response to regional and global trade. Mobile and malleable, a crackdown on one zone only results in capital and illicit activities moving to other areas. This type of zone is therefore best conceptualized as a form of assemblage that connects various actors while moving in and out and in various directions and scales rather than an "ideal type" of economic zone as typically portrayed in the literature about SEZs. More importantly, among the key players that contribute to the working and continuation of these shadow zone are the state and its quasi-state counterparts, which have often been left out of analyses of illegal trade and activities in the region.

References

Agnew, John (1994) The territorial trap: The geographical assumptions of international relations theory. *Review of International Political Economy*. 1(1): 53–80.

Agnew, John (2009) *Globalization and Sovereignty*. Lanham: Rowman and Littlefield.

ASEAN Now (2023) Fourteen Chinese casino workers intercepted crossing into Thailand – Three Thai drivers arrested. *ASEAN Now*, 5 March. https://aseannow.com/topic/1288342-fourteen-chinese-casino-workers-intercepted-crossing-thailand-three-thai-drivers-arrested/. Accessed 31 March 2023.

Auge, Marc (1995) *Non-Places: Introduction to an Anthropology of Supermodernity*. John Howe, trans. London and New York: Verso.

Bogard, William (2006) Surveillance Assemblages and Lines of Flight. In David Lyon (ed.), *Theorizing Surveillance: The Panopticon and Beyond*. London: Willan, pp. 97–122.

Camba, Alvin (2020) The Sino-centric capital export regime: State-backed and flexible capital in the Philippines. *Development and Change*, 51(4): 970–997. DOI: 10.1111/dech.12604.

Castells, Manuel (2010) *End of Millennium, The Information Age: Economy, Society and Culture Vol. III*. Malden, MA and Oxford, UK: Blackwell.

Chen, Jun (2023) Detained gambling tycoon Shé Zhijiang faces rendition to China. *Radio Free Asia*, https://www.rfa.org/english/news/china/myanmar-tycoon-06202023145223.html

Deleuze, Gilles and Felix Guattari (2004a) *A Thousand Plateaus: Capitalism and Schizophrenia*. Translated by Brian Massumi. London and New York: Continuum.

Deleuze, Gilles and Felix Guattari (2004b) *Anti-Oedipus: Capitalism and Schizophrenia*. Translated by Robert Hurley, Mark Seem and Helen R. Lane. London and New York: Continuum.

Deleuze, Gilles and Felix Guattari (2012) *Kafka: Toward A Minor Literature*. D. Polan, tr.). Minneapolis: University of Minnesota Press.

Easterling, Keller (2014) *Extrastatecraft: The power of infrastructure space.* London: Verso.

Farrelly, Nicholas, Alice Dawkins and Patrick Deegan (2022) *Sihanoukville: A hub of environmental crime convergence.* Global Initiative Against Transnational Organized Crime.

Figiaconi, Fabio. and Claudia Adele Lodetti (2020) South-East Asian Special Economic Zones Are Becoming Geopolitical. ISPI 90. https://www.ispionline.it/en/publication/south-east-asian-special-economic-zones-are-becoming-geopolitical-26958

Frontier (2022) Scam City: How the coup brought Shwe Kokko back to life (https://www.frontiermyanmar.net/en/scam-city-how-the-coup-brought-shwe-kokko-back-to-life/) Accessed 2 October 2022.

Global Times (2023) China, Myanmar eye greater cooperation in fight against cross-border internet fraud, gambling. 24 March. https://www.globaltimes.cn/page/202303/1287893.shtml?fbclid=IwAR3y2r85YHy18gT8ddMY8wSyDDc1p6EIbm-VUy0NCVl2DZHeBbbQsKFXrj0. Accessed 31 March 2023.

Gribkoff, Elizabeth (2022) Chemical recycling grows – along with concerns about its environmental impacts, *Environmental Health News*. https://www.ehn.org/chemical-recycling-grows-along-with-concerns-about-its-environmental-impacts-2658348681/what-is-chemical-recycling. Accessed 2 July 2022.

Holden, Chris (2017) Graduated Sovereignty and Global Governance Gaps: Special economic zones and the illicit trade in tobacco products. *Polit Geogr*. 59: 72–81. doi:10.1016/j.polgeo.2017.03.002.

Karen Peace Support Network (KPSN) (2020) Gambling away our lands: Naypyidaw's 'battlefields to casinos' strategy in Shwe Kokko. March. https://progressivevoicemyanmar.org/wp-content/uploads/2020/03/Gambling-Away-Our-Lands-English.pdf

Kennedy, Lindsey. and Nathan Paul Southern (2022) Inside Southeast Asia's casino scam archipelago. *The Diplomat*. https://thediplomat.com/2022/08/inside-southeast-asias-casino-scam-archipelago/

King, Grace (2020) Shwe Kokko (Yatai) Special Economic Zone. https://www.youtube.com/watch?v=8dudGWjqahg

Kyaw Ye Lynn (2020) Chinese dominated Myanmar's unregulated gambling business. AA https://www.aa.com.tr/en/asia-pacific/chinese-dominated-myanmar-s-unregulated-gambling-business/1943799

Lee, Ching Kwan (2018) *The Specter of Global China: Politics, Labor, and Foreign Investment in Africa*. Chicago: University of Chicago Press.

Minter, Adam (2014) Plastic, poverty and pollution in China's recycling dead zone, *The Guardian*, 16 July. https://www.theguardian.com/lifeandstyle/2014/jul/16/plastic-poverty-pollution-china-recycling-dead-zone. Accessed 20 September 2022.

Naing, Yang (2022) Controversial China-Backed new city is Myanmar's human trafficking hub, *The Irrawaddy*, 6 September. https://www.irrawaddy.com/opinion/guest-column/controversial-china-backed-new-city-is-myanmars-human-trafficking-hub.html. Accessed 20 November 2022.

Oakes, Tim (2021) The Belt and Road as method: Geopolitics, technopolitics and power through an infrastructure lens. *Asia Pacific Viewpoint*, 62(3): 281–285. DOI:10.1111/apv.12319.

Ong, Andrew (2020) Shadow Capital at Myanmar's Margins: Shwe Kokko New City and its Predecessors. *ISEAS Perspective*, 136: 1–9.

Pauly, Louis W. and Edgar Grande (2005) Reconstituting political authority: Sovereignty, effectiveness, and legitimacy in a transnational order. In Edgar Grande and Louis Pauly (eds) *Complex sovereignty: Reconstituting political authority in the twenty-first century*. Toronto: University of Toronto Press, pp. 3–21.

Radio Free Asia (2023) Four Laotian trafficking victims freed from Myanmar casino faced regular beatings. *Radio Free Asia* 16 February. https://www.rfa.org/english/news/laos/casino-02162023163151.html. Accessed 31 March 2023

Raymond, Gregory (2021) Jagged sphere: China's quest for infrastructure and influence in Mainland Southeast Asia. Lowy Institute Analysis. https://papers.ssrn.com/sol3/papers.cfm?abstract_id=3927622

Rosenau, James N. (2003) *Distant Proximities: Dynamics beyond Globalization*. Princeton: Princeton University Press.

Ruggie, John Gerard (1993) Territoriality and beyond: Problematizing modernity in international relations. *International Organization*, 47(1): 139–174.

Serlet, Thibault (2019) The 7 Deadly Sins of Special Economic Zones. *Economic Zones*. https://www.adrianoplegroup.com/post/the-7-deadly-sins-of-special-economic-zones

Thomas, Phil Crockett (2020) Crime as an Assemblage, *Journal of Theoretical & Philosophical Criminology*. New York: SSRN. https://ssrn.com/abstract=3706257

Tower, Jason and Priscilla A. Clapp (2020) *Myanmar's Casino Cities: The Role of China and Transnational Criminal Networks*. USIP Special Report.

US Department of the Treasury (2020) Press release: Treasury Sanctions Corrupt Actors in Africa and Asia. https://home.treasury.gov/news/press-releases/sm1206.

7 The Belt and Road Initiative in Myanmar: A Review

Ta-Wei Chu

Abstract

Since 2017, research on China's Belt and Road Initiative (BRI) in Myanmar has been growing. However, no systematic review of this body of research has been published until now. The objective in this article is to review the research on the BRI in Myanmar. I argue that the research has made three central contributions: it has captured much of the complexity of BRI projects, filled a notable research gap in BRI studies, and has raised awareness of local voices. Because the concept of state transformation involves multiple intersecting actors, future research that incorporates this concept could advance our understanding of China's BRI in Myanmar by exploring two sets of analytically meaningful contested relations: (1) the contested relations between China's Ministry of Foreign Affairs and prospective Chinese BRI investors and (2) the contested relations between the Myanmar government and local anti-BRI groups.

Keywords

China – Myanmar – the BRI – the China-Myanmar Economic Corridor – state transformation

Introduction

The Belt and Road Initiative (BRI) or One Belt, One Road, is the Chinese government's attempt to resolve domestic economic problems through international ties (Blanchard and Flint 2017;

Li 2020; Jones and Hameiri 2020; Ye 2021). Beginning in the early 2000s, China encountered the twin dilemmas of industrial oversupply and surplus capital. In response, policy experts and others suggested that "financing more infrastructure projects in other countries would be the only way to ease the overcapacity problem" (Li 2020: 174). The leadership in China's party–state apparatus accepted this suggestion, and President Xi Jinping proposed two components of the BRI: the Silk Road Economic Belt in September 2013 and the Maritime Silk Road Initiative in October 2013. In China, the National Development and Reform Commission, the Ministry of Foreign Affairs, and the Ministry of Commerce are responsible for implementing the BRI and have turned it "into policy frameworks" that "guide the wider party–state" (Jones and Hameiri 2020: 6–7). Chinese state-owned enterprises (SOEs) are key actors in the implementation of BRI investment projects overseas, and policy banks including the China Development Bank and the Export–Import Bank of China supplement SOEs with development financing (Blanchard 2018; Hameiri and Jones 2018). BRI infrastructure projects run the gamut from railways and seaports to gas and oil pipelines and hydropower dams.

In 2011, Myanmar's twenty-two-year-long military dictatorship ceded power to a semi-civilian government that led the country until late 2015. The president during this transitional government was Thein Sein, a former general in Myanmar's armed forces (commonly known as *Tatmadaw*). The Thein Sein government rhetorically welcomed the BRI but offered it little in the way of practical assistance (Jones and Khin Ma Ma Myo 2021). On 8 November 2015, the National League for Democracy (NLD), a liberal political party led by the reformer Aung San Suu Kyi, became Myanmar's ruling party following a landslide electoral victory. Unlike the Thein Sein government, the NLD government extended considerable practical support to the BRI. For example, in September 2018, the NLD government created the BRI Steering Committee, chaired by Suu Kyi, and signed a memorandum of understanding with China for the joint construction of the 1,700-kilometer China–Myanmar Economic Corridor (CMEC), which had originally been proposed in early 2010. In January 2020, when Xi Jinping visited Myanmar, the NLD government signed 33 memorandums of understanding with China. After another landslide victory in the 2020 elections, the NLD held 258 seats in the lower house (*Pyithu Hluttaw*) and 138 seats in the upper house (*Amyotha Hluttaw*) (Taylor 2021: 211). Myanmar's military, led by General Min Aung Hlaing, claimed that the election had been compromised by widespread fraud, and on these grounds, the general and his supporters staged a coup on 1 February 2021. After the coup, the Min Aung Hlaing regime stated its intention to continue Myanmar's full participation in BRI projects (*The Irrawaddy* 2021).

In Myanmar, the BRI projects are centered on the CMEC. On a map, the CMEC takes the form of an upside-down "Y" (Kobayashi and King 2022: 1019): extending south from China's Yunnan Province to Myanmar's centrally located and second-largest city, Mandalay, the CMEC then branches off in two directions, with one branch ending in the south-westerly coastal township of Kyaukphyu (in Rakhine State, formerly known as Arakan State), and the other branch ending in the southern city of Yangon.

Five prominent projects in the CMEC have attracted the attention of scholars and the media. The first project, regarded as "pioneering" with respect to the BRI, encompasses a gas pipeline (est. 2013) and an oil pipeline (est. 2017) linking Kyaukphyu to the Chinese city of Kunming (BRI Monitor 2021a). The main investor in the pipelines is the China National Petroleum Corporation. The second project is the Kyaukphyu Special Economic Zone (KSEZ), consisting of a deep seaport, an industrial park, and a residential project (BRI Monitor 2021b). In September 2014, a consortium led by China International Investment Corporation and consisting of China Harbour Engineering, China Merchants Holdings, TEDA Holding, Yunnan Construction Engineering Group, and the Thai company Charoen Pokphand Group, won the international tender to develop both a deep-sea port and an industrial zone in Kyaukphyu. The third project is the Kyaukphyu–Kunming Railway, which, when completed, will link Yunnan Province's main cities of Kunming, Dali, and Ruili to northern Myanmar's main cities of Muse, Lashio, Mandalay, and Kyaukphyu. A potential investor in this railway is the China Railway Eryuan Engineering Group Company (CREEC), a subsidiary of China Railway Group Limited. In fact, regarding the Kyaukphyu–Kunming Railway, CREEC signed an initial memorandum of understanding with the Thein Sein government in 2011, but it lapsed in 2014. In January 2021, however, CREEC and the NLD government signed a new memorandum of understanding, this time concerning a proposed railway from Mandalay to Kyaukphyu. The fourth project is the New Yangon Development Project. In 2018, the New Yangon Development Company (owned by the Yangon Region Government) and the Beijing-based China Communications Construction Co. (CCCC) signed an agreement to undertake the New Yangon Development Project, valued at US$5 billion. The fifth project consists of three border economic zones respectively located in Kanpiketi (in Kachin State), Muse (in Shan State), and Chinshwehaw (also in Shan State) (*The Irrawaddy* 2019a). The NLD government approved the economic zones in July 2018 and has called for investment (*The Irrawaddy* 2018).

Since 2017, the research literature on the BRI in Myanmar has grown substantially, but no systematic review of this corpus has been published before now. The objective of this article is to review the academic literature on the BRI in Myanmar. I argue that the existing literature makes three central contributions: (1) the research captures much of the complexity of the BRI–Myanmar projects, (2) the research helps fill knowledge gaps regarding BRI projects in host states and host states' relations with China, and (3) the research showcases local voices. I suggest that future research on the BRI–Myanmar topic would do well to explore two sets of analytically significant contested relations: (1) the contested relations between the Chinese Ministry of Foreign Affairs and prospective Chinese BRI investors; and (2) the contested relations between the Myanmar central government and local anti-BRI groups. The first set of contested relations is at odds with a prevailing tendency in the research to regard the Chinese state as "highly coherent" (Hameiri and Jones 2016: 81). The second set of contested relations reflects a lacuna in the research, which focuses on the "agency" attributable to the Myanmar government in its dealings with the Chinese state and, more specifically, with BRI projects. These two sets of contested relations suggest that neither China nor Myanmar are coherent actors. I argue that state transformation, as an analytical framework, might facilitate efforts to examine the contested relations. I have two reasons. First, the concept of state transformation transcends the concept of state centrism by emphasizing how changes in the international political economy, at least since the 1970s, have helped "disaggregate" states that, at first glance, appear quite centralized. Second, the concept of disaggregated statehood can strengthen analyses of the political system in China and the political-economic dynamics in Myanmar, in turn helping shed light on the contested relations between the two countries.

I divide this review article into four sections plus the introduction and conclusion. In the first section, I summarize and discuss the research according to three themes: (1) China's interests in the BRI in Myanmar, (2) the Myanmar government's handling of domestic

BRI projects, and (3) the local Myanmar population's responses to domestic BRI projects. In the second section, I discuss the major contributions of the existing research. In the third section, I discuss the two analytically meaningful contested relations outlined above. In the fourth section, I explain the concept of state transformation and its usefulness as an analytical framework for future studies on the BRI in Myanmar.

Research on the BRI in Myanmar

China's interests in the BRI in Myanmar

In "Myanmar's Role in China's Maritime Silk Road Initiative" (2018), J. Mohan Malik argues that Myanmar has played a key role in the Maritime Silk Road Initiative. For China, this initiative has served chiefly as a way for the country to resolve potential problems besetting its energy security. China has been heavily reliant on the Strait of Malacca for imports of oil, liquefied natural gas, and other resources. Former Chinese President Hu Jintao (2003–2013) described this dependency as "the Malacca dilemma." In using the CMEC's infrastructure to deliver oil, gas, and goods to China from Kyaukphyu, the Chinese state seeks to mitigate the Malacca dilemma. What is more, China could link the port in Kyaukphyu with ports in Bangladesh, Sri Lanka, the Maldives, and Pakistan in order to "thwart any encirclement by a concert of hostile powers," including most obviously the United States (p. 372). Malik also mentions that infrastructure projects promoted and organized by China are like "a Trojan horse for extending geopolitical clout and dumping excess capacity abroad as China's economy flags" (p. 373). The author further argues that Chinese investments have usually created problems with "imported Chinese labor, poor environmental standards and debt accumulation by host governments" (p. 373). Two intriguing assertions in the above study are that the people of Myanmar have tended to regard the BRI as China's economic colonial strategy to plunder "not just their forests, but their resources," and that the Myanmar government has been quite careful to avoid the potential debt-trap (p. 376).

In their article "China's OBOR Initiative and Myanmar's Political Economy" (2018), Chenyang Li and Shaojun Song argue that Myanmar's geographical location is strategically important for China. According to the two scholars, "Myanmar is the most convenient land pass for China to reach the Indian Ocean, open up the South and Southeast Asia, and diversify its resource import market, especially energy" (p. 319). In addition, Li and Song argue that after joining the BRI in 2015, Myanmar was able to receive more investments from China to address its energy-shortages. However, Myanmar's historical experience as a colonized state has left the country suspicious of China's motivations (p. 324). Thus, the authors suggest that China should expand its energy, agriculture, and tourism ties to Myanmar (pp. 326–327).

A more recent article on this topic is "Understanding the Belt and Road Initiative in Myanmar" by Xue Gong (2020). She shows that, upon its inception in 2013, the BRI attracted a lukewarm response from Myanmar given "China's past invasions and prior support for the Burmese Communist Party," "China's intervention in [Myanmar's] ethnic issues," and the Myanmar public's generally negative opinion of so-called collaborative Chinese projects (pp. 7–8). However, the Rohingya crisis, the state's persecution of a Muslim ethnic minority, created friction between Myanmar and the West, pushing Myanmar closer to China. China used this burgeoning alliance to launch the CMEC and to rebrand and resume some suspended projects, including the Muse–Mandalay–Kyaukphyu railway, which had lapsed in 2014. Most importantly, the Chinese state adopted an "adaptive approach" to interacting with Myanmar NGOs and Myanmar citizens, while Chinese (SOEs) presented themselves as socially responsible corporate entities (pp. 12–13). Nevertheless, many NGOs and citizens in Myanmar continue to harbor strong anti-Chinese sentiments and thus concerns about Chinese-led projects. They have criticized the Chinese government's deceitfulness, the opacity of BRI projects, and the Chinese investors' disregard for locals (pp. 14–18). Thus, Gong argues, "the effectiveness of such adaptation is constrained by socio-politico-economic dimensions of the Chinese capitalist in Myanmar" (p. 3).

In "China's Policy towards Myanmar" (2022), Sumie Yoshikawa focuses on the energy pipelines and the Myanmar–China Border Economic Cooperation Zone. Yoshikawa examines how BRI projects took shape in response to the interactions among local Chinese governments, the central Chinese government, and Chinese SOEs. Because the energy pipelines aligned with Beijing's energy strategy, Beijing approved and upgraded the pipelines to a national project within two years (pp. 148–151). However, the Border Economic Cooperation Zone interested neither Beijing nor SOEs, so the proposal took two decades to become a national project (pp. 141–154). Regardless of whether two years or two decades were needed, the task of realizing the BRI projects has been highly contested because the involved actors – the Chinese SOEs (the China National Petroleum Corporation and the China Petroleum & Chemical Corporation) in the pipeline project and the Chinese municipalities (Ruili, Houqiao, and Mengding) in the Border Economic Cooperation Zone – used the projects to enhance their interests and to marginalize others.

Myanmar government's handling of domestic BRI projects

In "Managing the Belt and Road" (2021), Linda Calabrese and Yue Cao explore Cambodia's and Myanmar's responses to the BRI. The authors emphasize the agency exercised by the two governments when dealing with China. The Royal Government of Cambodia has pursued a diversification strategy in response to Chinese investments in the country, seeking to attract a balanced set of development partners. Thanks in part to this strategy, Cambodia has a "low risk of debt distress" and a high level of development success in infrastructure construction and industrialization (pp. 5–6). In Myanmar, the NLD government adopted a strategy of impartiality, emphasizing the rule of law and transparency in development projects. The government along with Chinese investors re-negotiated the conditions of both the Kyaukphyu Special Economic Zone and its deep-sea port. In November 2018, the NLD government not only reduced the total number of berths in the seaport from ten to two but also slashed funding for the projects from US\$7.5 billion to \$1.3 billion (pp. 7–8). The government also created a policy bank capable of screening, selecting, and prioritizing projects whose funding would exceed US\$1.5 million (p. 9). This "two-pronged approach" reflects Myanmar's agency in reducing "the economic risks associated with the BRI projects" (p. 9).

Lee Jones and Khin Ma Ma Myo's article "Explaining Myanmar's Response to China's Belt and Road Initiative" (2021) explores why the Thein Sein government and the NLD government differed substantially from each other regarding their respective attitudes toward the BRI. Seeking to cultivate his democratic authority through popular reforms and specifically to distinguish himself from the former military junta, Thein Sein suspended Chinese megaprojects and expressed a distinct lack of enthusiasm for the BRI (pp. 311–314). Conversely, the NLD government wielded a good degree of democratic legitimacy in the eyes of the people, and Aung San Suu Kyi enjoyed unparalleled popularity domestically, as well as abroad. In addition, the NLD government negotiated with Chinese investors to downsize some projects and created strict regulations to reduce the negative impacts of the BRI projects on Myanmar (p. 314–319). Thus, the NLD not only embraced the BRI but also attempted to exploit it to the benefit of local communities in ways that enhanced the NLD's authority.

With a hedging strategy, a state tries to maximize its profits and minimize its costs (Soong and Kyaw Htet Aung 2021: 28) by following "a middle way between the two poles of bandwagoning and balancing" (Kobayashi and King 2022: 1014). Two articles address the Myanmar government's responses to the BRI through the lens of hedging strategies: "Myanmar's Perception and Strategy toward China's BRI Expansion on Three Major Projects Development" by Jenn-Jaw Soong and Kyaw Htet Aung (2021) and "Myanmar's Strategy in the China–Myanmar Economic Corridor" by Yuka Kobayashi and Josephine King (2022). Soong and Aung analyze the Kyaukphyu deep-sea port, the Myitsone Dam, and the New Yangon development projects in the context of interactions between the state, markets, and society. The authors argue that Myanmar's populace has been quite concerned about BRI projects' capacity for environmental degradation, corruption, insufficient profits, and creating a debt-trap (2021: 28–32). According to Soong and Aung, the Myanmar government has been well-aware of this widespread skepticism and has made extensive use of hedging strategies to protect the country's national interests without squandering the potential benefits of Chinese development projects.

Kobayashi and King agree that the NLD government adopted a hedging strategy against China, cautiously considering Chinese investments, diversifying its economic partners, and expanding its diplomatic relations (2022: 1022). However, they argue that the NLD government's reliance on this strategy was compromised by domestic fragmentation and instability (p. 1031). For example, the NLD's over-reliance on China for assistance in resolving the Rohingya crisis and shielding the Myanmar government from international criticism narrowed the space in which the NLD government could maneuver, thus undermining the effectiveness of the hedging strategy (pp. 1025–1030).

The local population's responses to domestic BRI projects

Three recent journal articles cover local responses to the BRI projects in Myanmar. In "Sharing the Spoils: Winners and losers in the Belt and Road Initiative in Myanmar," SiuSue Mark, Indra Overland, and Roman Vakulchuk (2020) explore "how the BRI has already transformed and may further transform the allocation of economic benefits and losses among actors in Myanmar" (p. 382). The researchers' fieldwork included interviews with local businessmen, politicians, and members of civil society and found that the BRI projects in Myanmar have greatly benefited Myanmar-based companies, which tend to be run mostly by citizens of Myanmar who are ethnic Chinese and who have close relations with the Chinese government as well as with Myanmar's political elites (p. 389). However, problems such as opaque decision-making processes may tarnish BRI projects in the eyes of local Myanmar communities. Mark, Overland, and Vakulchuk note a particularly interesting factor undermining the BRI projects: marginalized ethnic groups that have taken up arms against the Myanmar government have been excluded from the projects' decision-making processes (p. 390).

Debby Sze Wan Chan and Ngai Pun's (2020) article "Renegotiating Belt and Road Cooperation" focuses on the Letpadaung Copper Mine, located in the Sagaing Division's Salingyi Township. According to Chan and Pun, a state in political transition may encounter resistance to bilateral agreements to which the state is bound. If the resistance is intense enough, the signatories may have to renegotiate the agreements. In the Letpadaung Copper Mine case study, local villagers successfully protested the project, gaining nationwide support which compelled the Thein Sein government to suspend the project (pp. 2117–2118). The suspension was accompanied by Thein Sein's decision to create a parliamentary committee chaired by Aung San Suu Kyi and tasked with investigating the project's feasibility. After four months, the Thein Sein government negotiated a new contract with the mine's two main investors: Myanmar Wanbao Mining Copper, which is a subsidiary of China North Industries Corporation, and the military-backed Union of Myanmar Economic Holdings. The new contract ensured that the Letpadaung Copper Mine would resume in 2015, but 2% of future revenue would now go to local villages. Suu Kyi in particular supported a resumption of the mine's operations, as she "stressed that Myanmar should honour international obligations and maintain cordial relations with China" (cited in Chan and Pun 2020: 2119, 2121).

In "Sovereign Anxiety in Myanmar: An emotional geopolitics of China's Belt and Road Initiative," Mary Mostafanezhad, Robert A. Farnan, and Shona Loong (2022) develop the concept of "sovereign anxiety" to express the considerable unease and even fear that the BRI projects have provoked among the people of Myanmar. The term "sovereign anxiety" refers to "a generalized unease over the security of one's political community" (p. 133). Through interviews with members of Myanmar's civil society and representatives of the Myanmar government, these researchers found that the people's anxiety over the BRI was due to the nature of the BRI projects: they lack transparency and seemed likely to increase Chinese dominance over Myanmar while having adverse environmental and social effects (pp. 137–143). This anxiety is, according to the study, "rooted in collective memories of insecurity and subjugation" originating from British colonization and pre-BRI experiences with Chinese investments (pp. 140–141). Notably, however, Myanmar's Bamar and Kachin ethnic groups' anxieties were attributed to the groups' respective histories. For example, many members of the Bamar community – Myanmar's largest ethnic group – expressed the view that the Chinese state had destabilized Myanmar's sovereignty by supporting the Kachin Independence Organization. Similarly, the Kachin community seems to have opposed BRI projects because the Chinese and Myanmar governments have limited its political autonomy (p. 143).

Research contributions

The literature reviewed above has contributed to our understanding of the BRI in Myanmar in several ways. First, it has captured much of the complexity of these BRI projects. Contributing to this complexity are several basic facts: to begin with, at least ten Chinese SOEs have been involved in Myanmar's BRI projects; in addition, all the projects, except the New Yangon Development Projects have been rebranded under the CMEC heading; and all the projects have triggered local concerns and protests.

A second way in which previous studies of the BRI projects in Myanmar have enriched the literature is by filling important research gaps. Take, for instance, the Maritime Silk Road Initiative (MSRI) in Southeast Asia. Commenting on this literature, Jean-Marc F. Blanchard suggested that scholars could "delve into specific MSRI dyads or country pairs" and could "undertake in-depth examinations of specific MSRI projects to uncover their drivers, challenges, and narrow and wider implications" (2018: 342). These suggestions reflected lacunae in research on the MSRI in Southeast Asia five years ago. Subsequent research on the BRI in Myanmar has gone a long way towards filling these gaps. Some articles address China's interests in extending the BRI to Myanmar (Gong 2020; Li and Song 2018; Malik 2018) and others emphasize the Myanmar government's responses to BRI projects, thus bringing China–Myanmar relations to the forefront (Kobayashi and King 2022; Soong and Kyaw Htet Aung 2021).

Third, the research focusing on local responses to the BRI projects in Myanmar has shed some light on traditionally neglected local voices. The three studies that achieved this goal (Mark et al. 2020; Chan and Pun 2020; Mostafanezhad et al. 2022) pay particular attention to local people's anxieties about and grievances against the governance of BRI projects in Myanmar. These strengths in the existing research point to its vitality.

New research themes

Two analytically meaningful topics related to the BRI in Myanmar are worth exploring. The first topic concerns the contested relations among relevant actors in China. Since 2017, high-ranking officials in China's Ministry of Foreign Affairs, including the minister, the vice-minister, and the ambassador to Myanmar, have persistently supported and promoted CMEC projects (*The Irrawaddy* 2020a). In 2018, the Myanmar Investment Commission approved the Shwe Kokko Special Economic Zone (SKSEZ) in Myawaddy Township, Karen State, close to the Thai border. Development of the SKSEZ is a joint venture between Hong Kong-registered Yatai International Holdings Group (YIHG) and Chit Lin Myaing Company (CLMC). The YIHG's chair is Zhijiang Shé. The CLMC is owned by a

Myanmar military-backed armed group known as the Border Guard Force, led by Colonel Saw Chit Thu. Multiple Chinese SOEs including China Railway 20th Bureau Group, Metallurgical Company of China International, and Dongmei Company, have also invested in and helped construct the SKSEZ (Tower and Clapp 2020). The estimated cost of the SKSEZ has been set at US$15 billion, which will cover luxury housing, hotels, casinos, shopping centers, golf courses, an industrial zone with a cargo depot, and an airport. The YIHG claimed that the SKSEZ is part of the BRI (*The Irrawaddy* 2020b). Interestingly, the Chinese embassy in Myanmar denied this claim and voiced support for the Myanmar government to investigate possible irregularities surrounding the project (*The Irrawaddy* 2020b), which could directly affect YIHG's and the SOEs' interests. However, the YIHG continued to advertise the SKSEZ as part of the BRI.

The case of the SKSEZ problematizes the findings of those scholars (e.g., Kobayashi and King 2022; Li and Song 2018; Malik 2018; Soong and Kyaw Htet Aung 2021) who treat China as "a highly coherent state" (Hameiri and Jones 2016: 81). From their perspectives, Chinese actors are closely synchronized in their efforts to achieve China's strategic and economic ambitions. The Rohingya crisis, as mentioned earlier, is a good example of the Chinese state acting coherently. During the crisis, the Chinese Ministry of Foreign Affairs expressed its support for the NLD government and assisted it materially in ways that indirectly favored the development of Myanmar's BRI projects, invested in by SOEs (Kobayashi and King 2022). The contested relations between the Chinese Ministry of Foreign Affairs and potential BRI investors in the SKSEZ case raises an interesting question: how should we make sense of the incoherent and fragmented nature of the Chinese state?

The second analytically meaningful topic is the contested relations between the Myanmar government and local anti-BRI groups. Consider, for example, the local resistance to the Kyaukphyu SEZ and deep seaport, which persists despite the NLD government's decision to downsize the two projects. In November 2018, more than 1,000 activists with the Arakan Natural Resources and Environmental Network, an alliance of thirty local civil-society organizations, protested the current mega-development projects including Kyaukphyu SEZ and the deep seaport in Rakhine State. The activists demanded their right to "decide which development projects should be pursued in the region" (Radio Free Asia 2018). Consider, as well, the example of the celebrated pro-democracy activist and stateswoman, Aung San Suu Kyi: as an opposition leader, she opposed not only military rule but also the Myitsone Dam; however, after becoming State Counselor, she changed her position and embraced the dam. Suu Kyi explained her change of heart with a general aphorism: "We should not think based on one perspective. If we think from only one perspective, we could make the wrong decision" (*The Irrawaddy* 2019b). Despite Suu Kyi's reversal, local communities, civil society organizations, and the Kachin Independent organization continued to oppose the dam and its possible rebranding under the BRI umbrella (*The Irrawaddy* 2019c). A third example of contested relations between the Myanmar government and local anti-BRI groups is the Letpadaung Copper Mine, where opposition intensified after the 2021 coup. In fact, many miners joined the anti-coup movement to resist the project (Radio Free Asia 2022). Because the mine has been a key revenue source for the *Tatmadaw*, the military junta has aggressively and successfully defended the mine (Naing 2022).

These types of contested relations are not reflected in existing BRI literature. With respect to BRI projects, the research (e.g. Calabrese and Cao 2021; Kobayashi and King 2022; Soong and

Aung 2021) has shown that the Myanmar government's agency is manifest in its keen effort to preserve the country's national sovereignty and security through adopting hedging strategies against China and through domestic improvements in BRI governance. Interestingly, though perhaps not surprisingly, the three examples of contested relations cited above reveal that the Myanmar government's governance of the BRI has been limited, selective, and profit-driven; in other words, the agency displayed by the Myanmar government does not necessarily guarantee local people's rights and security. Future research in this field should fill this gap by probing both the Myanmar government's BRI governance and local responses to BRI projects.

The fact that the research has neglected these two types of contested relations reflects a somewhat lopsided focus on states – either the Chinese state or the Myanmar state – and their relations with each other. Of the four articles focusing on China's interests in the BRI, only Yoshikawa (2022) discusses subnational actors. Fortunately, the research focusing on Myanmar is more diverse: of the seven articles, three discuss local responses to BRI projects (Chan and Pun 2020; Mark et al. 2020; Mostafanezhad et al. 2022). However, only Chan and Pun's and Mostafanezhad et al.'s articles probe the dynamics of the relations between the Myanmar government and local critics. Likewise, Calabrese and Cao (2021), Kobayashi and King (2022), Soong and Aung (2021), and other studies reviewed above focus on the agency of the Myanmar government rather than the agency of local and relatively marginal actors. My point is not that the state-centric focus is obsolete: but rather that while it is necessary, it is not sufficient on its own. More comprehensive research is required go beyond state centrism and uncover the many diverse actors in China and Myanmar. Moreover, the literature should refine its analysis of states' political systems (especially China's) and the oftentimes contested relations between these systems and local political-economic factors in Myanmar.

Suggestions for an alternative framework

An alternative framework for analyzing Myanmar-based BRI projects should start by acknowledging that contemporary states can act in decentralized and fragmented ways, especially when dealing with international matters. Soon after the Second World War, many states engaged in economic planning and designed international monetary arrangements according to a "hierarchical, command-and-control system" (Jones and Hameiri 2022: 1029). This approach presumed that state apparatuses were precisely structured mechanisms capable of eliminating incoherence and destructive fragmentation from government activities, yet in the early 1970s, the collapse of the Bretton Woods system and the crisis of global capitalism prompted central states to shift from a top-down form of direct-intervention governance to "regulatory" governance based merely on "broad targets and regulations for diverse public and private actors" (Hameiri and Jones 2016: 73). In short, state governance is often revealed to be selective, fragmented, and even incoherent.

In the 1970s, China transformed from "Maoist state 'socialism' to state-managed capitalism" (Hameiri and Jones 2016: 82), and the Chinese Communist Party dispersed "authority to numerous, often overlapping, agencies, ministries and quasi-independent regulators" (Jones and Zeng 2019: 1419). The result was a shift away from a simple top-down system of government, party, and SOEs "towards a Chinese-style regulatory state model" (Jones and Zou 2017: 744). In this model, China's party–state leadership offers general directions and broadly semantic slogans instead of orders (Jones and Zou 2017; Jones and Zeng 2019). The vagueness and broadness of this governance, coupled with the multiplicity of government agencies, have generated inter-agency competition and squabbles over budgets, resources, and other sources of power: China's national interests are not always the principal focus of government operations (Jones and Hameiri 2021; Jones and Zeng 2019; Jones and Zou 2017). In other words, governmental agencies, provincial governments, and SOEs have considerable interpretive leeway in their application of foreign policy locally, as can be seen in, for example, the Greater Mekong Subregion economic initiative (Tubilewicz and Jayasuriya 2015), water diplomacy in the Mekong (Zhang and Li 2020), South China Sea policy (Li 2019a), and the BRI (Jones and Zeng 2019; Li 2019b). Scholars who acknowledge and examine this phenomenon argue that "China is now a 'de facto federal' system, with constant bargaining between governmental tiers" (Jones and Zou 2017: 745).

State transformation also occurred in Myanmar, despite its different developmental trajectory from China. Conservative factions in the junta resisted economic liberalization in the 1990s by expanding the country's state-sponsored enterprises which came to dominate the domestic economy (Jones 2014: 149). These pro-junta firms, overseen by pro-junta entrepreneurs, were heavily involved in extractive industries, infrastructure, and cash-crop plantations (Global Witness 2015; Woods 2011). All this state-orchestrated economic activity "constrained the privatization process" (Jones 2014: 149) and enriched military leaders and their cronies. Interestingly, most of the junta's foreign business partners were from China and included provincial governments, SOEs, and private actors (Woods 2011), by-products of state transformation in China. Thus, the state transformation in China has impacted Myanmar.

Interestingly, some Myanmar-based businesses and organizations that opposed the junta nevertheless partnered with junta-led business ventures (Woods 2011). Since its independence in 1948, Myanmar has been plagued by ethnic conflicts. In fact, despite being resource challenged, ethnic armed organizations (EAOs) in Myanmar act like miniature regional states, establishing governance regimes in the areas of health, law enforcement, and education (South 2008). The existence of these administrations operating parallel to the national government has decentralized Myanmar, a process reinforced by the 2015 National Ceasefire Agreement, which provided limited recognition of the insurgent administrations in several ethnic states (ibid.). In the 1990s, the junta enticed some ethnic armed organizations to sign ceasefire agreements and participate in state-sponsored joint ventures (Woods 2011). The leaders of these organizations, by collaborating with the junta, stoked the ire of young progressives, civil-society organizations, and grassroots activists, particularly when it became evident that the benefits from these collaborative projects were not trickling down to the people even though the projects were generating significant environmental and social ills (Brenner 2017; South 2008). The junta's "ceasefire capitalism" (Wood 2011) has turned many ethnic minority groups against both Chinese investors and ethnic Bamar people. The contested relations among the junta, ethnic armed organizations, and local communities have contributed to the highly fragmented nature of the Myanmar state.

Because the concept of state transformation goes beyond a simple preoccupation with state centrism, researchers who analyze relations between the Chinese and Myanmar states through the lens of the state-transformation concept can account for multiple actors operating in disaggregated contexts. In China, these actors include the Ministry of Foreign Affairs, SOEs, and provincial governments. In Myanmar, the actors include EAOs, their grassroots supporters, and military-backed enterprises. An awareness of the disaggregated nature of states can open researchers to the subtle and sometimes counter-intuitive truths surrounding China's and Myanmar's contested relations. In China, the Ministry of Foreign Affairs and SOEs have pursued significantly different interests and goals from each other: the main task of the Ministry of Foreign Affairs has been to protect China's national interests internationally, while SOEs pursue profits, which sometimes involves quasi-autonomous, arbitrary behavior that creates problems for the Ministry of Foreign Affairs (Jones and Hameiri 2021; Jones and Zou 2017). The disaggregated nature of the Chinese state explains why the Ministry of Foreign Affairs promoted CMEC projects but opposed the SKSEZ. In Myanmar, disaggregated statehood reflects inequalities between the Bamar majority and ethnic minorities. By using the country's BRI projects, the Myanmar government – from Thein Sein to the NLD and Min Aung Hlaing – maintained and enhanced its power, as Jones and Khin Ma Ma Myo (2021) demonstrate. However, the BRI projects have lacked transparency and have presented numerous environmental and social liabilities. Thus, the BRI in Myanmar has not addressed inequality but reinforced it, which complicates the Myanmar government's BRI governance and helps explain the contested relations between the Myanmar government and domestic opposition.

Conclusion

In this article, I have reviewed the research literature on the BRI in Myanmar. I identified three contributions of the research: it has captured much of the complexity of BRI projects, filled a notable research gap in BRI studies, and raised awareness of local voices. To advance our understanding of the BRI in Myanmar, researchers should explore two sets of contested relations: those between the Chinese Ministry of Foreign Affairs and prospective Chinese BRI investors and those between the Myanmar government and domestic opponents. These two topics are analytically meaningful because the former reflects China as a fractured actor, in contrast to portrayals of the Chinese state in most existing research, and because the latter indicates a prominent lacuna in the existing research. I suggest that the concept of state transformation can help researchers grasp the disaggregated nature of contemporary states, including the Chinese and Myanmar states. Once acknowledged, this characteristic of disaggregation can open researchers' eyes to the many types of actors contributing to the political-economic dynamics in the BRI-based relations between Myanmar and China.

In recent years, scholars in the Murdoch School have adopted the concept of state transformation to refine their analyses of the BRI (e.g., Jones and Hameiri 2020; Jones and Zeng 2019). China's disaggregated statehood is a political-economic asset that actors in and outside China have used to enhance their power, often at the expense of other actors. This explanation of the inner-working of BRI projects challenges the conventional realist, state-centric view that the BRI is a sophisticated and top-down grand strategy devised by China with the aim of eclipsing the world's current predominant powers (i.e., the United States and its Western allies) (e.g., Aoyama 2016; Beeson 2018). Thus, armed with the concept of state transformation, future research on the BRI in Myanmar may yield findings that stimulate theoretical and empirical debates specific to this topic and beyond.

References

Aoyama, Rumi (2016) 'One Belt, One Road': China's New Global Strategy. *Journal of Contemporary East Asia Studies*, 5(2): 3–22.

Beeson, Mark (2018) Geoeconomics with Chinese Characteristics: The BRI and China's evolving grand strategy. *Economic and Political Studies*, 6(3): 240–256.

Blanchard, Jean-Marc F. (2018) China's Maritime Silk Road Initiative (MSRI) and Southeast Asia: A Chinese 'pond' not 'lake' in the works. *Journal of Contemporary China*, 27(111): 329–343.

Blanchard, Jean-Marc F. and Colin Flint (2017) The Geopolitics of China's Maritime Silk Road Initiative. *Geopolitics*, 22(2): 223–245.

Brenner, David (2017) Authority in Rebel Groups: Identity, recognition and the struggle over legitimacy. *Contemporary Politics*, 23(4): 408–426.

BRI Monitor (2021a) *Belt and Road Monitoring Project: Myanmar-China Oil and Gas Pipeline Projects*. https://www.brimonitor.org/wp-content/uploads/2022/02/MyanmarPipe.pdf

BRI Monitor (2021b) *Kyaukphyu Special Economic Zone*. https://www.brimonitor.org/wp-content/uploads/2021/08/CS_KPSEZ.pdf

Calabrese, Linda and Yue Cao (2021) Managing the Belt and Road: Agency and development in Cambodia and Myanmar. *World Development*, 141: 1–13.

Chan, Debby Sze Wan and Ngai Pun (2020) Renegotiating Belt and Road Cooperation: Social Resistance in a Sino-Myanmar Copper Mine. *Third World Quarterly*, 41(12): 2109–2129.

Global Witness (2015) *Jade: Myanmar's Big State Secret*. London: Global Witness.

Gong, Xue (2020) Understanding the Belt and Road Initiative in Myanmar: A Socio-Politico and Economic Approach. *China and the World: Ancient and Modern Silk Road*, 3(4): 1–25.

Hameiri, Shahar and Lee Jones (2016) Rising Powers and State Transformation: The case of China. *European Journal of International Relations*, 22(1): 72–98.

Hameiri, Shahar and Lee Jones (2018) China Challenges Global Governance? The case of Chinese international development finance and the Asian Infrastructure Investment Bank. *International Affairs*, 94(3): 573–593.

The Irrawaddy (2018) Govt approves sites for 3 new economic zones along China border, 13 July. https://www.irrawaddy.com/business/govt-approves-sites-3-new-economic-zones-along-china-border.html/. Accessed 1 May 2023.

The Irrawaddy (2019a) China's six Belt and Road Projects in Myanmar to watch in 2019, 24 January. https://www.irrawaddy.com/specials/chinas-six-belt-road-projects-myanmar-watch-2019.html/. Accessed 1 May 2023.

The Irrawaddy (2019b) Suu Kyi repeats call for 'wider perspective' on Myitsone Dam, 14 March. https://www.irrawaddy.com/news/burma/suu-kyi-repeats-call-wider-perspective-myitsone-dam.html/. Accessed 1 May 2023

The Irrawaddy (2019c) Thousands of downstream villagers protest against Myitsone Dam, 22 April. https://www.irrawaddy.com/news/burma/thousands-downstream-villagers-protest-myitsone-dam.html/. Accessed 1 May 2023.

The Irrawaddy (2020a) Timeline: China-Myanmar Relations, 13 January. https://www.irrawaddy.com/news/burma/timeline-china-myanmar-relations.html/. Accessed 1 May 2023.

The Irrawaddy (2020b) China backs Myanmar probe of controversial border 'new city' backed by Chinese investors, 26 August. https://www.irrawaddy.com/news/burma/china-backs-myanmar-probe-controversial-border-new-city-backed-chinese-investors.html/. Accessed 1 May 2023.

The Irrawaddy (2021) Myanmar Regime reorganizes committees to press ahead with BRI projects, 18 May. https://www.irrawaddy.com/opinion/guest-column/myanmar-junta-sells-resources-to-neighbors-in-exchange-for-legitimacy./ Accessed 1 May 2023.

Jones, Lee (2014) The political economy of Myanmar's transition. *Journal of Contemporary Asia*, 44(1): 144–170.

Jones, Lee and Jinghan Zeng (2019) Understanding China's Belt and Road Initiative: Beyond 'grand strategy' to a state transformation analysis. *Third World Quarterly*, 40(8): 1415–1439.

Jones, Lee and Khin Ma Ma Myo (2021) Explaining Myanmar's response to China's Belt and Road Initiative: From disengagement to embrace. *Asian Perspective*, 45(2): 301–324.

Jones, Lee and Shahar Hameiri (2020) *Debunking the Myth of 'Debt-trap Diplomacy': How recipient countries shape China's Belt and Road Initiative*. London: Chatham House.

Jones, Lee and Shahar Hameiri (2021) *Fractured China: How state transformation is shaping China's rise*. Cambridge: Cambridge University Press.

Jones, Lee and Shahar Hameiri (2022) COVID-19 and the failure of the neoliberal regulatory state. *Review of International Political Economy*, 29(4): 1027–1052.

Jones, Lee and Yizheng Zou (2017) Rethinking the role of state-owned enterprises in China's rise. *New Political Economy*, 22(6): 743–760.

Kobayashi, Yuka and Josephine King (2022) Myanmar's strategy in the China-Myanmar economic corridor: A failure in hedging? *International Affairs*, 98(3): 1013–1032.

Li, Chenyang and Shaojun Song (2018) China's OBOR initiative and Myanmar's political economy. *The Chinese Economy*, 51(4): 318–332. DOI: 10.1080/10971475.2018.1457324.

Li, Mingjiang (2019a) Hainan Province in China's South China Sea Policy: What role does the local government play? *Asian Politics & Policy*, 11(4): 623–642.

Li, Mingjiang (2019b) China's Economic Power in Asia: The Belt and Road Initiative and the local Guangxi government's role. *Asian Perspective*, 43(2): 273–295.

Li, Mingjiang (2020) The Belt and Road Initiative: Geo-economics and Indo-Pacific Security Competition. *International Affairs* 96(1): 169–187.

Malik, J. Mohan (2018) Myanmar's Role in China's Maritime Silk Road Initiative. *Journal of Contemporary China*, 27(111): 362–378.

Mark, SiuSue, Indra Overland and Roman Vakulchuk (2020) Sharing the Spoils: Winners and losers in the Belt and Road Initiative in Myanmar. *Journal of Current Southeast Asian Affairs*, 39(3): 381–404.

Mostafanezhad, Mary, Robert A. Farnan, and Shona Loong (2022) Sovereign Anxiety in Myanmar: An emotional geopolitics of China's Belt and Road Initiative. *Transactions of the Institute of British Geographers*, 48(1): 132–148.

Radio Free Asia (2018) Activists Stage Protest to Demand Right to Control Resources in Myanmar's Rakhine, 27 November. https://www.rfa.org/english/news/myanmar/activists-stage-protest-to-demand-right-11272018165100.html. Accessed 1 May 2023.

Radio Free Asia (2022) Myanmar's Junta Vows to Defend China-Backed Copper Mine after PDF Threats, 2 May. https://www.rfa.org/english/news/myanmar/mine-05022022095603.html. Accessed 1 May 2023

Soong, Jenn-Jaw and Kyaw Htet Aung (2021) Myanmar's Perception and Strategy toward China's BRI Expansion on Three Major Projects Development: Hedging strategic framework with state-market-society analysis. *The Chinese Economy*, 51(1): 20–34.

South, Ashley (2008) *Ethnic Politics in Burma: State of Conflict*. Oxon: Routledge.

South, Ashley (2018) 'Hybrid Governance' and the Politics of Legitimacy in the Myanmar Peace Process. *Journal of Contemporary Asia*, 48(1): 50–66.

Taylor, Robert H. (2021) Myanmar in 2020: Aung San Suu Kyi once more triumphant. Southeast Asian Affairs 2021: 205–222.

Tower, Jason and Priscilla A. Clapp (2020) *Myanmar's Casino Cities: The Role of China and Transnational Criminal Networks*. The United States Institute of Peace.

Tubilewicz, Czeslaw and Kanishika Jayasuriya (2015) Internationalisation of the Chinese Subnational State and Capital. *Australian Journal of International Affairs*, 69(2): 185–204.

Woods, Kevin (2011) Ceasefire Capitalism: Military-private partnerships, resource concessions and military-state building in the Burma-China borderlands. *The Journal of Peasant Studies*, 38(4): 747–770.

Ye, Min (2021) Fragmented motives and policies: The Belt and Road Initiative in China. *Journal of East Asian Studies* 21: 193–217.

Yoshikawa, Sumie (2022) China's Policy towards Myanmar: Yunnan's commitment to Sino-Myanmar oil and gas pipelines and border economic cooperation zone. *Journal of Contemporary East Asia Studies*, 11(1): 143–161.

Zhang, Hongzhou and Mingjiang Li (2020) China's Water Diplomacy in the Mekong: a paradigm shift and the role of Yunnan provincial government. *Water International*, 45(4): 347–364.

8 | The Belt and Road Initiative from the Perspectives of Political Economy and Business Transnationalism

Hong Liu

Abstract

As a modest effort to critically review the growing literature on the Belt and Road Initiative (BRI) which was launched in 2013, this chapter argues for the importance of approaching the BRI from the perspectives of political economy and business transnationalism. The chapter is composed of three main parts. It starts with an overview of recent studies on the BRI in the context of the changing political economy of Southeast Asia, a key region for the BRI. It calls for the systemic integration of political economy and business transnationalism approaches in deciphering the BRI. The second part of the chapter discusses Singapore's engagement with the BRI since 2013, with a focus on various policy initiatives after 2020, when the Covid-19 pandemic struck the world. The third part presents two case studies of Sino-Singaporean business transnationalism which incorporate the role of the state and ethnicity in shaping the BRI development in the region. It is hoped that the case studies of Singapore-Chinese businesses operating in China have demonstrated how the state, ethnicity, and culture – which is a vital connection for the Chinese business community's participation in the BRI – continue to remain crucial to the strategies of Southeast Asian (Chinese) businesses as they capitalize on new opportunities and navigate challenges amid technological and geopolitical transformations.

Keywords

Belt and Road Initiative – political economy – business transnationalism – Singapore – China

Perspectives on the Belt and Road Initiative

The BRI at 12: A brief review

In 2013, Chinese President Xi Jinping announced the Belt and Road Initiative (BRI), which has since become China's foremost diplomatic and economic strategy for engaging with neighboring countries and beyond. According to the Refinitiv BRI Database, there were 2,631 projects with a combined value of US$3.7 trillion in 2019, mostly in developing nations. The number of enterprises involved in the signature project stands at nearly 2,600, of which more than 55% are non-Chinese companies (cited in Liu 2022a).

Since its inception, numerous views have been expressed on the BRI by both the scholarly and policy communities (e.g., Zhao 2020; Blanchard 2021; Liow, Liu and Gong 2021a; Yu 2024; Khanal and Zhang 2024; Santasombat et al. in the Introduction to this volume): is the BRI informed by altruism (as per China's declared intentions to uplift the economies of its neighbors on the principle of 'win-win cooperation' and 'the human-wide community of shared destiny') or pragmatic realism (seeking to enhance Chinese security, particularly of access to crucial energy resources)? Or does the BRI represent China's effort to reshape the international order? One group of analysts assert that the BRI will dramatically increase Beijing's global influence, particularly in China's neighborhood. As a multifaceted initiative centered on six economic corridors – China-Pakistan, New Eurasia Land Bridge, China-Mongolia-Russia, China-Indochina Peninsula, Bangladesh-China-India-Myanmar, and China-Central Asia-West Asia –

the BRI involves economic, trade, geopolitical, diplomatic and geostrategic dimensions that have the potential to fundamentally transform the interactions between states and economies in Asia and beyond. Another group expects the BRI will fail because insurmountable challenges can be expected to overstretch China. The latter points out that even before the Covid-19 pandemic, there were already problems with financing (for details, see Liow, Liu and Gong 2021b).

With the growing geo-political tensions between China and the West, the latter has launched a number of new initiatives over the past two years to counterbalance the BRI, such as the US-led Indo-Pacific Economic Framework launched by Joe Biden in June 2022 and the EU's €300 billion Global Gateway Initiative (European Commission 2021). These initiatives highlight key differences with the BRI, such as the focus on sustainability, transparency, good governance, and gender equity etc. But they also face structural challenges such as insufficient funding, lack of strategic clarity and inadequate economic incentives for ASEAN nations (cf. Forough 2022).

Scholars have also analyzed knowledge production associated to the BRI. A recent study (Liu and Bennet 2022) examines Chinese and international literature on the geopolitics and subjectivities embedded in the BRI's environmental studies. It finds widespread agreement on: 1) the need for a greener BRI; 2) the need for more diversified governance that engages non-state actors; and 3) the need for host country context and capacity to influence the BRI's implementation. Others have highlighted disagreements on 1) the severity of the BRI's potential impacts; 2) investors' and non-profit organizations' intentions and appropriate roles; and 3) whether China should export its norms and standards or adopt international ones (Sun, Lewis and Urpelainen 2023; Liu and Benett 2022).

While most studies of the BRI have focused on economy and geopolitics, some recent studies have approached it from the perspective of international business (IB). Lewin and Witt (2022) outlines the domestic and geopolitical objectives of the BRI, linking them to new IB research questions. Domestically, they stress the importance of the BRI for the legitimacy of Chinese Communist Party rule in the context of slowing growth and overcapacity. Internationally, they explore the BRI's role in advancing China's geopolitical position, not least vis-à-vis the United States, as well as its potential to provide a nucleus around which a new, alternative world economic order might form (Liu and Benett 2022; Lewin and Witt 2022). Li et al. (2022a; 2022b) call for a close examination of "organizational heterogeneity under the BRI theme," which includes "a variety of players like the governments of the host countries, non-government institutions, firms with different ownership structures, managers with different backgrounds, and their idiosyncratic characteristics." From an IB perspective, the authors suggest the examination of different aspects of IB activities, such as innovation, entrepreneurship, and corporate social responsibility (for more details on the status of IB studies, see Liu and Goh 2024).

In short, numerous studies embedded in different knowledge ecosystems have reached a diverse range of often contradictory conclusions about the BRI. It is beyond the scope of this chapter to systemically examine and review this vast literature (cf. Khanal and Zhang 2024). This chapter intends to connect the region's political economy with international business by offering some cases from Singapore's growing investment in and trade with China under the broad umbrella of the BRI.

Political economy and Southeast Asia[1]

While the above perspectives have advanced our knowledge of the BRI, it is essential to approach the BRI from the perspective of the international political economy, especially in the context of small and middle powers in Southeast Asia, arguably the most important region for the BRI in terms of economy, trade, and geopolitics. According to the McKinsey Global Institute, "Asia is becoming more Asian as intraregional flows expand – moving within the region are 60% of goods traded by Asian economies, 59% of foreign direct investment, 74% of Asian air travelers, and 71% of Asian investment in start-ups" (cited in Liu 2022a). Rapidly growing intra-Asian trade and economic activities which now account for more than 50% of East Asia's total trade, a substantial increase from the late 1970s when only 20% of total exports were to each other by the Asian economies (Liu 2022a; Tanaka 2020).

China-ASEAN trade, economic and social ties deepened significantly following the commencement of the ASEAN-China Dialogue Relations in 1991 (Ren and Liu 2022). In 2011, ASEAN was China's third-largest trading partner, and in 2019 it overtook the USA as the second largest. Since early 2020, ASEAN has replaced the European Union as China's largest trading partner. According to the Statista reports, in 2019, the total value of exports from the ASEAN region to China amounted to approximately US$202.46 billion. This represented a dramatic increase from 2010, when the total value of exports from the ASEAN region to China amounted to just over US$112.5 billion. The total value of imports from China to the ASEAN region in 2019 amounted to approximately US$305.39 billion, a big increase from 2010, when the total value of imports from China to the ASEAN region amounted to US$122.94 billion (ASEANstats n.d.). Despite

---

1 This section mainly draws from Introduction to Liu (2022a).

the Covid-19 pandemic, two-way trade hit new highs, reaching US$798.4 billion in the first ten months of 2022, up by 13.8% year-on-year (Li Keqiang 2022).

The formation of the China–ASEAN Free Trade Area in 2010 created an economic entity with a combined GDP of US$6.6 trillion, 1.9 billion people, and total trade of US$4.3 trillion. China has constituted a significant source of investment in ASEAN, with Chinese foreign direct investment (FDI) to the region more than doubling from US$7 billion in 2013 to $18.65 billion in 2022. By the end of 2022, China had established more than 6,500 directly-invested companies in ASEAN, employing more than 660,000 foreign employees. As of 2022, cumulative two-way investment between China and ASEAN exceeded US$380 billion (Huld 2023).

Refuting the zero-sum judgement that China's economic rise has been at the expense of Southeast Asia, Anne Booth argues: "it is clear that the economies of both Southeast Asia and China have gained from their interaction" (cited in Liu 2022a). According to the CIMB ASEAN Research Institute, BRI projects in ASEAN countries amount to more than US$739 billion, including $98.5 billion in Malaysia, $70.1 billion in Singapore, and $9.4 billion in the Philippines (cited in Liu 2022a; see also Liu, Tan and Lim 2022).

At the height of the Covid-19 disruption of global supply chains and the growing tendency towards deglobalization, ten members of ASEAN, China, Japan, Korea, Australia, and New Zealand signed the Regional Comprehensive Economic Partnership (RCEP) in November 2020. As the largest trading bloc in the world, RCEP member countries make up nearly one-third of the global population and account for about 30% of global GDP. Once fully implemented, RCEP will eliminate tariffs for at least 92% of goods, with additional preferential market access for exports, thus significantly expediting and expanding the flow of goods (as well as capital and population). At the virtual signing ceremony, Singapore's Prime Minister Lee Hsien Loong declared, "It signals our collective commitment to maintaining open and connected supply chains, and to promoting freer trade and closer interdependence especially in the face of Covid-19 when countries are turning inwards and are under protectionist pressures" (Ng 2020).

While inspired by previous research, this author and his collaborators have forged an unconventional path by proposing a political economy approach to the BRI (cf., Liow, Liu and Gong 2021; Liu, Tan and Lim 2022; Liu 2022a; Liu and Lim 2023; Liu, Xu and Lim 2024; Ren and Liu 2022), focused on how it has been structurally embedded in the Southeast Asia (regional, national and local) political economy, which has, at the same time, been shaped by the changing global geo-political environment. The so-called "perfect storm" – the escalation of the US-China confrontation, the Covid-19 pandemic, global supply chain disruption, and the Russia-Ukraine war – has greatly complicated the development of the BRI and clouded its prospects, both in Southeast Asia and beyond. Wang and Fu (2022), for example, demonstrate how Southeast Asian countries' domestic socio-political factors influence their foreign policy, which in turn affect the BRI projects in Southeast Asia. Their empirical study finds that the Philippines' "populist" type of foreign policymaking engenders the highest level of risks (both political and societal) for BRI projects, while Singapore's "procedural" type produces the lowest. Malaysia's "arbitrary" type and Indonesia's "democratic" type, meanwhile, generate mid-level political and societal risks. They underscore the salience of meso-level BRI studies from recipient countries' perspectives, as the success (or failure) of the BRI projects significantly depend upon engagement with and responses from recipient countries.

Twelve years after the BRI commenced, there remains relatively little research on how small- to medium-sized states, such as those from Southeast Asia, engage with the BRI to advance their own national interests. Most published studies are either China-centric or focused on a singular issue (such as diplomacy or trade, or a particular academic discipline). Most of the literature has presumed that the BRI is an effective strategy to promote trade, build infrastructure, improve FDI flows and therefore GDP growth (e.g. Kratz and Pavlićević 2019; Mitchell 2020; Yu 2024). The World Bank (2019) estimates that BRI transport projects in Asia would boost the GDP of participating countries by up to 3.4% (on average). Other studies examine international relations, environmental studies, science and technology, law and political science, many focused almost exclusively on the interests and strategies of Chinese political and economic actors (Liou 2014; Nordin and Weissmann 2018). From the vantage point of the populace in many countries outside China, BRI is largely construed as a Chinese initiative to engage in bilateral trade and infrastructural expansions (Voon and Xu 2020).

Extending Liu and Lim's (2019; 2023) work on Malaysia as well as Kratz and Pavlićević's (2019) work on Indonesia, this chapter studies how a small (yet important) state such as Singapore skillfully incorporates domestic political economy factors with business transnationalism to manages China's growing presence in the region. Our central argument is that Chinese capital, especially that related to infrastructure, has been increasingly embedded into the host state's political fabric, which in turn shapes Chinese capital's business strategies. In the meantime, Singapore Chinese businesses have also expanded their regional connections and transactions under the framework of the BRI and increasing transnationalism. This chapter highlights the critical importance of the agency of domestic interest groups, not least in engaging with the BRI to advance key projects and pursue their own agendas.

The changing role of the state is a crucial issue for understanding the BRI from political economy and business transnationalism perspectives. Recent transformations in the global economy have reignited interest in the role of the state. Such transformations include a resurgence of various forms of state-led development, especially in the Global South (Alami and Dixon 2020). Among the most notable findings of research in this field is the ways that China, as a pacesetter in the developing world, is challenging established market assumptions. For Massot (2021), China's emergence is challenging market belief in three ways: "the continued resilience of China's authoritarian state-led capitalist economic model, China's positioning around notions of power and fairness in the global economy, and China's mixed preferences regarding global markets." Massot (2021) proposes "an institutionally grounded definition of markets" by emphasizing the ways in which markets vary along "different institutional features such as the behavior of market stakeholders, its shape, the nature of the interactions among market actors, its governance structures, power relations and embeddedness features." In a similar vein, in her study of Chinese investment in Africa, Ching Kwan Lee (2017: xiii) explores the question "Is Chinese state capital a different kind of capital?" and treats "capital, labor, and state as processes and relations of power, not as quantifiable amounts of money, economic inputs, or aggregates of policies and policy makers" (see also Lee 2022).

Building on such works, this author (along with his collaborators) has advocated a "transnational state capitalism" framework to discern how state activism is moving across borders and shaping development outcomes. It also sheds light on infrastructure, a pivotal issue for developing countries, distinguishing itself from earlier studies' focus on financial institutions such as sovereign wealth funds and their investment in emerging market equities and other investments abroad. We argue that a transnational state capitalism with four key characteristics is emerging in Southeast Asia: it is state-centric in that major decision-making and resource allocation comes from the government and/or state-owned enterprises (SOEs); it is driven by *both* an economic logic of expanding market share and profits and a geopolitical agenda of boosting Chinese influence; it has strategic and institutionalized linkages with ethnic Chinese business networks established long before the BRI; and it is tied to a set of inherent dilemmas (such as inefficient resource allocation) that are exacerbated by its complex intertwining with the host country's political economy. We have also argued (Liu and Lim 2023; Liu 2022b) that with the rise of non-Western economies such as China and the other BRICS countries over the past decade, it is imperative to depart from West-centrism in order to investigate the economic dynamics and market mechanisms of emerging economies. By focusing on China's growing economic influence and its engagement with Southeast Asia, our study represents a modest attempt to answer Feldmann's (2019) plea for a global varieties of capitalism (VOC) approach which could "shed light on the functioning of capitalism and the structure of economic institutions in the Global South."

A missing link: Chinese diaspora networks and the BRI

Numerous studies have examined the important role of the Chinese diaspora since China's 1978 reforms, with ethnic Chinese from outside of mainland China contributing about 70% of China's foreign direct investment and international trade (Peterson 2013; Martínez-Zarzoso and Rudolf 2020). Analyzing the response of Chinese business associations in Southeast Asia to the BRI, this chapter reveals emerging characteristics of ethnic Chinese transnational networks in the new era.

I have argued that "Transnational Asia" (Liu 2022a) has a profound historical and cultural foundation. An important characteristic of Chinese associations in post-war Southeast Asia has been their centrality in facilitating transnational flows of goods, capital and ideas. Transnational engagement with China and across the diaspora has played an important role in the globalization of Southeast Asia. J. M. Liu (2022) finds that since the 2010s, China has shifted away from soliciting the diaspora's support for domestic economic growth and national unification in favor of working with Chinese abroad to expand China's soft power. While the Chinese associations in Southeast Asia have been studied from many perspectives, they have seldom been considered in the context of the BRI and the greater Chinese diaspora. Collectively, Southeast Asian Chinese account for about 80% of the world's diasporic Chinese population. They comprise only about 6% of the Southeast Asian population, but their contribution to the region's economic and trade activities is much larger. Illuminating the integration of ethnicity, business, investment and the political economy, therefore, will reveal the changing characteristics of not only a rising China in Southeast Asia but also the diaspora Chinese (Liu and Ren 2023; Guo 2022).

From a theoretical perspective, this chapter engages the growing literature on transnationalism and its critique. Since the 1990s transnationalism has been a central paradigm in migrant studies, helping to understand the lives of refugees, immigrant entrepreneurs, highly skilled Chinese in the OECD, migrant networks, and the particulars of social and cultural capital in a diaspora (e.g., Ren and Liu 2015; 2019). More recently, the role of immigrant organizations has been a focal point of transnationalism studies.

Ethnic Chinese business associations were well-placed to get involved as the BRI began making inroads into Southeast Asia, thanks in part to their ethnic and cultural connections with the (ancestral) homeland. Both Chinese and Southeast Asian governments have engaged Chinese business associations as interlocutors to seize opportunities presented by the BRI. As will be detailed later, this has in turn led to establishing and reinforcing various mechanisms and structures.

It must be noted that Southeast Asian states encouraged their local Chinese communities to engage with China through the BRI in pursuit of their own interests: taking maximum advantage of the economic opportunities presented by a rising China. In Singapore, for example, the government has established a set of effective institutions and mechanisms which include both government agencies, the private sector, and Chinese business associations to facilitate its engagement with China and the BRI (Liu, Fan and Lim 2021).

Singapore and the Belt and Road Initiative

Continuation of the whole-of-nation approach

While there are many similarities in how the diverse nations of Southeast Asia engage with the BRI, Singapore's unique development experience (i.e., the uninterrupted governance of a single dominant party and being the largest source of FDI in China since 2014) suggests that the state is likely to play a larger role in governance affairs than other states. Importantly, the Singaporean state is a "networked state," which communicates with various key players through existing and new institutional mechanisms. These institutions coordinate and manage the often-diverse interests and agendas of key stakeholders, establishing effective and broad-based partnerships (Liu 2022a). This highly coordinated governance style is highly effective at mediating policy disputes about cross-border resources and exchange vis-à-vis other economies (e.g., FDI and trade of goods and services).

Singapore is one of the first countries to publicly express support for the BRI. During the 11th China-ASEAN EXPO Opening Ceremony in September 2014, Prime Minister Lee Hsien Loong affirmed China's desire to play a larger role in both the regional and broader international setting. Some of the initiatives Lee explicitly supported were upgrading the ASEAN-China Free Trade Agreement (FTA), establishing the Asian Infrastructure Investment Bank (AIIB), and promoting the 21st Century Maritime Silk Road. Contributing US$250 million towards the US$100 billion capital of the AIIB, Singapore enjoys a 0.2585% stake in the bank, giving it 0.4365% voting rights. According to Singapore's representative, the then Senior Minister of State for Finance and Transport Josephine Teo, this move was "to support further economic development in the region, by working with all founding members to build up the AIIB as a first-class multilateral financial institution" (cited in Liu, Fan and Lim 2021).

Building on its multilateral efforts, Singapore has also implemented several policies to strengthen bilateral cooperation. During the First Belt and Road Forum for International Cooperation, held on 14 and 15 May 2017 in Beijing, Singapore and China signed a memorandum of understanding (MOU), which was subsequently fine-tuned to focus collaboration in three areas: infrastructure connectivity, project financing, and joint undertaking of projects in third countries.

Impact of Covid-19 and US-China tensions

No country or project escaped the devastating impact of the Covid-19 pandemic. Wang Xiaolong, Director-General of the Chinese Ministry of Foreign Affairs' International Economic Affairs Department, said in Beijing on 19 June 2020 that about 20% of projects under BRI had been "seriously affected" by the Covid-19 pandemic. According to a survey by the Ministry, about 40% of projects had suffered little adverse impact, and another 30–40% were somewhat affected (cited in Liow, Liu and Gong 2021a).

During the first Trump administration, US competition with China in the ICT sector became more acute as the White House adopted a whole-of-government approach to countering and containing China's technological development (Liu and Miao 2024). This confrontational approach has been continued by the Biden administration, with the passage of the *Chips and Science Act* in August 2022, investing billions of dollars aiming to reduce costs, create jobs, sustain global supply chains, and perhaps most importantly, contain China (White House 2022). The *Chip 4 Alliance* of the USA, Japan, South Korea and Taiwan was subsequently formed to institutionalize these strategies.

All these changes impacted the BRI in Southeast Asia. For Southeast Asian governments and business communities, however, China remains an economic powerhouse that cannot be ignored (Liu and Goh 2024). As Singapore Prime Minister Lee Hsien Loong remarked in May 2022, one "'cannot afford not to do business with China' given the sheer size of opportunities and markets, with China being the 'biggest trading partner of nearly every country in Asia'" (*Nikkei Asia* 2022). Reflecting upon his official visit to China in early December 2023, Lawrence Wong, Singapore's Deputy Prime Minister and the designated successor to Lee Hsien Loong, remarked candidly: "Never bet on the decline of China, because China's economy is of such tremendous scale (with) so many different areas of strength… and on top of that, they have such a huge market" (Oh 2023).

The outbreak of Covid-19 did not stop Singapore's engagement with the BRI, although during the ensuing years it has been focusing much greater attention on the Digital Silk Road, in accordance with the country's focus on the digital economy.[2]

Table 8.1 summarizes Singapore's main engagement with the BRI between 2020 and 2023, which updates my earlier study of the country's engagement with the BRI (Liu, Fan and Lim 2021; see also Ji 2023).

The examples cited in Table 8.1 reveal Singapore's continuing "whole-of-nation" approach toward the BRI and its engagement with China, in the context of regional collaboration and changing geopolitics. The council meetings cited have been co-chaired by senior officials of both countries. Reflecting Singapore's renewed political leadership, it is fitting that its next generation of politicians (commonly known as fourth-generation leaders) are co-chairing several of these bilateral cooperation councils.

Ethnicity contributes to transnationality in both Singapore and China. Since the 1990s, the Singapore government has consistently emphasized the importance of culture and ethnicity to the success of Singaporean Chinese businesses (Liu and Goh 2024). In

---

2 According to the government's *Singapore Digital Economy Report 2023*: "We have defined Singapore's digital economy as comprising both the value-added (VA) of the Information & Communications (I&C) sector and the VA from digitalisation in the rest of the economy. The size of SGDE with Singapore's digital economy is about 17.3% of Singapore's gross domestic product (GDP) in 2022, up from 13% of GDP in 2017. Overall, SGDE with Singapore's digital economy grew at a compound annual growth rate (CAGR) of about 12.9% p.a. since 2017, outpacing the overall economy." (Infocomm 2023)

Table 8.1 Singapore's engagement with the BRI from 2020 to 2023

When	Who	What	Where
9 Dec 2020	Deputy Prime Minister Heng Swee Keat and Health Minister Gan Kim Yong	As the relationship between Singapore and China evolves, the two countries are working together in new areas such as public health and coming up with ways to deepen connectivity. Ten memorandums of understanding (MOUs) and agreements on health, food safety and the environment, among other things, were signed yesterday at the apex meeting held virtually.	16th Joint Council for Bilateral Cooperation between Singapore and China
11 Mar 2021	Chief Justice Sundaresh Menon	"While we might reasonably expect a lull in enthusiasm for new projects in the immediate aftermath of the pandemic, the crisis seems certain to drive a spike in disputes arising from existing projects as construction programmes are delayed, suspended, re-negotiated or even terminated." "We should build on these advantages, and think about new ways in which the SICC can better address the needs of users in this sector."	The Chief Justice was addressing about 300 participants, including judges and local and international experts, at a virtual symposium to discuss the latest trends and developments in international commercial litigation.
9 Jun 2021	Vivian Balakrishnan, Foreign Minister	"Particularly for Singapore, (we have) our China-Singapore Chongqing Connectivity Initiative and the International Land-Sea Trade Corridor (ILSTC). And how this concept links the Belt and the Road to South-east Asia and beyond," he said, describing this as an area for "fertile discussion with much to look forward to."	Special meeting of ASEAN and China's foreign ministers, Beijing
17 Sep 2021	Tan See Leng, Minister for Manpower	Bilateral trade between Singapore and China's Sichuan province grew more than 10% year on year between January and June this year, despite the Covid-19 pandemic.	Singapore-Sichuan Trade and Investment Committee meeting
30 Nov 2021	Deputy Prime Minister Heng Swee Keat	The United States and China must find a new equilibrium for there to be peace and prosperity, but this may take some time. China's economic success has been a boon for the region; ASEAN and China are each other's biggest trading partners. China's Belt and Road Initiative is an important effort for greater economic integration and mutual gains.	12th S. Rajaratnam Lecture

When	Who	What	Where
30 Dec 2021	DPM Heng Swee Keat	Touching on working together in a post-Covid-19 world, Mr Heng said the economy would have to be more resilient, more digitalized and much more reliant on technology and innovation. Agreement reached on a total of 14 projects 1. Urban Governance 2. Garden City in Tianjin 3. Nature conservation 4. Cultural cooperation 5. Customs 6. Green development 7. Competition Law 8. Maritime digitalization 9. Internationalization Corridor 10. Research Translation	17th Joint Council for Bilateral Cooperation between Singapore and China
31 Aug 2022	Deputy Prime Minister Heng Swee Keat	"Peace has become more brittle in Asia" and it is important to preserve the stability that has enabled the region to prosper in the past few decades. Collaboration on the following: 1. Bankability, responsibility, and interconnectedness 2. Infrastructure Asia to co-create infrastructure solutions and promote collaboration in the region. 3. environmentally responsible development along the Belt and Road. 4. clean energy and decarbonization solutions 5. Digital Economy Partnership Agreement and ASEAN Data Management Framework	7th Belt and Road Summit Policy Dialogue, Hong Kong
1 Nov 2022	Deputy Prime Minister Heng Swee Keat	• Digital domain and green economy • The foundations and prospects for regional cooperation are strong, especially with the ASEAN-China Comprehensive Strategic Partnership established the previous year • We can also work closely on third party projects, through platforms like the Belt and Road Initiative. The development needs and potential of Southeast Asia are large • 19 MOUs and agreements announced	18th Joint Council for Bilateral Cooperation (JCBC) between Singapore and China – the first to be held in person since the outbreak of the pandemic.
25 Nov 2022	Deputy Prime Minister Heng Swee Keat	• The story of the Nanyang Centre for Public Administration is one of building bridges • These people-to-people exchanges are foundational for further cooperation and learning	Speech at NTU's Nanyang Centre for Public Administration's "Mayors' Class" 30th Anniversary Gala Dinner

Table 8.1 Singapore's engagement with the BRI from 2020 to 2023 *(continued)*

When	Who	What	Where
30 Mar 2023	Prime Minister Lee Hsien Loong	• China has become the largest trading partner for almost every country in Asia. It has launched regional and global initiatives, such as the Asian Infrastructure Investment Bank (AIIB), the Belt and Road Initiative (BRI), and the Global Development Initiative (GDI) • And we look forward to participating in new growth opportunities in China's dynamic economy • Singapore's ties with China are doing well. We are updating and improving the China-Singapore FTA, and raising overall relations to a higher level	Speech by PM Lee Hsien Loong at the Boao Forum for Asia (BFA) Annual Conference. PM Lee was on an official visit to China from 27 March to 1 April 2023
17 May 2023	Deputy Prime Minister Lawrence Wong	• Reaffirming the long-standing relationship between the two countries which had recently upgraded to an "All-Round High-Quality Future-Oriented Partnership"	Meeting with Chinese Premier Li Qiang, Beijing
11 Aug 2023	Deputy Prime Minister Lawrence Wong	• Expressed in-principal support for China's interest to join the Comprehensive and Progressive Agreement for Trans-Pacific Partnership (CPTPP)	Meeting with visiting Chinese Foreign Minister Wang Yi
7 Dec 2023	Deputy Prime Minister Lawrence Wong	• 19th JCBC saw 24 MOUs and agreements announced • The 19th JCBC meeting reviewed the progress of bilateral cooperation in a wide range of areas, including the Belt and Road Initiative (BRI), trade, sustainability, agriculture, food security, digital economy, smart cities, green economy, science and innovation, renewable energy, finance, public health, as well as the China-Singapore Guangzhou Knowledge City, which is a State-Level Bilateral Cooperation Project. • Under the China-Singapore Free Trade Agreement (CSFTA) Further Upgrade Protocol, Singapore will secure greater market access to China's services sectors • Singapore, China to mutually extend visa-free travel to 30 days from 2024	19th Joint Council for Bilateral Cooperation (JCBC) in China

Sources: Collated by the author from the *Straits Times* and the Prime Minister's Office Singapore (PMO) website.

launching the Global Hua Yuan Collaborative Network in 2016, Minister Chan Chun Sing declared that "networks by Chinese community groups can play a new role in connecting Singapore with the rest of the world." Noting the boundless market and business opportunities arising from China's growth, Minister Ong Ye Kung pointed to the need for students to "experience the local culture (of China) and build up their network of contacts" through immersion programs (cf., Liu 2022c; Ren and Liu 2022).

As mentioned, Southeast Asian states have encouraged local Chinese to engage with the BRI to take advantage of the economic opportunities presented by a rising China. In Singapore, the government has established effective institutions and mechanisms to connect Singapore's government agencies, the private sector, and Chinese business associations to China through the BRI (Liu and Goh 2024). To strengthen connections with diasporic Chinese business communities, the Chinese government has dispatched large numbers of delegations across the region. According to the Singapore Chinese Chamber of Commerce (SCCCI) annual reports, the SCCCI received 116 delegations from Chinese government agencies and commercial organizations between 2015 and 2018.

Since 2017 the SCCCI and Singapore government agencies have jointly organized a series of overseas market workshops and customized training courses for Singaporean enterprises and professionals. "These workshops are intended to provide a deeper understanding of the overseas markets, particularly in China, and to develop specialized market knowledge, establish networks, and help their companies' internationalization efforts" (Ren and Liu 2022). Eleven overseas workshops in 2017 and 2018 addressed topics such as: trends in the smart-gadget industry, developments in the food catering industry, and the general state of mind of the new Chinese economy. These workshops were typically week-long and held in different cities, including Shenzhen, Guangzhou, Beijing, Shanghai, Chongqing and Qingdao. Workshop participants visited local key enterprises and met with local entrepreneurs and officials.

It should be noted, however, that while being supportive of the local-Chinese' interactions with China, the Singaporean state has taken various steps to ensure that their engagement is confined to the economic arena and not at the expenses of their national identity and loyalties (Ren and Liu 2022). As Lee Hsien Loong wrote for *Foreign Affairs* in June 2020, the presence of significant numbers of ethnic Chinese in Southeast Asia is a politically sensitive issue and, as such, an "obstacle that would prevent China from taking over the security role currently played by the United States." He highlights specifically the delicate challenges faced by Singapore:

> Singapore is the only Southeast Asian country whose multiracial population is majority ethnic Chinese. In fact, it is the only sovereign state in the world with such demographics other than China itself. But Singapore has made enormous efforts to build a multiracial national identity and not a Chinese one. And it has also been extremely careful to avoid doing anything that could be misperceived as allowing itself to be used as a cat's-paw by China. For this reason, Singapore did not establish diplomatic relations with China until 1990, making it the final Southeast Asian country, except for Brunei, to do so. (Lee 2020)

Business and economic connections

Singapore's small- and medium-sized private firms are important players in the country's engagement with the BRI. As a result of decades of experience operating in both China *and* Southeast Asia, they have developed innovative capabilities and place-specific cultural nuances, competitive advantages that are difficult to replicate. This makes them "natural partners" for Chinese firms entering the region (especially those lacking experience outside China) as well as Western and Japanese TNCs eager to tap into the opportunities opened by the BRI.

Their proactiveness is evidenced by how swiftly business associations/federations associate their major events and forums with the BRI to raise awareness, generate discussions, and build understanding of the BRI among their members. Examples of such associations in Singapore include Business China (a semi-official organization established in 2007 by the Singapore government and business sector), Singapore Chinese Chamber of Commerce (SCCCI), and Singapore Business Federation (SBF). Beyond business-related discussions, these associations have also played a significant role in strengthening cultural and personal exchanges with China's business chambers. In this respect, the SBF is particularly noteworthy.[3] The SBF and *Lianhe Zaobao*, the Chinese language flagship newspaper of Singapore Press Holdings, jointly launched a BRI-themed portal in 2016. The portal is Southeast Asia's first bilingual (Chinese and English) comprehensive website to focus on the BRI, offering a Southeast Asian perspective and promoting BRI-related business activities between Singapore, Southeast Asia, and China. It presents an overview of the BRI, its latest developments, news, business opportunities, analyses, commentaries, and a calendar showcasing BRI-related activities in the region.

---

3   The SBF is the city-state's leading business chamber representing as many as 25,800 (mostly small- and medium-) firms. It also represents smaller local and foreign business chambers.

Sino-Singaporean business transnationalism

We have discussed various approaches to transnationalism, especially the role of institutionalized transnationalism in which the state plays an indispensable role. By using the new concept of business transnationalism for this chapter, we draw upon the expanding field of transnational studies and its emphasis on the regularity and multiple impact of cross-border connections. The following pages are devoted to a brief case study of two companies from Singapore in their engagement with the BRI.[4]

Reengaging the global supply chain: Pacific International Lines (PIL)

Teo Woon Tiong (1918–2020) was born in China's Fujian province and sailed to Singapore in 1937. In 1967, Teo set up Pacific International Lines (PIL) with share capital of SGD10,000,000 and four vessels. PIL's early entry into China's market was facilitated by Teo's close relationship with government officials, shipping agents, and customers. In 2017, PIL was ranked the 15th largest shipping line in the world, based on shipping capacity. Its multinational clients include China National Petroleum Corporation, Exxon Mobil Chemical Asia Pacific, Sinochem International (Overseas) Pte Ltd., and Wilmar International Limited. Based on its share capital, the company has a value of USD376 million in 2017 (cited in Liu and Goh 2024). PIL remains a privately-owned firm based in Singapore. After 2018, PIL was managed and led by Teo Siong Seng, son of Teo Woon Tiong.

PIL's business interests lie not only in shipping, but also in the related areas of container manufacturing and logistics through its ownership of PIL Logistics Pte. Ltd. and Singamas Container

---

4 Data for this section are drawn from Liu and Goh (2024).

Holdings, the world's second largest container manufacturer. Following debt restructuring and cost rationalization, PIL sold its shares in Singamas to the China Ocean Shipping Co. in 2019.

During the 2010s, PIL was directly involved in China's BRI, which "struck a chord" with the Teos, who saw it as "just a repeat" of how the elder Teo sailed on a boat from Xiamen to Singapore in 1937. To the younger Teo, Singapore's competitive business environment, supported by strong and efficient government as well as bilateral and multilateral trade agreements, made the city-state an attractive partner for the BRI. Another key attraction was Singapore's position as the world's second largest RMB offshore trading center, a boon for China-based corporations wanting to invest here. However, Singapore's biggest competitive advantage, according to the younger Teo, is the capability of its people to straddle between different cultural environments. With business experience in a "East-meets-West" destination, Singapore companies could partner Chinese firms seeking to expand into third countries in Southeast Asia.

As a shipping company with decades of experience in China, PIL was and remains closely involved in Sino-Singapore trade initiatives. It was part of a consortium that developed China's Southern Transport Corridor in 2017, which formed a key component of the Chongqing Connectivity Initiative between China and Singapore (Zhu et al. 2023). That same year, PIL invested SGD206 million in the construction of an integrated logistics park in Guangxi. To further strengthen collaboration in shipping and logistics between China and Southeast Asia, PIL signed an MOU with the ASEAN Federation of Forwarders Association in support of the Chongqing-centered International Land-Sea Trade Corridor, and with China's Hodo Group to jointly develop logistics and supply chains. In response to Covid-19's global supply chain disruption, PIL signed an agreement in December 2022 with the local state-owned enterprise (International Land-Sea New Connectivity Co.) to construct a global supply chain linking China's domestic logistics networks with international networks.[5]

PIL has invested in new technologies in response to the Fourth Industrial Revolution. It worked with Port of Singapore Authority International and IBM on a blockchain-based supply chain platform to track and trace cargo shipped from Chongqing to Singapore. It signed another agreement in July 2021 with Singapore's Infocomm Media Development Authority and a group of banks, ports, shipping companies, and commodity exporters to launch the Singapore Trade Data Exchange, which would enhance the secure sharing of data and optimize cargo handling and operations (for details, see Liu and Goh 2024).

The new industrial revolution: Nanofilm Technologies International (NTI)

The founder of NTI, Shi Xu, was born in Shanghai in 1964. After receiving his PhD in thin film technology from the University of Reading in the UK in 1991, he joined a Singapore university as its youngest lecturer at the time and received tenure shortly after. In 1993, Shi embarked on a project with Cambridge University on Filtered Cathodic Vacuum Arc (FCVA) technology, which transforms carbon into thin diamond films that significantly improve the durability of products such as hard drives and semiconductors. He left the university and founded NTI in 1999.

NTI has been listed on the mainboard of the Singapore Stock Exchange since 2020, with an equity value of SGD465.86 million in January 2024. It provides three main services. First, it supplies FCVA-based surface solutions to key components and parts of

---

5 http://cq.china.com.cn/2022-12/14/content_42203620.html.

the global supply chain. Second, it produces nanoproducts that are essential in the manufacture of certain end-products such as optical imaging lenses. Third, it provides coating and auxiliary equipment, spare parts, and after-sales support to customers. These services have been provided to more than 300 corporate clients from different industries. Many of them have long-standing working relationships with NTI. Fuji Xerox, Nikon and Canon have been NTI customers for more than 10 years. NTI has also serviced Microsoft for five years, and Huawei for four years.

Although NTI operates in the high-tech sector, there is a strong overlap between family ownership and management in the company. As of December 2023, Shi Xu and his wife owned a controlling stake of 53% of shares. In comparison with PIL, NTI's corporate structure is flatter, reflecting the decentralization trend typical of the Fourth Industrial Revolution. NTI's China-based ventures are located in Shanghai, Shi Xu's birthplace, illustrating the continuing relevance of family and place ties in its organizational structure. At the start of the 21st century, in 2002, Shi Xu founded Nanofilm Vacuum Coating (Shanghai), focusing on vacuum coating services using FCVA technology and related services. He subsequently established Nanofilm Renewable Energy Technology (Shanghai) in 2011, with more than 1,000 staff supplying coating systems for high performance photovoltaic modules at low cost. NVC was granted the status of a high-tech company by the Shanghai government in 2011. "With our business expansion, we will speed up the setup of research and development in China," Shi said. "We strive to forge synergies and promote more interactions between our operations in Singapore and China and excel in their respective areas. By leveraging our international platform in Singapore, Nanofilm will bring more technologies, equipment and talented people into China and help it develop core competency in vacuum coating technology" (cited in Liu and Goh 2024).

Through its subsidiaries, Witzure Technologies (Yizheng) Co. and Yizheng Nahuan Technologies Co., NTI collaborates with business partners in China and the USA, namely the Yizheng Piston Ring Factory and ASMICO company. Alongside private entities, NTI also works with the Singapore state through Sydrogen, a joint venture owned by NTI (65%) and Temasek Holdings (35%). This venture seeks to apply NTI's vacuum coating technologies in the new hydrogen economy, aiming to increase the affordability and performance of fuel cells.

Shi also participates in institutionalized social and business networks through the Singapore Huayuan Association, which has been heavily involved in the BRI, where he was formerly its vice-president. Formed by China-born professionals in 2001, this association is a medium for Chinese migrant businessmen and Singapore-born entrepreneurs to connect with each other through organized activities such as investment talks, business trips and networking meets, as well as integrating with local society through events organized with the local People's Association (Liu 2022c).

In sum, these two companies represent two distinct economic sectors, shipping (PIL) and high technology manufacturing (NTI). In the context of the BRI, both companies offer flexible operating units through flat corporate structures. Both companies are Singapore-based and founded by China-born businessmen. While NTI was formed in the 1990s after China's opening-up, PIL started operations in 1967. The two differ not only in age, but also their ownership and management. NTI is owned and managed by first-generation migrants (or *xinyimin*) from China since the early 1990s, whereas PIL is managed by a second-generation ethnic Chinese businessman born in Singapore.

Gordon Redding observed that Chinese family companies have yet to shift towards the "professionalism and public ownership" that characterized the "Western economic revolution." We see that in these two cases: Even as they adopt and adapt to international models, their "fundamentals" remain unchanged in terms of family ownership and management (Redding 2000). The cases of PIL (before restructuring) and NTI indicate continuities in business familism amid a rising China through the BRI over the past decade, as both companies are owned and controlled by founding families.

Apart from Sino-Singaporean business transnationalism discussed previously through the cases of Singaporean investments in Greater China, there is also a pattern of institutionalized business transnationalism in Southeast Asia, evidenced by numerous things: First, business associations set up sub-committees specially to deal with increasing economic interactions with China. Second, BRI-specific business associations or affiliated agencies were created to promote and coordinate the BRI projects. The Singapore Business Federation (SBF), a multi-ethnic business federation with a heavy Chinese orientation in membership and leadership, set up a BRI portal in conjunction with the *Lianhe Zaobao* newspaper in 2016. Third, new modes of regional business organizations have been formed in response to the increasing number of economic interactions between Southeast Asia and specific places in China. They included the Singapore Guangdong Enterprise Association which focuses on business links between Singapore and Guangdong, and the Malaysian Shamchun Chamber of Commerce, which aims to promote relationships between Malaysia and Shenzhen. These associations are mostly made up of entrepreneurs originating from, or having business ties with, the specific locations in China (Ren and Liu 2022).

Concluding remarks

This chapter has highlighted the importance of approaching the BRI from the perspective of political economy and business transnationalism in Southeast Asia, the most dynamic region along the BRI routes. The key arguments are the embeddedness of the BRI in the local political economy, which is in turn shaped by diaspora business transnationalism in the context of a rising China and complex global geopolitics.

It is hoped that the case studies of the Singapore government's engagement with the BRI between 2020 and 2023, as well as PIL and NTI outlined above, have demonstrated how the state, ethnicity, and culture – a key asset for the Chinese business community in its participation in the BRI – continue to remain crucial to the strategies of Singaporean Chinese businesses as they capitalize on new opportunities and navigate challenges amid technological and geopolitical developments. Our case studies reinforce the main characteristics of political transnationalism, showing how businesses continue to be conditioned by political forces. The growth of PIL and NTI occurred in the context of the strategic support provided by the governments of Singapore and China. The state plays a central role in expanding business transnationalism not only in terms of policy, but also through direct participation in the transnational ventures of Chinese companies.

Finally, as demonstrated elsewhere (Liu and Goh 2024), business transnationalism is an increasingly important phenomenon that has not been given adequate attention in either international business studies or the transnationalism literature, especially with reference to the Chinese diaspora and their connection to the BRI. It is hoped that this chapter can contribute to greater understanding of the significance of political economy and business transnationalism in the context of the BRI and China's increasing influence in Southeast Asia.

References

Alami, Ilias and Adam D. Dixon (2020) "State capitalism(s) redux? Theories, tensions, controversies." *Competition & Change*, 24(1): 70–94.

Blanchard, Jean-Marc F. (2021) Belt and Road Initiative (BRI) Blues: Powering BRI research back on track to avoid choppy seas. *Journal of Chinese Political Science*, 26: 235–255.

Feldmann, Matthew (2019) Global varieties of capitalism. *World Politics*, 71(1): 162–196.

Forough, Mohammadbagher (2022) America's pivot to Asia 2.0: The Indo-Pacific economic framework. *The Diplomat*, May 26.

Guo, Shibao (2022) Reimagining Chinese diasporas in a transnational world: toward a new research agenda. *Journal of Ethnic and Migration Studies*, 48(4): 847–872.

Huang, Yanzhong (2022) The health silk road: How China adapts the Belt and Road Initiative to the Covid-19 pandemic. *American Journal of Public Health*, 112(4): 567–569.

Ji, Xianbai (2023) Stay Useful, Stay Relevant: Singapore's institutional diplomacy toward China's Belt and Road Initiative. *Asian Perspective*, 47(4): 553–577.

Kratz, Agatha and Dragan Pavlićević (2019) Norm-making, norm-taking or norm-shifting? A case study of Sino–Japanese competition in the Jakarta–Bandung high-speed rail project. *Third World Quarterly*, 40(6): 1107–1126.

Lai, Karen P. Y., Shaun Lin, And James D. Sidaway (2020) Financing the Belt and Road Initiative (BRI): Research agendas beyond the 'debt-trap' discourse. *Eurasian Geography and Economics*, 61(2): 109–124.

Lee, Ching Kwan (2017) *The Specter of Global China: Politics, Labor, and Foreign Investment in Africa*. Chicago: University of Chicago Press.

Lee, Ching Kwan (2022) Global China at 20: Why, how and so what? *The China Quarterly*, 250: 313–331.

Lee, Hsien Loong (2020) The Endangered Asian Century: America, China, and the perils of confrontation. *Foreign Affairs*, 99(4).

Lewin, Arie Y., and Michael A. Witt (2022) China's Belt and Road Initiative and international business: The overlooked centrality of politics. *Journal of International Business Policy*, 5: 135–151.

Li, Jiatao, Ari Van Assche, Xiaolan Fu, Lee Li and Gongming Qian (2022b) The Belt and Road Initiative and international business policy: A kaleidoscopic perspective. *Journal of International Business Policy*, 5(2): 135–151.

Li, Jiatao, Gongming Qian, Kevin Zheng Zhou, Jane Lu and Bun Liu (2022a) Belt and Road Initiative, globalization and institutional changes: Implications for firms in Asia. *Asia Pacific Journal of Management*, 39(3): 843–856.

Lim, Guanie, Chen Li and Emirza Adi Syailendra (2021) Why is it so hard to push Chinese railway projects in Southeast Asia? The role of domestic politics in Malaysia and Indonesia. *World Development*, 138: 105272.

Liou, Chih-shian (2014) Rent-seeking at home, capturing market share abroad: The domestic determinants of the transnationalization of China State Construction Engineering Corporation. *World Development*, 54: 220–231.

Liow, Joseph Chinyong, Hong Liu and Gong Xue (eds) (2021a) *Research Handbook on the Belt-and-Road Initiative*. Cheltenham: Edward Elgar.

Liow, Joseph Chinyong, Hong Liu and Gong Xu (2021b) Introduction. In Joseph Chinyong Liow, Hong Liu and Gong Xu (eds) *Research Handbook on the Belt and Road Initiative*. Cheltenham: Edward Elgar, pp. xx–xxii.

Liu, Hong, Kong Yam Tan and Guanie Lim (eds) (2022) *The Political Economy of Regionalism, Trade, and Infrastructure: Southeast Asia and the Belt and Road Initiative in a New Era*. Singapore: World Scientific Publishing.

Liu, Hong (2022a) *The Political Economy of Transnational Governance: China and Southeast Asia in the 21st Century*. London: Routledge.

Liu, Hong (2022b) China engages the Global South: From Bandung to the Belt and Road Initiative. *Global Policy*, 13 (S1): 11–22.

Liu, Hong (2022c) Identity, politics, and transnationalism: Deciphering new Chinese diaspora in Singapore, 2010–2020. In Yos Santasombat (ed.) *Transnational Chinese Diaspora in Southeast Asia*. Singapore: Springer, pp. 125–152.

Liu, Hong and Guanie Lim, G. (2023) When the state goes transnational: The political economy of China's engagement with Indonesia. *Competition & Change*, 27(2): 402–421.

Liu, Hong and Chunzie Miao (2024) Digital geopolitics in a VUCA world: China encounters a new global order. *Global Policy*, 15(S6): 67–83.

Liu, Hong and Na Ren (2023) Between positionality and nudging: A rising China and Chinese voluntary associations in Southeast Asia, *Asia Pacific Viewpoint*, 64(3): 304–316.

Liu, Hong and Jeremy Goh (2024) Emerging business transnationalism in Singapore and greater China: Governance, networks, and strategies. *Asia and Pacific Business Review*, 30(4): 640–666.

Liu, Hong and Guanie Lim (2019) The political economy of a rising China in Southeast Asia: Malaysia's response to the Belt and Road Initiative. *Journal of Contemporary China*, 28(116): 216–231.

Liu, Hong, Xin Fan and Guanie Lim (2021) Singapore engages the Belt and Road Initiative: Perceptions, policies, and institutions. *Singapore Economic Review*, 66 (1): 219–241.

Liu, Hong, Chengwei Xu and Guanie Lim (2024) The China effect on regional economic integration: A longitudinal study of Central, South, and Southeast Asia. *Journal of the Asia Pacific Economy*, 29(4): 2110–2132.

Liu, Jiaqi M. (2022) When diaspora politics meet global ambitions: Diaspora institutions amid China's geopolitical transformations. *International Migration Review*, 56(4): 1255–1279.

Liu, Xiaofeng and Mia M. Bennett (2022) The geopolitics of knowledge communities: Situating Chinese and foreign studies of the Green Belt and Road Initiative. *Geoforum*, 128: 168–180.

Khanal, Shaleen, and Hongzhou Zhang (2024) Ten years of China's Belt and Road Initiative: A bibliometric review. *Journal of Chinese Political Science*, 29(2): 361–395.

Martínez-Zarzoso, Inmaculada and Robert Rudolf (2020) The trade facilitation impact of the Chinese diaspora. *The World Economy*, 43(9): 2411–2436.

Massot, Pascale (2021) The state of the study of the market in political economy: China's rise shines light on conceptual shortcomings. *Competition & Change*, 25(5): 534–560.

Mitchell, David (2020) Making or breaking regions: China's Belt Road Initiative and the meaning for regional dynamics. *Geopolitics*, 26(5): 1400–1420.

Negara, Siwage and Leo Suryadinata (2022) The Flying Geese and China's BRI in Indonesia. In Hong Liu, Kong Yam Tan and Guanie Lim (eds), *The Political Economy of Regionalism, Trade, and Infrastructure: Southeast Asia and the Belt and Road Initiative in a New Era*. Singapore: World Scientific, pp. 301–324.

Ng, Charmaine (2020) 15 countries, including Singapore, sign RCEP, the world's largest trade pact. *Straits Times*, November 16. https://www.straitstimes.com/singapore/politics/15-countries-including-singapore-sign-rcep-the-worlds-largest-trade-pact

Nikkei Asia (2022) Q&A with Singapore's Lee: Nations 'Big and Small' Must Play by Rules. https://asia.nikkei.com/Editor-s-Picks/Interview/Q-A-with-Singapore-s-Lee-Nations-big-and-small-must-play-by-rules.

Nordin, Astrid H. M. and Mikael Weissmann (2018) Will Trump make China great again? The Belt and Road Initiative and international order. *International Affairs* 94(20): 231–249.

Oh, Tessa (2023). Forecasts of China's slowing growth have no impact on collaboration with Singapore: DPM Wong. *Business Times*, December 8. https://www.businesstimes.com.sg/international/global/forecasts-chinas-slowing-growth-have-no-impact-collaboration-singapore-dpm

Peterson, Glen (2013) *Overseas Chinese in the People's Republic of China*. London: Routledge.

Portes, Alejandro (1995) Economic sociology and the sociology of immigration. In Alejandro Portes (ed) *The Economic Sociology of Immigration*. New York: Russell Sage Foundation, pp. 1–41.

Portes, Alejandro, Luis E. Guarnizo and Patricia Landolt (1999) The study of transnationalism: Pitfalls and promise of an emergent research field. *Ethnic and Racial Studies*, 22(2): 217–237.

Redding, Gordon (2000) What is Chinese about Chinese family business and how much is family and how much is business? In Henry Wai-chung Yeung and Kris Olds (eds) *Globalization of Chinese Family Firms*. London: MacMillan Press, pp. 31–54.

Ren, Na and Hong Liu (2015) Traversing between transnationalism and integration: Dual embeddedness of new Chinese immigrant entrepreneurs in Singapore. *Asian and Pacific Migration Journal*, 24(3): 298–326.

Ren, Na and Hong Liu (2019) Domesticating 'transnational cultural capital': The Chinese state and diasporic technopreneur returnees. *Journal of Ethnic and Migration Studies*, 45(13): 2308–2327.

Ren, Na and Hong Liu (2022) Southeast Asian Chinese engage a rising China: Business associations, institutionalised transnationalism, and the networked state. *Journal of Ethnic and Migration Studies*, 48(4): 873–892.

Sun, Yixian, Joanna I. Lewis and Johannes Urpelainen (2023) Environmental governance of China's Belt and Road Initiative. *Environmental Politics*, 32(7): 1109–1116.

Tanaka, Hitoshi (ed) (2020) *Historical Narratives of East Asia in the 21st Century: Overcoming the Politics of National Identity*. London: Routledge.

Voon, Jan P. and Xinpeng Xu (2020) Impact of the Belt and Road Initiative on China's soft power: Preliminary evidence. *Asia-Pacific Journal of Accounting & Economics*, 27(1): 120–131.

Waldinger, Roger and David Fitzgerald (2004) Transnationalism in question. *American Journal of Sociology*, 109(5): 1177–1195.

Wang, Zhaohui and Yuheng Fu (2022) Local politics and fluctuating engagement with China: Analysing the Belt and Road Initiative in maritime Southeast Asia. *The Chinese Journal of International Politics*, 15(2): 163–182.

World Bank (2019) *Belt and Road Economics: Opportunities and Risks of Transport Corridors*. https://www.worldbank.org/en/topic/regional-integration/publication/belt-and-road-economics-opportunities-and-risks-of-transport-corridors

World Bank (2021) https://data.worldbank.org/indicator/NY.GDP.MKTP.CD?locations=CN

Yoshimatsu, Hidetaka (2018) New dynamics in Sino-Japanese rivalry: Sustaining infrastructure development in Asia. *Journal of Contemporary China*, 27 (113): 719–734.

Yu, Hong (2024) *Understanding China's Belt and Road Initiative*. Singapore: Springer Nature.

Zhao, Suisheng (ed) (2020) *China's New Global Strategy: The Belt and Road Initiative (BRI) and Asian Infrastructure Investment Bank (AIIB)*. Volume 1. Oxon: Routledge.

Zhu, Siying, Yutong Cai, Mengtong Wang, Hua Wang and Qiang Meng (2023). How will China–Singapore international land–sea trade corridor affect route choice behaviour? A discrete choice model. *Transport Policy*, 144: 11–22.

9 | Maximizing the Benefits of the Mekong Subregional Cooperation Frameworks[1]

Romyen Kosaikanont

Abstract

Development in the Mekong subregion has become increasingly important in the early 21st century, both as a necessity for a prosperous ASEAN Community and as a site of geopolitical competition among super and emerging powers. Following China's announcement of the Belt and Road Initiative in 2013 and its subsequent launch of Lancang Mekong Special Funds of USD300 million and new mechanisms for Lancang-Mekong Cooperation (LMC) in 2016, the US reformed the Lower Mekong Initiative (LMI) into the expanded Mekong-US Partnership (MUSP) in 2020. This paper treats the multilateral cooperation frameworks LMC and MUSP as the smallest unit of analysis and uses the concept of "reciprocal influence" to examine geopolitical competition between China and the US in the Mekong subregion. Under the BRI, China has worked with Mekong member countries to address their needs for economic development through LMC Special Funds and by participating in subregional multilateral venues for consultation, seeking to position itself as "a responsible great power" prioritizing development. Through the MUSP, the US formed the Friends

---

1 This research is funded by TSRI. The researcher also received the Fulbright US ASEAN Scholarship to conduct a field study in Washington DC from 23 May–30 August 2022. The author would like to express the deepest appreciation to both funders and host institution the Stimson Center for all their kind support.

of the Mekong to improve donor country cooperation and coordination in promoting so-called "universal values" – good governance, respect for a rules-based order, and respect for human rights – while providing development assistance in the Mekong subregion, seeking to ensure the region's autonomy and to contain China. My argument is that the Mekong subregion and its member states are not passive by-standers in this competition but rather active agents negotiating for "reciprocal influence," navigating the US-China rivalry to maximize their respective benefits from the geopolitical competition. The small states in the Mekong subregion hedge, bandwagon, resist, and selectively engage with the major powers in both bilateral and multilateral frameworks.

Keywords

US-China rivalry – reciprocal influence – hedging – bandwagoning – selective engagement – Belt and Road Initiative

Introduction

The Southeast Asian region is diverse, complex, and has become a hotly contested site of the US-China rivalry (Shambaugh 2021; Amitav 2021; Paradorn Rangsimaporn 2023). Geographically, the region is divided into maritime Southeast Asia (Singapore, Indonesia, Malaysia, Philippines, Brunei, and Timor-Leste) and mainland Southeast Asia or the Mekong subregion (Cambodia, Lao PDR, Myanmar, Thailand, and Vietnam). The US-China rivalry in Southeast Asia is most commonly discussed in terms of security and conflict in the South China Sea, but those are certainly not the only sites of competition between the two powers. In the early 21st century, the Mekong subregion has become the venue for intense US-China competition (Middleton 2018; Poowin Bunyavejchewin 2016; Pongphisoot Busbarat 2018, 2020; Biba 2019; Grunwald

2021; Ho and Hoo 2016; Lampton, Ho, and Kuik 2021; Paradorn Rangsimaporn 2023).

The most intense competition centers on two main sets of issues that trouble the region: (1) Water security and water governance. Some 20% of the Mekong River's headwaters is in China, feeding Chinese claims that it is a Chinese national river. The river's flow to the lower four countries is directly affected by upstream river management. (2) Infrastructure and economic development. The Mekong subregion has great needs for infrastructural investment. There are competing views on how best to finance and build this infrastructure. A fundamental point of difference between China and the US are that the former prioritizes development before individual rights while for the latter, universal values come before development. The interesting recent development is that both the US and China and to some extent other middle powers engage in this region compete for their influences through competing multilateral regional mechanisms, namely the Mekong-US Partnership (MUSP) and China's Lancang-Mekong Cooperation (LMC).

On the surface, LMC is seen as an extension of the BRI with a specific geographical focus in the highly strategic immediate neighboring countries along the southern border of China. But I argue that the LMC should be addressed with special attention considering that it was originally initiated by Thailand as "Mekong Lancang Cooperation (MLC)" in 2012, and then China took the lead in 2016 proposing concrete mechanisms for cooperation, launching the USD300 million LMC Special Funds, and reenforcing a needs-based approach and its funding model. This needs-based allocation of available funding means that the member countries' demands for development can be responded to quickly without universal value conditions. China's leadership in LMC is to demonstrate their commitment and the concrete impact it can have in the international development arena.

The launch of LMC Special Funds came at a time when the BRI was being heavily criticized for its lack of transparency, the absence of any sustainability requirement or environmental and social safeguards, and was accused of being a debt trap. China's attempt to take over the LMC was an effort to gain support from the Mekong subregion countries for an alternative approach to multilateral cooperation and development. China offered assurances that the LMC development would be consulted with the Mekong subregion countries. They also emphasized that agreed projects could be swiftly implemented because the funds were already available – which they call outcome-oriented development.

The question is why China wants to invest in this region. There could be different reasons including (1) pragmatic reason of providing development to China's neighboring countries, (2) interdependency in terms of economic engagement, and (3) security reasons. However, I argue that China's enhanced engagement with LMC and the Mekong subregion is aimed at something bigger. Xi Jinping announced "China's Dream" in November 2012 when he became a leader of the Chinese Communist Party. And in order to achieve China's Dream of the great rejuvenation of the Chinese nation, he proposed building the Community with a Shared Future. From this perspective, the BRI is a community-building tool. But as a response to the BRI's harshest critics, the investment in LMC can be seen as an experiment which, if successful, will provide proof that China is a responsible power. At the same time, China's approach to development is welcome because it allows quick positive responses to the needs of participating countries. Gradually, this development mechanism is intended to establish China's reputation as a responsible power, not a regional hegemon.

The US has criticized China for aggressively expanding its influence on water security issues in the Mekong subregion as well as investing in the infrastructural projects without safeguarding against negative environmental and social impacts. As China does not interfere with internal matters nor require participating countries to promote democracy and human rights or strengthen the rule of laws, it has also been criticized for the increased risk of corruption in project management and implementation. The US sees its role, in contrast, as a responsible superpower seeking to protect "universal values" and empower the Mekong member states through the MUSP.[2] The unique branding of the MUSP is on human development, capacity building, science diplomacy and policy dialogue to ensure that member states and civil societies can uphold the international rules-based order while safeguarding the environment, society, and human rights. MUSP is an important US vehicle for containing China's influence in the Mekong subregion.

Against the backdrop of this rivalry, the important question is how the subregion maximizes the situation of great power competition for its benefits. Lampton, Ho, and Kuik (2022) introduce the concept of "reciprocal influence," arguing that regional actors have agency to react to both China and the US, rejecting, bandwagoning, and hedging to maximize benefits while reducing risk. In this case, they may choose to use bilateral or multilateral frameworks through which to negotiate reciprocal influence. Their respective abilities to negotiate, however, depend on various factors including the size of the economy and country, their location, and state capacity.

This paper presents a conceptual overview of the China-US rivalry in the Mekong subregion through their respective multilateral mechanisms. The main research questions are: (1) What are the rationales and objectives of the US and China in

---

2   For details on the Lower Mekong Initiative, see https://mekonguspartnership. org/2012/07/13/fact-sheet-lower-mekong-initiative. For details on the US-Mekong Partnership, see https://mekonguspartnership.org.

engaging with the Mekong subregional member countries through their respective multilateral mechanisms? (2) How influential are the MUSP and LMC in the Mekong subregion? and (3) How do the Mekong subregion and member states navigate the situation and maximize their benefits?

This paper is presented in four sections, including this introduction. The next section outlines the development of the China-US rivalry in the Mekong subregion. The third section introduces the concept of "reciprocal influence" to help understand the agency of the member countries in their dealings with the China and US presence in the region. The final section concludes the discussion.

China-US rivalry in the Mekong subregion

This section is in two parts. The first part presents the background of the Mekong subregion and its evolution from a "development area" to a "site of geopolitical competition" between the US and China. The second part maps the crowded field of the Mekong subregion's multilateral development cooperation frameworks.

The Mekong subregion: From "development area" to "site of geopolitical competition"

The Mekong subregion

The Mekong subregion is a geographical area in Southeast Asia comprising five countries: Cambodia, Lao PDR, Myanmar, Thailand, and Vietnam and two provinces of China, namely Yunnan and Guangxi. In the early 1990s, after the cold war ended, four of the five countries in the subregion embarked on ambitious reform programs: the New Economic Mechanism (NEM) of Lao PDR, the Doi Moi reform of Vietnam, liberalization policies in Cambodia, and the triple reform (political, economic, and social reform) of Myanmar. In all four cases, the reforms were intended to transform the country's centrally planned economy to a more liberalized market-based economy. It should be noted, however, that the political regimes remain quite diverse and dynamic, with one-party states in Lao PDR and Vietnam, a constitutional monarchy with varying degrees of political stability and military control in Thailand, and unique regimes in Cambodia and Myanmar.

The Mekong subregion's wealth of natural resources has the potential to generate great economic wealth. Substantial hardware and software infrastructures are required, however, before this wealth can be realized. Until the early 1990s or the end of the cold war, except for Thailand, infrastructures such as roads, ports, and airports were poor to nonexistent throughout the region. In 1993, the Asian Development Bank (ADB) launched the Greater Mekong Subregion (GMS) Economic Cooperation Program, which has funded numerous infrastructure projects in pursuit of the GMS's vision of Connectivity, Competitiveness and Community. When the GMS was launched, there was limited presence of extra-regional powers in the region beyond Japan's presence in Thailand as a foreign investor. Japan is seeking to expand its investments in Thailand's neighboring countries to offset the rising costs of production in Thailand. At the time, China was totally focused on their own infrastructural development, building roads, and railways to connect the countries' diverse regions. Zawacki (2019) pointed out that after the cold war, the US pulled out of the region and left a vacuum. Pranee Thiparat (2022) disagreed, claiming that "the US has never left the region, but they just ignore us."

The reengagement of the US: The containment of the rise of China

In 2005, the American Council on Foreign Relations commissioned an independent task force to conduct a study of US-China relations 35 years after their normalization. The Council identified five points of concern: (1) The rapid growth of China's economy and its trade surplus with the US; (2) That political reform had not followed economic reform in China, China did not promote Western democracy, rule of law, or universal human rights; (3) China's growing influence, especially in Southeast Asia, was perceived as a challenge to the US's global leadership; (4) Its significant defense spending and increasingly modernized military; and (5) China's ascent while the US engaged in its "war on terrorism."

In 2007, another report, "U.S.-China Relations: An Affirmative Agenda, A Responsible Course," made a series of recommendation. For our purposes, the most relevant was the recommendation to enhance security relations by working more closely with China's neighbors and regional architecture such as ASEAN (Jannuzzi 2007). Following the publication of this report, the US appointed an ambassador to ASEAN, signed the Treaty of Amity and Cooperation with ASEAN, and joined the East Asia Summit. In 2009, President Barack Obama launched Pivot Asia as a strategic move to reengage with the region. Following a visit by Secretary of State Hilary Clinton, the Lower Mekong Initiative (LMI) – renamed Mekong-US Partnership in 2020 – was launched to foster cooperation with the countries of the ASEAN riparian states. This report indicates that the US's subsequent strategic engagement was driven by a felt need to counter the rise of China and its increasing influence in the region.

Michael Pillsbury (2022), a former intelligence officer, argues that China has always sought to rise to the top. Different strategies have been employed, including deception and Deng Xiaoping's low-key foreign policy approach. Responding to sanctions imposed following the Tiananmen Square protest, Deng issued guidelines for China's foreign policy: observe carefully, secure China's positions, calmly cope with the challenges, hide China's capacities and bide its time, be good at maintaining a low profile, and never claim leadership. The intention was to convince the world that China's rising prosperity and power could be achieved peacefully. But many scholars and strategists, not only in the US, have asked whether China's rise can be peaceful as it also has a great need for critical resources, especially energy, as well as a great desire for the power to influence others and exercise leadership on the global stage.

John J. Mearsheimer (2014) is among those who argue that the rise of China cannot be peaceful. He argues that, realistically, all powers must compete for power merely to survive and he rejects as overly idealistic the liberal belief that world peace might be achieved. And because the world has no central authority to protect the state, states will inevitably run into conflict despite their interdependent trade relationships. Although he agrees with the liberal "international institutions" that peace and prosperity are preferable to war, he maintains it is impossible to achieve.

Without a supra-national apparatus, states form the view that the only way to survive is to acquire power for themselves. How much power and how to acquire it are always in question. Some argue that power can only be acquired through military might, but others argue that soft power can also be acquired through development aid and public diplomacy, as China has demonstrated in Africa (Bräutigam and Huang 2023; Bräutigam 2009). From this perspective, superpower initiated multilateral mechanisms can be seen as a means of acquiring power to shape agendas and systems. Hence, LMC, I argue is a venue for China to gain support through soft power.

In terms of agenda setting, the US and China clash over development approaches and ideologies, which we might think of as the "Washington consensus" and "Beijing consensus." The Washington consensus embraces liberal thinking, freedom of speech, good governance, the rule of law, democracy, human rights and a free market, while the Beijing consensus respects the states' rights to design their own development policies/pathways, and state sovereignty free of foreign interference, especially in domestic politics and governance. These conflicting positions can help to understand the US's concerns about the rise of China and its motivation to contain China's growth and influence. In the Mekong subregion, the US strategically engages in both bilateral relations with individual states and in multilateral relations through the Mekong US Partnership. The latter efforts include "offshore balancing," strategically engaging likeminded middle powers – e.g., Australia, Japan, ROK – through the "Friends of the Mekong" to align their operations within the Mekong with the goal of containing China. We will return to this point later.

China: A responsible power of the neighboring Mekong subregion

Following its 1978 "reform and opening up," China has experienced rapid economic development reflected in its strong GDP growth rate, its economic resilience during the COVID-19 period, and strong foreign currency reserves. In the early 2000s, China made a strategic move to gradually engage on the global stage. Starting with joining the World Trade Organization in 2001, it began actively providing foreign aid to developing nations to address global issues such as climate change and sustainable development.

The BRI is China's ambitious transcontinental infrastructure initiative, complete with new financial institutions embedded with Chinese culture and ideology. The BRI's objective is to connect

China with Asia, Europe, and Africa, but its immediate neighbors have always been given high priority. This can be seen in the fact that, at the Chinese Communist Party conference "Peripheral Diplomacy Work" (24–25 October 2013), Xi Jinping personally chaired the meeting discussing the importance of the Southeast Asian region (Shambaugh 2021), where he first introduced "Periphery Diplomacy" (Jianwei Wang and Hoo Tiang Boon 2019). Xi told the gathering that China must create "an excellent peripheral environment for its development" and that the periphery regions "are strategically significant to our country in terms of geography, the environment, and relationships." China's foreign policy actors, Xi stressed must "enhance political good will; deepen regional economic integration; increase its cultural influence; and improve regional security cooperation" (Jianwei and Hoo 2019). The endurance of this policy position can be seen in the Chinese government's more recent publication, "Outlook on China's Foreign Policy on Its Neighborhood In the New Era" (Ministry of Foreign Affairs, PRC 2023), which highlights why China prioritizes the Mekong subregion.

Zhang WeiWei (2012), the eminent Chinese scholar, argues in *The China Wave: Rise of A Civilizational State*, that the world can trust the BRI because China is a civilized state with four exceptional characteristics: (1) China has an exceptionally large population which is a source of wealth and prosperity. A large population means a large pool of engineers to be deployed for developmental work around the world. Zhang claims that there are more engineers in China than in the US, Japan and Germany combined. Furthermore, the large population means large numbers of international travelers spending money around the world and boosting local GDPs. (2) China is physically an enormous country with great potential. The new Silk Road and Economic Belt, the BRI, will open more opportunities for growth and prosperity to

China, its neighboring countries, and the world. (3) China has an exceptionally long history and rich culture. Its Confucian ideology promotes peace and prosperity. Hence, according to Zhang, the world can rest assured that China's rise will be peaceful.

The claim that China is a peace-loving country has been politicized through its frequent repetition in the speeches of its leaders. Neil Thomas (2020) points out that the phrase "responsible great power" was used in a speech by Jiang Zemin in the early 1990s, soon after the leadership's decision to open the Chinese economy to the region and the world. He notes that it appears again, following the Global Financial Crisis in 2007–2009, when Hu Jintao used the term to reassure the region that China was trying to mitigate the impact of the crisis (ibid.). But what does the phrase "responsible great power" really mean to China?

In his report to the 19th Party Congress (18–24 October 2017), Xi emphasized that China would retain "socialism with Chinese characteristics" while offering a "Chinese solution" to humanity's problem. In a similar vein, Zhao Ting Yang, a prominent philosopher at the Chinese Academy of Social Sciences, sought to modernize the ancient worldview of *tianxia*, or "all under Heaven" (Callahan 2008). According to Zhao, the world's problems are not caused by failed states but by a failed world-system. The rules-based world order itself, Zhao argued is the problem, to which the Chinese worldview of *tianxia* offers a corrective.

Zhao argues that democracy creates chaos through its divisiveness, and hence we need a new world order constructed from the perspective that we are "all one people." He further argued that rather than a rule-based world system, we need a strong state that acts in the interests and for the benefits of all. While Western institutions identify three levels – individual, community, and nation-state – *tianxia* only identifies two levels of state and family, with the state governing top-down in the interests of all the families under Heaven. That is to say, China would be recognized as a "responsible great power" not only on the basis of its economic and military strengths, but by "offering new world concepts and a new world structure" (Callahan 2008). And to actualize *tianxia* as a system of global governance, Zhao argues that China needs to engage in multilateral relations at the regional and global levels.

From this perspective, China's creation of the Lancang-Mekong Cooperation as a multilateral institution is an expression of its self-appointed role as a "responsible great power." China is aiming to address the region's development gaps by constructing much needed infrastructure via its alternative "no strings attached" development model, in contrast to the Western model of tying aid to conditions of upholding "universal values." Thus, although LMC emphasizes the importance of "consultation" to ensure projects genuinely respond to member country needs, China is setting the agenda and establishing new norms for multilateral development cooperation.

Among the criticisms of China's efforts, Pal Nyiri (2006) notes that what is said in China's policy announcements and what is done in practice can be two quite different things. Pal Nyiri argues that China's development discourse portrays a civilizing mission dutifully accepted as a "yellow man's burden." It is aiming to construct civilization by improving the quality of the population through the modernization process. But many argue this is just another form of hegemony in the name of development and civilization, no different from the so-called "white man's burden" the Western colonial powers used to justify their "interventions" in other countries. That is to say that, although China claims to seek the status of a "responsible great power" and civilized state, in practice, this is mere rhetoric in a hegemonic contest disguised as a civilizing mission.

Mapping the cooperation frameworks and the US-China rivalry

The rise of China and development in the Mekong subregion is a focus of many developed nations, not only the US. Many nations engage in the region, both bilaterally and through multilateral mechanisms. Asia Foundation and Mekong Institute are two of the many organizations and individual scholars that attempt to map the many cooperation frameworks in the Mekong subregion. The Asia Foundation (2018) published findings that there is constant change in cooperation and development agreements. At the regional forum "Seeking Synergies on Mekong-ACMECS Cooperation" on 17 June 2022, the Mekong Institute reported that there were fourteen multilateral frameworks in the region, but this figure includes an expression of interest from Australia which has not yet been realized in any agreements.

Table 9.1 is a reconstruction of the Asia Foundation study which maps the cooperation frameworks in the Mekong subregion classified by areas of cooperation. The column represents twelve cooperation frameworks which can be distinguished into three categories: those initiated by extra regional powers (medium and large), intra regionally initiated cooperation frameworks, and intergovernmental organizations.

To be more specific, the large and rising powers' frameworks are the US led Mekong US Partnership (MUSP) and the China led Lancang Mekong Cooperation (LMC); the medium powers-led frameworks are the Indian led Mekong Ganga Cooperation (MGC), the Japan led Mekong Japan Cooperation (MJC), and the Republic of Korea led Mekong ROK. Intra-regionally initiated cooperation frameworks are the Ayeyarwady Chaophraya Mekong Economic Cooperation Strategy (ACMECS), Cambodia, Lao PDR, Myanmar and Vietnam (CLMV) and Cambodia, Lao PDR, and Vietnam (CLV). The four intergovernmental organizations are the Asian Development Bank's Greater Mekong Subregion (GMS), Mekong River Commission (MRC), the ASEAN Mekong Basin Development Cooperation (AMBDC) and Initiatives of ASEAN Integration (IAI). Apart from the twelve cooperation frameworks presented by Zawacki (2018), we should recognize the Mekong Institute as a regional organization contributing to the development of the subregion.

The rows in Table 9.1 list 28 areas of cooperation namely: connectivity, education, agriculture, development, trade and investment, communication ICT/digital, water, environment, health, tourism, energy, human resource development, SMEs, climate change, disaster reduction, culture, fish, poverty, human development, production capability, cross border cooperation, urban development, forestry, mining, financial cooperation, cyber security, customs and youth. The areas of cooperation can be summarized as extremely diverse and complex. While most powers want to brand their own initiatives as distinctive, there is significant overlap in their respective areas of cooperation. The most crowded field is in the area of "connectivity," with eleven out of twelve frameworks identifying as engaged with these issues in the subregion. However, connectivity means quite different things for different frameworks. For example, for an official of the Mekong US Partnership in Washington DC, "connectivity" would not mean support for a physical infrastructure construction project such as road or port building. Instead he means building state capacity, such as educating civil servants to be able to critically assess proposals and to ensure any physical infrastructure project is completed with good governance, to high standards, and is environmentally friendly (Interview, August 2022). The second most crowded area of cooperation is "education," identified by ten out of twelve frameworks. The two frameworks that do not include education in their plan are Mekong River Commission and

Table 9.1 Mapping cooperation frameworks in the Mekong subregion by areas of cooperation

	LMC	MUSP	MGC	MJC	ACMECS	MRC	Mekong ROK	GMS	CLMV	CLV	AMBDC	IAI
Connectivity			■				■		■			
Education	■					■	■					■
Agriculture	■		■		■		■				■	
Development					■		■			■		
Trade and Investment			■		■							
Communication ICT/digital	■						■					
Water						■	■					
Environment						■	■					
Health	■		■									■
Tourism					■							
Energy					■							
Human resource					■		■					
SMEs			■									
Climate change					■	■						
Disaster reduction					■	■						
Culture	■		■							■		
Fish						■						
Poverty	■											
Human development				■								
Production cap.	■											
Cross border cooperation	■											
Urban development								■				
Forestry											■	
Mining											■	
Financial cooperation						■						
Cyber security						■						
Customs	■											
Youth	■											

Source: Reconstructed from Zawacki (2018).

the AMBDC. Of course, education, too, is interpreted differently. For example, for MUSP, education means English language programs for civil servants but for India's Mekong-Ganga it means a scholarship program.

Some cooperation frameworks have identified unique areas of cooperation. For example, GMS is the only framework working on "urban development" and AMBDC focuses on "forestry" and "mining."

A comparative analysis of the areas in which the US and China engage reveals that China is engaged in more areas (13) of cooperation than the US (7). The two countries are both engaged in six areas, namely connectivity, education, agriculture, water, environment, and health. China's LMC is the only multilateral framework engaged in six other areas: communications ICT/digital, culture, poverty, production capacity, cross border cooperation, customs, and youth. Culture is identified as an activity area for China's LMC, the CLV, and India's MGC. The only area of cooperation that the MUSP is alone in is human development.

Importantly, though, we must note that this map is based on analysis of the respective plans and mission statements. What is happening on the ground is much more difficult to assess. One of the difficulties in getting a clear picture of what is really happening in the region, according to the Mekong Institute, is that the various cooperation frameworks' reports of investment and progress include bilateral projects between the respective extra regional powers and individual member countries of the Mekong subregion, thus inflating their self-reported effectiveness. Likewise, there is very little transparency about funding and the contributions of the lead countries in various frameworks. It is often not clear whether the figures cited refer to amounts pledged, allocated budgets or funds spent. It is even more difficult to ascertain how much of a multilateral organization's budget was allocated to a specific project. When we asked policy makers and project managers across the region to compare funding support from China and the US, though, they were typically of the view that China is both providing greater funding and is readier to commit. That is, once the parties agreed on a project, funds from China begin to flow almost immediately, in contrast to funding from the US, which must be approved via democratic processes and take much longer.

As mentioned, the US initiated Friends of the Mekong (FOM) group is an offshore balancing strategy – an attempt to recruit other extra regional powers (except China) to cooperate in the development of the subregion. FOM is basically a meeting mechanism to cooperate and coordinate on certain projects. For example, the US created the Japan US Mekong Power Partnership (JUMPP) to pursue energy security and enhanced regional energy trade and integration as shown in Figure 9.1. Such collaborative projects help to share responsibilities and to be more competitive with China's large-scale funding arrangements.

Of the intra regionally initiated cooperation frameworks – ACMECS, CLV and CLMV – ACMECS, led by Thailand, is engaged in more areas of cooperation than the others. In comparison, ACMECS identified sixteen areas of cooperation while CLMV and CLV identified eight and five respectively. Notably, ACMECS is the only framework highlighting cooperation in the areas of cyber security, fish and financial cooperation. It is important to emphasize the financial cooperation in the masterplan of ACMECS. The ACMECS Funds were created with Thailand's initial pledge of USD200 million and a request for member countries' contributions. ACMECS also seeks support from "development partners" – extra powers and the subregional member countries to put more money in the fund to implement the projects stipulated in the ACMECS Master Plan.

Figure 9.1 Mekong US Partnership at a glance   Source: MUSP 2020.

In summation, mapping the cooperation frameworks in the region highlights how fuzzy the picture is; that is, it remains unclear who is doing what in any given area of cooperation, how much funding has been allocated, how much was spent, and what it was spent on. Some areas of cooperation such as connectivity and education are foci for the majority of frameworks, while others are engaged in by only one multilateral organization. In interviews, government officials overseeing these frameworks both within and outside of the subregion, generally agreed that these crowded fields have created burdens on time and resources. Preparation and participation in the meetings of each framework consumes all their time and efforts. Perhaps the biggest challenge is how the diverse countries of the Mekong subregion can synergize their strategic position – the member countries have no shared view of how to engage with these extra-regional "partners." But more importantly for present purposes, these frameworks of cooperation clearly evidence the geopolitical competition of great and middle powers which the subregion and individual states must carefully negotiate.

ACMECS, the crowded field and reciprocal influence

Lampton et al. (2022) argue that the US typically looks at China through a mythical misconception through which it sees "an unconstrained great power bestriding a continent changing everything in its wake." For Lampton et al., this view is simply wrong; even small states in Southeast Asia have agency with which to affect the extent to which China can achieve its objectives. This is called "reciprocal influence" as opposed to "hegemonic imposition of power."

In *Rivers of Iron: Railroads and Chinese Power in Southeast Asia*, Lampton et al. (2022) conclude that: (1) China is big and influential, but it cannot just do whatever it pleases. China needs friends, and especially in neighboring countries like Southeast Asia, which both have resources China needs and share long borders which are important for China's security. (2) The purpose of China's engagement in the region is to create an economic influence and interdependency between Asia and China. China is taking advantage of the US leaving the region in vacuum for years after the cold war (see also, Zawacki 2019). (3) China's rise in both economic and military power is mutually reinforcing.

As mentioned, even small states have agency. Lampton et al. (2022) argue that the capability to negotiate with China depends on three factors. (1) Size, wealth, and location: taking a state as the unit of analysis, they demonstrate that different countries in Southeast Asia have different powers to negotiate depending on size, wealth and location. For example, the size of Indonesia's economy and its domestic political situation provide significant leverage to bargain with China on interest rates for infrastructure investment under the BRI. Geography gives Thailand and Laos a strategic advantage, as China cannot achieve its broader ambitions without routing BRI infrastructure through these two countries. Importantly, we must not forget that countries have their own visions and may choose to work with other countries or other sources of funding. This would impact China's ability to influence the member states in the region. (2) State and civil society capacity: State capacity refers to the robustness of government institutions, the rules of law, civil society, human resources, and the ability to regulate and monitor. For example, the Thai-based Rak Chiang Khong NGO is working in consortium with regional partners to engage in science diplomacy and disseminate knowledge about the impact of upstream dams on the lower Mekong. Singapore is an example of a country with high state capacity. The implication is that the higher the capacity, the higher the negotiation capability. (3) Domestic politics: public opinion and domestic politics significantly impact a state's capacity to negotiate with China.

The concept of "reciprocal influence" helps to understand how – through multilateral frameworks – countries in the Mekong subregion maximize their benefits from the competition between the two great powers in the region. Denny Roy (2013), a professor at the Asia Pacific Security Studies Center, identified four strategies for small states to deal with great powers, namely: (1) Hedging to create various options for the state; (2) Engaging or cooperating with persuasion for the advancer to comply with the universal rule of laws and enmeshment; (3) Balancing to counter the external force by self-empowerment through creating alliances with other countries; and (4) Bandwagoning through an alliance with a great power without resistance. In the case of ACMECS, various actors are involved, including China through LMC and the US via MUSP, as well as Japan, ROK, and others. Hence, this study focuses on a case study of ACMECS as a representative of multilateral cooperation in the Mekong subregion and its strategy to deal with the China-US rivalry.

Ayeyarwady Chaophraya Mekong Economic Cooperation Strategy (ACMECS) is a Thai initiative launched in 2003 during Thaksin Shinawatra's administration. Although the organization derives its name from the three main rivers in the region – the Ayeyarwady in Myanmar, the Chaophraya in Thailand and the Mekong, which runs through all five member countries – initially, Thailand's intention was to address challenges in the border areas. Anuson Chinvanno (2022), Thailand's ambassador to Vietnam at that time, recalls that ACMECS was originally created to bridge the development gap between Thailand and its neighbors. Connectivity projects and the Special Economic Zone at the border are examples of ACMECS flagship projects.

ACMECS has no permanent secretariat but a rotating Chair. A former Thai ambassador to the US has suggested that ACMECS has lost its momentum due to a lack of leadership from the Thai side (Interview, May 2022). A former official in charge of ACMECS at the Thai Ministry of Foreign Affairs suggested that its lack of a permanent secretariat and recurring funding issues may have contributed to its decline (Interview, August 2022). More significant, however, is that with many new donor countries engaged in the subregion, the member countries have alternative sources of development aid and financing through bilateral cooperation. Other initiatives like ADC have thus experienced similar declines.

Cognizant of the tensions between China and the US and its impact on development in the region, in 2018, while chairing the 8th ACMECS Summit Meeting, Thailand took the initiative to revive ACMECS, launching the ACMECS Fund and proposing an ACMECS Master Plan (2019–2023) aiming to position ACMECS as an intra subregional agenda setting body and thereby enhance the collective negotiating power of the countries in the region. ACMECS stated vision is to "connect the connectivity" and ultimately to bridge the development gap between the Mekong subregion and the maritime ASEAN countries. The Master Plan has three main pillars: (1) Seamless connectivity (2) Synchronize connectivity and (3) Smart connectivity.

Under this new agreement, Thailand pledged to contribute USD200 million into the ACMECS Fund (*Bangkok Post* 2020) and proposed establishing a permanent secretariat. In 2022, a Senior Official Meeting of ACMECS approved commissioning the Mekong Institute to serve as an interim secretariat. The interim secretariat would be situated at the Ministry of Foreign Affairs of Thailand. Cambodia pledged USD7 million to the Fund and ROK contributed USD1 million for a specific ACMECS branded project. In 2022, Australia also expressed interest in financially contributing to an ACMECS project (Humphreys 2022). But despite this expressed interest by ACMECS member countries and development partners to contribute to the Fund, no conclusions have been reached about how the fund will operate. According to an interview with a Thai government official at the Ministry of Foreign Affairs in charge of the Mekong Cooperation, there are two main challenges to the establishment of the fund: (1) how to ensure the shared ownership of the fund if it is operated by Thailand; and (2) there are practical legal issues about how the funds would be managed by Thailand. Hence, the ACMECS Fund is not yet available.

According to Ambassador Arunrung Photong Humphreys, Ambassador for Mekong Cooperation, ACMECS should be envisaged as a connector of the subregion. With a shared vision and agenda for the subregion – developed and agreed to by the member states – ACMECS can connect and synergize the efforts of all development partners in the region and ensure local control of the direction of development. That is, Thailand is attempting to build a regional mechanism to coordinate planning and realize a shared vision of the subregion and thereby enhance its negotiating power, based on the strategic value of its location and natural resources to China and the US.

By comparison, the other multilateral mechanisms in the region – CLV, CLMV, AMBDC and MRC – are less-well suited to play the role proposed for ACMECS. A Vietnamese diplomat suggested in an interview that CLM and CLMV would have difficulties because they do not include all the countries of the Mekong subregion. And although AMBDC includes all of the relevant countries, with Cambodia as Chair, little progress has been made. The MRC's focus is primarily Mekong River management, and it is not equipped to deal with broader political or development issues. Hence, ACMECS, with five member countries, a new vision, a master plan, an interim secretariat and a new funding mechanism appears to be the most promising multilateral cooperation framework to maximize benefits and minimize risk in this crowded field.

Conclusion

This paper discusses the Mekong subregion as a site of geopolitical competition. Amid the twelve cooperation frameworks, the US-China rivalry in this subregion is clear. For the US, engaging with the Mekong subregion is seen as necessary to contain China's influence. The Mekong US Partnership and the Friends of Mekong are agencies of the US's offshoring balancing strategy, promoting the "universal values" of good governance, a rules-based order, and respect for human rights in close collaboration with all extra regional partners and the Mekong subregion countries to pursue a vision of a better connected and economically integrated subregion. China is the only stakeholder in the region that is not a party to this "partnership."

China, meanwhile, is engaging in the region through the Lancang-Mekong Cooperation. Although it promotes LMC as a comprehensive development cooperation framework, I argue that one of China's driving objectives is to be recognized as a "responsible great power" on a civilizing mission to develop all aspects of life in the Mekong subregion. Through the LMC, China offers an alternative to the Western development model with ample funds to allocate as proof of the possibility of China's peaceful rise to great power status.

As the only Mekong subregional cooperation framework that includes all five subregional countries, ACMECS is perhaps the most promising connector and agenda setter for subregional development. And synchronizing the five-countries' hedging, engagement, balancing and bandwagoning strategies is perhaps the best way to maximize the benefits and minimize the costs of the US-China rivalry.

Key deliverables of the 8th ACMECS Summit in Bangkok (16 June 2018)

1. Engagement with Development Partners (DPs) Based on a principle of balance and inclusivity the Summit has endorsed the engagement of DPs group 1 namely Australia, Japan, USA, ROK, China and India with Thailand serving as coordinator. Subsequently, the Joint Development Plan on Cooperation between ACMECS and DPs;JDP has been drafted and under consideration.
2. Establishment of ACMECS Fund
3. Approval of the ACMECS Master Plan (2019–2023)

Key deliverables of the 9th ACMECS Summit (Virtual) (9 December 2020)

Three documents endorsed namely 1. ACMECS Development Fund (ACMDF) 2. Coordinating mechanism of ACMECS 3 pillars 3. List of 30 Prioritized Projects (6 projects for each member country)

Figure 9.2 One Page Summary: ACMECS
Ayeyawady-Chao Phraya-Mekong Economic Cooperation Strategy

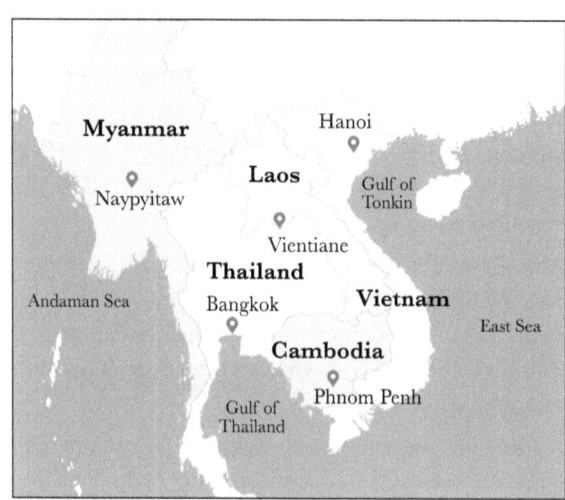

Population:
230 million

Area:
1.94 million square Meter

GDP:
225 million USD

Background
- Thailand's initiated and launched in 2003 with 5 members Cambodia, Lao PDR, Myanmar, Vietnam and Thailand
- Objective: Intra subregional consultation platform for sustainable development of the subregion

Three pillars under ACMECS Master Plan (2019–2023)
1) Seamless ACMECS
2) Synchronized ACMECS Economies
3) Smart and Sustainable ACMECS

- Hardware infrastructure: connecting missing logistic and transport links
- Digital infrastructure
- Energy infrastructure connectivity

- Software connectivity
- Trade, investment and industry: coherent rules and regulation, integrated value and supply chain
- Financial cooperation: financial connectivity and ACMECS funds

- Human resource development and utilisation of modern technology
- Environmental cooperation for sustainability
- Sustainable agriculture
- Tourism
- Public health

Source: Created by the author based on an interview with the Mekong Cooperation Unit, Ministry of Foreign Affairs, Thailand.

References

Amitav Acharya (2021) *ASEAN and regional order: Revisiting security community in Southeast Asia*. Oxfordshire: Routledge, Taylor & Francis Group.

Anuson Chinvanno (2022) Synergy or Centralised: ACMECS as an Architectural Connector of the Mekong Subregion. Paper presented to the 8th ACMECS Summit Meeting, organized by the Thailand Ministry of Foreign Affairs, 29 September 2022. Sukhosol Hotel, Bangkok

Asia Foundation (2018) ASEAN as the Architect for Regional Development Cooperation: Advancing ASEAN Centrality and Catalyzing Action for Sustainable Development. Asia Foundation. https://asiafoundation.org/wp-content/uploads/2018/09/ASEAN-as-the-Architect-for-Regional-Development-Cooperation.pdf

ASEAN (2019) ASEAN Outlook on Indo-Pacific. https://asean.org/wp-content/uploads/2019/06/ASEAN-Outlook-on-the-Indo-Pacific_FINAL_22062019.pdf. Accessed August 2022.

Bangkok Post (2020) Thailand gives virus vaccine pledge to ACMECS members. https://www.bangkokpost.com/thailand/general/2032763/thailand-gives-virus-vaccine-pledge-to-acmecs-members. Accessed 15 October 2024.

Bureau of East Asian and Pacific Affairs (2019) Lower Mekong Initiative. United States Department of State. 21 February. https://www.state.gov/lower-mekong-initiative/

Biba, Sebastian (2019) China's Hegemonic Choice in the Mekong Region. *East Asia Forum*, 30 August. https://eastasiaforum.org/2019/08/30/chinas-hegemonic-choice-in-the-mekong-region/

Brautigam, Deborah. (2009). *The Dragon's Gift: The Real Story of China in Africa*. Oxford University Press.

Brautigam, Deborah and Yufan Huang (2023). Integrating China into Multilateral Debt Relief: Progress and Problems in the G20 DSSI (Research Report 09/2023). Briefing Paper. https://www.econstor.eu/handle/10419/271579

Callahan, William A. (2008). Chinese Visions of World Order: Post-Hegemonic or A New Hegemony? *International Studies Review*, 10(4): 749–761. https://doi.org/10.1111/j.1468-2486.2008.00830.x

Chang, Felix K. (2013) The Lower Mekong Initiative & U. S. Foreign Policy in Southeast Asia: Energy, Environment & Power. *Orbis*, 57(2): 282–299. https://doi.org/10.1016/j.orbis.2013.02.005

Grunwald, Richard (2021) Lancang-Mekong Cooperation: Overcoming the Trust Deficit on the Mekong. ISEAS Yusof ISHAK Institute. *Perspectives* 89. https://www.iseas.edu.sg/articles-commentaries/iseas-perspective/2021-89-lancang-mekong-cooperation-overcoming-the-trust-deficit-on-the-mekong-by-richard-grunwald/ Accessed 18 January 2025.

Ho, Benjamin and Hoo Chiew-Ing (2018) Will China Be a Responsible Great Power? *RSIS Commentary*, 62, 3 April. https://www.rsis.edu.sg/wp-content/uploads/2018/04/CO18062.pdf

Humphreys, Arunrung Photong (2022) Synergy or Centralised: ACMECS as an Architectural Connector of the Mekong Subregion. Paper presented to the 8th ACMECS Summit Meeting, organized by the Thailand Ministry of Foreign Affairs, 29 September 2022. Sukhosol Hotel, Bangkok.

Jannuzi, Frank Sampson (2007) US-China Relations: An Affirmative Agenda, A Responsible Course. Independent Task Force Report No. 59. Washington D.C.: Council on Foreign Relations.

Jianwei Wang and Hoo Tiang Boon (2019) *China's Omnidirectional Peripheral Diplomacy*. Singapore and London: World Scientific Publishing.

Jong Woo Kang (2015) The Noodle Bowl Effect: Stumbling or Building Block. ADB Economic Working Paper Series No. 446 by https://www.adb.org/publications/noodle-bowl-effect-stumbling-building-block. Accessed January 2022.

Kawai, Masahiro and Ganeshan Wignaraja (2009) The Asian "Noodle Bowl:" Is it serious for Business? ADBI Working Paper Series, No. 136. https://www.adb.org/sites/default/files/publication/155991/adbi-wp136.pdf. Accessed January 2022.

Kuik, Cheng-Chwee (2021) Getting Hedging Right: A Small-State Perspective. *China International Strategy Review*, 3: 300–315.

Lampton, David S., Selina Ho and Cheng-Chwee Kuik (2020) *Rivers of Iron: Railroads and Chinese power in Southeast Asia*. Berkeley: University of California Press.

LMC (2022) Lancang-Mekong Cooperation homepage. http://www.lmcchina.org/eng/. Accessed June 2022.

Mearsheimer, John J. (2014) *The Tragedy of Great Power Politics*. New York: W. W. Norton

Mekong Institute (2022) Mekong-RoK Cooperation: Seeking synergies on Mekong-ACMECS Cooperation. Bangkok, 17 June 2022.

Mekong–US Partnership (2020) About Mekong–US Partnership. https://mekonguspartnership.org/about/

Middleton, Carl (2018) Reciprocal Transboundary Cooperation on the Lancang-Mekong River: Towards an Inclusive and Ecological Relationship. Center for Social Development Studies, Chulalongkorn University. Thailand.

MUSP (2009) [WWW] LMI Factsheet. https://mekonguspartnership.org/2012/07/13/fact-sheet-lower-mekong-initiative. Retrieved June 2022

Narut Charoensri (2010) Greater Mekong Subregion Economic Cooperation. Bangkok, Security Project Chulalongkorn University. Bangkok.

Ministry of Foreign Affairs, PRC (2023) Outlook on China's Foreign Policy on Its Neighborhood in The New Era. 24 October.

Pal Nyiri (2006) The Yellow Man's Burden: Chinese migrants on a civilizing mission. *The China Journal*, 56: 83–106

Paradorn Rangsimaporn (2023) A Tale of Two Regions: Geopolitics, hedging and regionalism in Central Asia and Southeast Asia. *Points of View*, no. 4, International Studies Center. Ministry of Foreign Affairs, Thailand.

Pillsbury, Michael (2022) *The Hundred-Year Marathon: China's Secret Strategy to Replace America as the Global Superpower*. New York: Holt.

Pongphisoot Busbarat (2018) Grabbing the Forgotten: China's leadership consolidation in mainland Southeast Asia through the Mekong-Lancang Cooperation. *Perspective*, 2018(7), ISEAS Yusof Ishak Institute.

Pongphisoot Busbarat (2020) Re-enmeshment in the Mekong: External Powers' Turn. *Perspective*, 2020(88). ISEAS Yusof Ishak Institute.

Poowin Bunyavejchewin (2016) The Lancang-Mekong Cooperation (LMC) Viewed in Light of the Potential Regional Leader Theory. *Journal of Mekong Societies*, 12(3): 49–64.

Pranee Thiparat (2022) *ASEAN Community: Myth and Reality*. Bangkok: P Press Publishing.

Roy, Denny (2013) *Return of The Dragon: Rising China and Regional Security*. Columbia University Press. https://doi.org/10.7312/roy-15900

Shambaugh, David (2021) *Where Great Powers Meet: America and China in Southeast Asia*. New York: Oxford University Press.

Thomas, Neil (2020) Great Power Responsibility: The Evolution of Chinese Foreign Policy. 11 May. *MacroPolo*. https://macropolo.org/china-great-power-foreign-policy-covid19/

Zawacki, Benjamin (2019) Implications of a Crowded Field: Sub-regional architecture in ACMECS Member States. Asia Foundation.

Zhang, WeiWei (2012). *The China Wave: Rise of A Civilizational State*. Hackensack: World Century.

Index

airport, 11, 90, 113–114, 175, 185, 194, 221, 273

anthropology *see* ethnography

of regionalization, 3, 23, 25, 36, 38, 44

ASEAN, 1, 18, 26, 32, 37, 41–43, 56, 58–59, 112–113, 199, 235, 237–238, 248–249, 255, 267, 274, 281, 289

Asian Infrastructure Investment Bank (AIIB), 33, 54–56, 115, 245, 250

Ayeyarwady Chaophraya Mekong Economic Cooperation Strategy (ACMECS), 19, 280, 282, 284, 286, 288–293
see Mekong Subregional Cooperation Frameworks

bandwagoning, 20, 108, 216, 268, 271, 288, 291

Belt and Road Initiative (BRI), xv–xvi, 1–34, 36–38, 41–44, 51–64, 67–72, 77–81, 83–84, 86–89, 92, 97–100, 105–107, 109–111, 114–116, 125, 128, 130, 137–138, 140–148, 150, 152, 159–160, 175, 178, 181–183, 185–186, 189, 191–192, 196, 201, 207–225, 227–228, 233–255, 258–260, 267–270, 276–287

bilateral, 9, 16, 26, 28, 51, 66–67, 71, 106, 218, 240, 245, 247–250, 255, 268, 271, 276, 280, 283, 289

border, 6–7, 43–44, 77–80, 82–84, 87, 93, 95–96, 114, 119–120, 138, 145, 161, 175–176, 179–181, 184, 187–188, 196–200, 210, 214, 220–221, 241, 269, 282, 287–288

cross-border, 6, 29, 77, 80–82, 147, 245, 254, 281–283

bridge, 55, 57, 138, 145, 234, 249, 288–289

business transnationalism, 16–18, 233–234, 240–241, 254, 259–260, 263

Cambodia, 20, 32, 64, 145, 181–183, 187, 215, 268, 272–273, 280, 289–290, 293

cattle trade, 6–7, 77–81, 83–84, 86–88, 92–94, 96–97, 99–100

actor, 6, 77, 79–82, 84, 87, 89, 98

broker, 6–7, 77–83, 87, 92–100

brokerage system, 6–7, 77, 79, 81–83, 92, 94–95, 97, 99–100

network, 6–7, 77, 79–89, 92–94, 97–98, 100

transnational-, 6, 77–81, 87, 92, 94, 99

China-ASEAN EXPO (CAEXPO), 30, 245

China dream, 15, 68, 270 *see* slogans

Chinese banks, 36, 55

Bank of China, 55, 58

China Development Bank, 208

China Export-Import Bank (China Exim Bank), 55, 115, 208

Industrial and Commercial Bank of China (ICBC), 55, 58
Chinese capitalism, 6–7, 11, 78, 80–81, 83, 92, 94, 99–100 *see* state-led capitalism
Chinese Communist Party (CCP), 37, 224, 236, 270, 277
Chinese communities, 155, 244, 251
Chinese developers
  China Communication Construction Company (CCCC), 58, 60–61, 210
  Country Garden, 58, 62
Chinese merchant, 78–79, 82, 93
China Railway 138–139
China Railway Construction Company, 58
China Railway Engineering Company, 58
China Railway Eryuan Engineering Group Company (CREEC), 210
community of shared destiny, 15, 234 *see* slogans
Covid-19, 1, 16, 23, 79, 188, 233, 235, 238–239, 246–249, 255, 276
creditor, 92–93, 95–96, 118–119
crime
  organized-, 12, 176, 180
  state-corporate-, 2, 11, 21
  transnational-, 176

domestic politics, 8–9, 52, 105, 110, 130, 276, 287–288

East Coast Rail Link (ECRL), 4–5, 51–53, 55, 57–61, 64, 67, 69–72, 143
Eastern Economic Corridor (EEC), 12, 175–177, 179–180, 183, 189, 193–194, 196, 200
engagement, 270, 274, 287, 291–292 *see* selective engagement
entrepreneurs, 6, 17, 139, 225, 236, 243, 252, 258–259
ethnography, 10–11, 24, 38, 137–138, 140, 142, 159–162, 166 *see* multi-sited ethnography
expressway, 111, 114, 120–123, 125, 127–129 *see* highway

foreign direct investment (FDI), 54, 56, 112, 119, 182, 192, 237–238, 240, 242, 244–245 *see* investment
foreign loans, 107, 115, 129
Forest City project, 4, 53, 67

geopolitical, 2, 16, 18–21, 27–28, 34, 141, 149, 212, 233, 235–236, 239, 242, 260, 267–268, 272, 286, 291
geopolitics, 12, 18, 175, 178, 218, 235–237, 247, 260
government-linked companies (GLCs), 55, 57
Greater Mekong Subregion (Scheme) (GMS), 13–14, 30, 113, 225, 273, 281–283

Index   301

hedging, 7–8, 20, 105, 108–109, 120, 268, 271, 288, 291
  strategy, 7–8, 15, 105, 108–109, 116, 120, 130, 216–217, 223
highway, 11, 57, 113, 115, 120–123, 126, 128–130, 138, 143, 155, 158, 175 *see* expressway
Hu Jintao, 212, 278
Indonesia, 29, 35–36, 42, 68, 112, 117, 140, 144, 239–240, 268, 287
infrastructure
  immobile and material, 7, 100
  mobile, 78, 84, 87
  mobile and immaterial, 6–7, 84, 87, 100
  temporality, 78, 80, 89–92, 94, 97–98, 100, 153, 156
  transport, 9, 105, 107, 111, 113, 121, 130
  urbanism, 176, 192
investment, 7, 9, 14, 17, 20, 29, 32, 36, 42, 51–54, 56–59, 61–62, 64–66, 69, 106, 108, 110–114, 116–118, 120–122, 125–126, 128–130, 141, 144, 155, 176, 178–179, 181–183, 186, 189, 194, 208, 210, 212–213, 215–216, 219, 236–238, 241–243, 258–259, 269–270, 273, 281–283, 287, 293 *see* foreign direct investment

KK Park, 175–177, 180, 184–186, 188, 194, 199–200
Kyaukphyu-Kunming Railway (KKR), 15, 210

Lancang Mekong Cooperation (LMC), 18–19, 267, 269–270, 272, 275, 279–280, 282–283, 288, 291

Laos, 6–7, 9–10, 20, 38, 65, 78, 81, 83–84, 87, 93, 98–100, 137–138, 140–143, 145–147, 149, 152–153, 155, 159, 161, 163–164, 166, 178, 181–182, 187, 198–199, 287, 293
  Laos-China Railway (LCR), 138, 140–141, 143–147, 160
Lee Hsien Loong, 239, 245–246, 250, 252
Lower Mekong Initiative, 19, 267, 271, 274

Mahathir Mohamad, 63–68, 143
Malaysia, xv, 4–5, 32, 36, 38, 42, 51–72, 112, 140, 143, 238–240, 259, 268
  1Malaysia Development Berhad (1MDB), 4–5, 52, 64, 69, 71
  Malaysia-China Kuantan Industrial Park (MCKIP), 58, 65–66, 71
  Persatuan Persahabatan Malaysia–China (PPMC), 32
  Sino-Malaysia relations, 51–52
Maoist state socialism, 13, 224
Marx, Karl, 80, 84–86, 88, 90–91
Mekong, 6, 13, 18–20, 81, 114, 138, 225, 267–271, 276, 280–284, 287–291, 293
  subregion, 19–20, 267–273, 276–277, 280, 282–283, 286, 288–291

subregional cooperation framework, 19, 291 *see* ACMECS

Mekong US Partnership (MUSP), 18–19, 267, 269, 271–272, 274, 276, 280–283, 285, 288, 291

migrant, 17, 243, 258

misconduct, 51–52

multilateral, 8, 17–18, 27, 105, 107, 109, 192, 245–255, 267–272, 275–276, 279–280, 283, 286, 288, 290–291

multi-sited ethnography, 2–4, 21, 23–25, 39, 44, 161, 164

mutual benefit, 15, 152 *see* slogans

mutual dependency, 5, 72

Myanmar, 6–7, 13–16, 20, 29, 33–34, 36, 38, 81, 83–84, 87, 93, 95, 100, 175–176, 179–182, 184–185, 187, 196–199, 207–228, 234, 268, 272–273, 280, 288, 293

China-Myanmar Economic Corridor (CMEC), 207, 209, 212–213, 216, 219–220, 227

Najib Tun Razak, 52, 57, 60, 63–66, 68–69, 143

Nanofilm Technologies International (NTI,), 16–18, 256–260

NGO, 150, 214, 287

Official Development Assistance (ODA), 9, 117, 120–121, 129–130

Pacific International Lines (PIL), 16–18, 254–260

perception, 4, 26, 30–31, 35, 43, 52, 61–62, 67, 119, 140, 147, 164–165, 216

Philippines, 33, 35–36, 42, 112, 144, 179, 187, 238–239, 268

political economy, 2, 16, 18, 21, 27, 80, 86, 211, 213, 233–234, 236–237, 239–243, 259–260

port, 11, 31, 55–60, 66, 98, 106, 113–115, 117, 138, 175, 188, 208–210, 212, 215–216, 222, 256, 273, 281

public-private partnership (PPP), 66, 113, 121–122, 125, 129

railway/railroad, 9–11, 20, 57, 59–60, 98, 106, 111, 115–117, 126, 128, 137–162, 164–167, 175, 208, 210, 213, 273

reciprocal influence, 19–20, 267–268, 271–272, 286, 288

recycling industry, 12, 175–176, 180, 183, 193, 195, 200

road, 85, 88, 98, 106, 113–114, 120–121, 126–127, 138, 151, 155, 160, 191, 194, 207, 273, 281

selective engagement, 268
 see engagement

shadow zone, 11–12, 175–176, 179–183, 192–195, 197–198, 200–201

Silk Road, 27, 54, 56, 68, 142–143, 208, 245, 247, 277

China's New Silk Road, 106

China's New Silk Route Initiative, 26

Index 303

Maritime Silk Road Construction (MSR), 32
Maritime Silk Road Initiative (MSRI), 208, 212, 219–220
Singapore, xv, 16–18, 35, 60, 62–63, 143, 147, 233–234, 236, 238–240, 244–260, 268, 287
  Sino-Singapore, 16, 233, 254–255, 259
slogans, 13–15, 65, 224
South China Sea, 13, 21, 105, 225, 268
sovereignty, 1, 4–5, 9, 12, 32–33, 41, 65, 70–71, 109, 125, 127, 176, 180, 184, 191, 195–197, 200, 219, 223, 276
  flexible sovereignty, 176, 196
special economic zone (SEZ), xv, 11, 20, 155, 175, 177–178, 184, 189, 191, 196, 288
  Eastern Economic Corridor (EEC), 12, 175–177, 179–180, 183, 189, 193–194, 196, 200
  Golden Triangle SEZ, 178, 181, 183, 198–199
  Kyaukphyu SEZ, 15, 38, 184, 209–210, 212–213, 215–216, 222
  Mong Cai, 38, 111
  Shwe Kokko SEZ, 12, 38, 175, 177, 180–181, 184–188, 196–200, 220
  Sihanoukville SEZ, 181, 183, 185, 187
Sri Lanka, 31, 64, 212
state-led capitalism/state-managed capitalism, 13, 37, 224
  see Chinese capitalism

state-owned enterprises (SOE), 14–15, 17, 35, 53–55, 57–58, 83, 116, 143, 153, 208, 214, 219, 221, 224–227, 242
state transformation, 13–14, 207, 211–212, 225–226, 228
station, 6, 83, 138–139, 144–145, 147–149, 153–154, 161, 183

Thailand, xv–xvi, 6–7, 9–10, 20, 32, 38, 43, 60, 78–79, 81–84, 93, 95, 98, 100, 112, 137–138, 140–144, 146–149, 153, 155, 159–160, 163–166, 175, 177, 179–184, 188–190, 196, 198–199, 268–269, 272–273, 284, 287–290, 292–293
  State Railway of Thailand (SRT), 139, 146–147, 158–159, 163
  Thailand-China Railway (TCR), 138–139, 141, 143, 146–147
top-down, 1, 13, 15, 27–28, 34, 44, 84, 224, 228, 278

US-China rivalry, 18, 20, 144, 268, 280, 291–292
US Partnership
  see Mekong US Partnership

Vietnam, 7–9, 20, 29, 33, 38, 81, 105–130, 182, 268, 272–273, 280, 288, 290, 293
voice approach, 3, 23–24, 37, 41, 43–44

Xi Jinping, 23, 37, 52, 54, 208–209, 234, 270, 277